Bravo!

Bravo!

THE NZSO AT 50

JOY TONKS

EXISLE
PUBLISHING

ISBN 0-908988-05-2

First published April 1996.
Exisle Publishing Limited
PO Box 8077, Auckland
New Zealand.
Ph: 64-9-303 3698; Fax: 64-9-309 0191.
e-mail: exisle@cybernet.co.nz

Printed by Colorcraft Ltd, Hong Kong.

Designed by C. Humberstone.

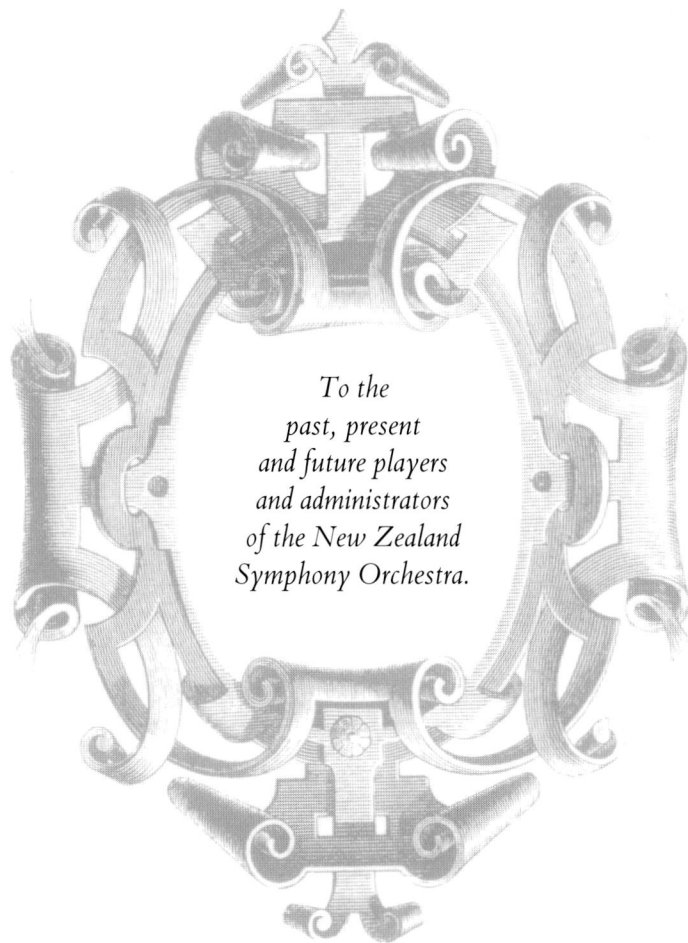

*To the
past, present
and future players
and administrators
of the New Zealand
Symphony Orchestra.*

Acknowledgements

Taped interviews have provided the basis for much of the material contained in *Bravo!* Interviews with these past and present players, management, conductors and soloists began with the Supporters Club newsletter, continued with *Concert Pitch* magazine, and for the orchestral history in 1986, with a further 50 interviews conducted in 1995. My sincere thanks to all who have taken part. There was not time to interview everyone who could have made a valuable contribution to the orchestra's story, nor was it possible to quote all those who gave their valuable time to talk with me, but whose recollections helped to give me a broader picture of the unique musical organisation that is the NZSO.

A special thanks to my NZSO colleagues: Mark Keyworth, who patiently answered my questions and read the manuscript; Anita Woods, for preparing the Appendices; Murray Alford, for updating the list of conductors, soloists and composers; and to Joy Aberdein, Brian Morris, Rosemary Brown, Elenoa Eyles and Glenn Young for their help and interest in the project.

Selecting illustrations was a pleasure with such excellent professional photographs available from Tom Shanahan, the orchestra's former trombonist, whose collection spanning 30 years was a feature of the last book. Graeme Browne, principal bass trombone, provided more recent photographs, as did Stephen Harker. Thank you to all the photographers whose work appears on these pages, and to those who submitted material.

My thanks also to designer Craig Humberstone for his commitment to helping produce a book worthy of its subject.

Wendy Allardice, Les Austin, Vivien Chisholm, John Gray, Ashley Heenan and Michael Vinten have helped and advised; Michael Monaghan has been an inspiration, and other friends and family, especially Ralph, have been totally supportive. My daughter Karen devoted six precious weeks in the final stages of the manuscript's preparation to work as my one-person support team – secretary, editor, critic and encourager: a very special time that I will always remember with much love.

Joy Tonks

Foreword

The 50th Anniversary! Congratulations, and of course, grateful thanks to all those people who have given so much to ensure this orchestra has flourished for half a century.

When I became conductor of the National Orchestra in 1957, letters questioning the use of public funds for the orchestra still appeared in the press from time to time. Gradually the immense value of a national orchestra was accepted and Joy Tonks' book shows how enormous the orchestra's contribution has been to New Zealand's musical life. It is hard to imagine how music could have fared without it.

I have a painting by Peter McIntyre of the orchestra rehearsing in the Wellington Town Hall about 1960. It is a constant joy to be reminded of those who were there in the early days – Bill Barsby, Peter Glen, Neil Dixon, Mott Connors, Bill McLean, Carol McKenzie – all 'captured' in action by the artist. These and many more fine musicians were the backbone of the orchestra. They were a sure foundation for what was, in 1946, a very ambitious post-war project of the New Zealand Government. Peter Glen often told how the players from all over New Zealand gathered in Wellington for the first rehearsal. The customary official speeches having been made, the Governor General said: "Well, play something!" Peter said it sounded awful!

Not so today: the orchestra has shown itself to be most adept in performing a large variety of music at a consistently high level. May this continue in the next 50 years.

John Hopkins
Sydney, March 1996

Introduction

Bravo! The NZSO At 50 was written to celebrate the orchestra's 50th birthday and update its history in the decade following the publication of *The New Zealand Symphony Orchestra: The First Forty Years*. It is also my personal thank you to the orchestra for an association of over 20 years.

Although these pages celebrate a half-century, the focus is on the last decade. Two chapters cover the major, non-musical events after 1986: Pack-out and Run-out are based on typical days in the life of the NZSO in Symphony House and on tour to Auckland; Players, Maestros, Seville, Concert-masters, Music Making and Guest Artists are for dipping into; Timeband covers all five decades.

Writing in 1995, the orchestra's *annus horribilis*, created special problems, with events changing by the day. The story is still developing and ultimately will have to be told by future writers who will have the luxury of a longer perspective.

Most readers will be aware of the orchestra's difficult transition to life as a Crown-Owned Entity and limited liability company. Reduced funding has affected every aspect of its operation, prompting drastic measures to continue to fulfil its role as the national orchestra for all centres; a commitment vigorously endorsed by players.

It is the players who have been most affected by financial restraints that have resulted in "run-out" concerts and longer hours spent in recording. Occupational health, maintaining musical integrity and conductor standards are issues that demand closer involvement by the players in their own destiny. A vast pool of musical knowledge and experience exists in the orchestra and players' participation in the artistic, health and safety and other committees effectively taps into that.

An orchestra may take years to reach international level, and many never do. The New Zealand Symphony Orchestra is at that level now, and ready to take the next step. My hope is that this book will help to focus attention on the contribution the orchestra has already made to our cultural life and what it can make in the future, representing New Zealand at home and overseas.

Joy Tonks
Wellington, March 1996

Contents

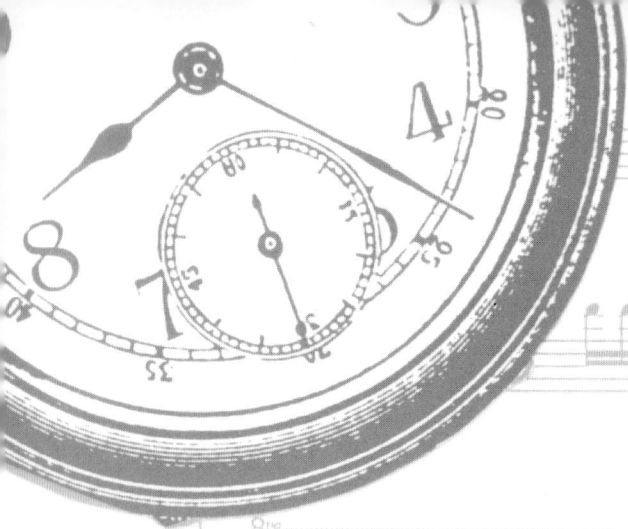

Timeband

1865	First Exhibition Orchestra, George West's Philharmonic Society, 50 players, Dunedin.[1]	*Early Days*
1882	Wellington Orchestral Society formed. Other orchestral societies and orchestral unions in main cities follow later in decade.	
1906/07	First professional orchestra: New Zealand International Exhibition Orchestra, Christchurch. Conductor: Alfred Hill, 55 players. An outstanding success at the Exhibition for the country's celebrations on becoming a Dominion. The orchestra is retained for a national tour, but Government declines to continue its funding as a national orchestra and it disbands.	
1920	Visit of the first overseas orchestra: Henri Verbrugghen's New South Wales State Orchestra; almost 100 players. Conceived on an 'Australasian basis'[2] it tours again in 1922 with 80 players, then disbands.	
1925	Radio Broadcasting Company of New Zealand founded (British Broadcasting Company founded 1922; Australian Broadcasting Company 1929). Broadcasting studio orchestras formed in main centres in late 1920s.	
	Conductors Alfred Hill, Sir Bernard Heinz and Sir Malcolm Sargent advise New	*The Thirties*

Zealand Government on setting up a National Orchestra in New Zealand, a move parallelled by the ABC (Australian Broadcasting Commission, established 1932).

1936   National Broadcasting Service set up; Professor James Shelley, director.

1939   1 December: National Broadcasting Service String Orchestra launched at Centennial Exhibition of New Zealand, Wellington. First performance 13 December. English violinist Maurice Clare engaged to audition, conduct and train the 12-piece orchestra. Leader: Vincent Aspey.

The Forties   1940   Centennial Symphony Orchestra formed from nucleus of NBS String Orchestra. Performs at New Zealand Centennial Exhibition, Wellington and also in the week-long Centennial Music Festivals in Auckland, Christchurch and Dunedin, augmented by NBS studio orchestras to 65 players. Conductor: English composer and pianist Andersen Tyrer; leader: Maurice Clare. Soloists include Isobel Baillie and New Zealand bass Oscar Natzke.

The Centennial Orchestra, planned to become New Zealand's first permanent national orchestra, is unsustainable during World War II and disbands when the Centennial Music Festival concludes in June.

Broadcasting retains the NBS String Orchestra throughout the war under Maurice Clare; leader Vincent Aspey.

1941   Maurice Clare departs on military service, composer Douglas Lilburn guest conducts for three months, followed by Andersen Tyrer.

1943   Andersen Tyrer's contract expires in July, and the NBS String Orchestra is split into the NBS String Quartet (leader: Vincent Aspey), and NBS Light Orchestra under Harry Ellwood.

1945   War in the Pacific ends. Professor James Shelley, with support of Prime Minister Peter Fraser, revives plans for a fulltime national orchestra.

1946   Appointment of Andersen Tyrer as conductor creates controversy. Auditions for players commence in February and are held throughout the country. Orchestra formally announced by Prime Minister Peter Fraser, 25 June.

October 24: National Symphony Orchestra of New Zealand launched by New Zealand Broadcasting Service (NZBS), a government department. Musical director and conductor: Andersen Tyrer; leader: Vincent Aspey; principals from

the NBS String Orchestra and Royal New Zealand Air Force Central Band, 65 players. Concert manager: John Proudfoot. First rehearsal held at NZBS studios, Waring Taylor Street, in the presence of the Governor General Sir Bernard Freyberg, VC, and Deputy Prime Minister, Walter Nash.

Based in Wellington, the National Orchestra rehearses together until November when it divides into four groups to work with NBS Studio Orchestras in Wellington, Auckland, Christchurch and Dunedin for three months each year.

1947   March 6: First concert of the National Symphony Orchestra, at Wellington Town Hall. Conductor: Andersen Tyrer; leader: Vincent Aspey; 65 players, no soloists; in the presence of the Prime Minister, members of Cabinet and the diplomatic corps. The Governor General attends a special dress rehearsal two nights earlier. First schools concerts, 14 and 21 March. Inaugural symphony and schools concerts in Christchurch, Dunedin and Auckland commence in April.

First work by New Zealand composer performed by the Orchestra: *Song of the Antipodes* by Douglas Lilburn.

1948   NZBS production of Bizet's opera *Carmen* is accompanied by National Orchestra, giving 33 performances in a four-month tour, to Dunedin, Christchurch, Wellington and Auckland. First visits to Invercargill and Wanganui.

1949   International (Italian) Grand Opera Company tours New Zealand accompanied by National Orchestra.

First major tour of provincial centres, North Island: New Plymouth, Hawera, Palmerston North, Hastings, Napier, Gisborne, Hamilton, Masterton, Wanganui and Rotorua. South Island: Ashburton, Oamaru, Timaru, Greymouth, Hokitika, Westport, Nelson and Blenheim.

Andersen Tyrer resigns and returns to England.

1950   Irishman Michael Bowles appointed resident conductor.

First New Zealand/Australian exchange of conductors: Michael Bowles, NZBS/ Sir Bernard Heinz, ABC.

First visits to Lower Hutt and Levin.

Last year of group system. The orchestra becomes fully based in Wellington from 1951. Several players leave for this reason.

1951   New rehearsal rooms: St Paul's Sunday School in Sydney Street East, Thorndon.

February: First outdoor concerts, Auckland's 111th Birthday Carnival at Epsom

The Fifties

THE
NATIONAL ORCHESTRA
of the
NEW ZEALAND BROADCASTING SERVICE

Programme

GOD SAVE THE KING

Overture: " Carnival " . . . . . Dvorak

Symphony No. 2 in D . . . . . Brahms
  Allegro non troppo
  Adagio non troppo
  Allegretto grazioso—Presto ma non assai
  Allegro con spirito

INTERVAL

Rhapsody: " Shropshire Lad " . . Butterworth
Roumanian Rhapsody No. 1 . . . . Enesco
Prelude and Love's Death (" Tristan ") . Wagner
Tone Poem " Till Eulenspiegel " . Richard Strauss

Town Hall   Thursday, 6 March
Wellington   1947

Conductor   -   Andersen Tyrer
Leader   -   Vincent Aspey

GRAND OPERA HOUSE,   WELLINGTON, N.Z.
J. C. Williamson Theatres Limited
Managing Directors: Frank S. Tait, John H. Tait, J. Nevin Tait (London).

Grand Opera Season
Organised and presented by
J. C. WILLIAMSON THEATRES LTD.
by arrangement with the
NEW ZEALAND BROADCASTING SERVICE
FRIDAY EVENING, APRIL 1, 1949
(PREMIERE)

"Tosca"

Showgrounds (open-air serenade concerts). Conductor: Michael Bowles. First Subscription series of concerts in Wellington. First visits to Cambridge and Tauranga.

1952   February: First Proms concerts (five) in Wellington. Extended to Auckland, Christchurch and Dunedin in 1953.

1953   Michael Bowles declines re-engagement. New Zealand-born international conductor Warwick Braithwaite appointed principal conductor.

1954   January: First Royal Concert for Queen Elizabeth and Prince Philip at Dunedin Town Hall. Conductor: Warwick Braithwaite; soloist: New Zealand pianist Richard Farrell.

Englishman James Robertson appointed resident conductor; he re-auditions the orchestra, resulting in several seating and personnel changes. Former principal cello Claude Tanner takes his complaint to Parliament.

= LODGE MAKES HIS CONTRIBUTION TO THE NATIONAL ORCHESTRA'S TENTH BIRTHDAY. =

NEVILLE LODGE, 1956

1955	James Robertson holds the first workshops for composers, concerto soloists and conductors.
1958	Englishman John Hopkins, aged 29, appointed resident conductor.
1959	First commercial recording *Festive Overtures*, EMI, conductor: John Hopkins. First concert for a major international conference, South East Asian Treaty Organisation (SEATO), Wellington, 200 delegates. September: National Youth Orchestra launched by John Hopkins. Two performances: Lower Hutt (with violinist Igor Ozim) and Wellington (with pianist Ilse von Alpenheim). Leader: Vincent Aspey Jnr; 65 players. Czech Philharmonic Orchestra tour, 110 players. First professional symphony orchestra heard live by many members of the National Orchestra, including leader Vincent Aspey.
1961	November: Igor Stravinsky, aged 79, conducts two concerts of his own compositions in Wellington and Auckland, shares conducting with his assistant Robert Craft. National Orchestra Trainees (later Schola Musica), an orchestral training scheme, founded by John Hopkins. First intake: nine trainees. Musical director: Ashley Heenan. First schools concert: Wellington Girls' College, four months after musicians assemble; first professional tour, first public concert at Waipukurau some months later. First visit to Te Puke.
1962	New Zealand Broadcasting Corporation (NZBC), a public corporation, replaces NZBS, a government department, as management of the orchestra. April: Concert Orchestra of the NZBC founded to accompany opera and ballet, and perform concerts in smaller centres. Conductor: James Robertson; leader: Ruth Pearl; 25 players. August: Royal Concert at the Civic Theatre, Christchurch, for state visit of King Bhumibol Adulyadej and Queen Sirikit of Thailand. Conductor: John Hopkins. First visit to Marton and Paeroa. National Orchestra re-auditioned.
1963	Orchestral Bursary schemes start for orchestra members to undertake advanced studies overseas. First recipient: Glynne Adams, viola, with Hungarian violinist Tibor Varga.

The Sixties

TUDEHOPE PHOTOGRAPHY

John Hopkins leaves NZ to become Federal Director of Music, ABC, Sydney.

1964	Name change: New Zealand Broadcasting Corporation Symphony Orchestra (NZBCSO).
	New home: 38 The Terrace, former Broadcasting Studios. The orchestra, concert section and orchestral trainees, housed under one roof for the first time.
	British composer Sir William Walton conducts the orchestra in seven performances of programmes of his own works.
	July: Juan Matteucci appointed resident conductor.
	September: Hungarian Laszlo Heltay appointed first associate conductor.
	November: Concert Orchestra disbanded. Many players absorbed into Symphony Orchestra.
1965	April: First television recording of the orchestra, filmed in Winter Show Buildings, Wellington. The orchestra mimes to sound pre-recorded at The Terrace Studio. Conducted by Juan Matteucci.
	July: Recruitment drive to Europe, North, Central and South America, by Juan Matteucci and BCNZ executive, Malcolm Rickard.
1966	Little Symphony Orchestra formed from within the expanded NZBCSO to play baroque, classical and modern repertoire and give concerts in smaller centres. Conductor: Henri Temianka. Leader: Eric Lawson; 35 players. First performance: Paramount Theatre, Wellington.
1967	Despite considerable success, notably 15 Proms, including two with Kiri Te Kanawa at the Festival of the Pines, New Plymouth, the Little Symphony disbands a few months later.
	Vincent Aspey retires after 21 years as leader of the National Orchestra in August, and takes a chair further back in the first violins section, the first time he had played in an orchestra of which he was not leader.
	August: Alex Lindsay appointed leader.
	Juan Matteucci's term as resident conductor expires. A new system of guest conductors is introduced. Planning starts for the orchestra's first overseas tour. Alex Lindsay becomes first concertmaster.
The Seventies 1970	Royal Concert in Dunedin, for Her Majesty the Queen; Prince Philip, Duke of Edinburgh; Prince Charles, the Prince of Wales and Princess Anne. Conductor: Walter Susskind; soloist: Kiri Te Kanawa.

1971	Frank Gurr, principal clarinet, performs in a World Symphony Orchestra in Washington; conductor: Arthur Fiedler.

1973   Englishman Brian Priestman appointed chief conductor.
Vincent Aspey MBE retires after working continuously with Broadcasting orchestras for over 40 years. He receives an Honorary Doctorate of Music from Victoria University in 1974.

1974   The Adam Report into Broadcasting recommends the restructuring of NZBC; the orchestra is to remain with Broadcasting Council, administered by Radio New Zealand.
November: First overseas tour to Australia; conductor: Brian Priestman, soloists: Kiri Te Kanawa and Michael Houstoun. Concerts in Sydney (seven), Canberra (one), Adelaide (one) – nine concerts, seven different programmes, (two repeated), in 11 days.
Concertmaster Alex Lindsay dies suddenly on 4 December at the age of 55. The Alex Lindsay Memorial Award for young musicians is established by his orchestral colleagues in 1975.
John Chisholm, aged 27, becomes acting concertmaster.
An Orchestral Supporters Club is started by cellist Wilfred Simenauer. Membership later exceeds 2000.

1975   Name change: New Zealand Symphony Orchestra (NZSO); Radio New Zealand assumes management.

1976   American Peter Schaffer is appointed concertmaster of the NZSO. The third leader in 30 years, and the first overseas musician.
Australian Opera Company presents Verdi's *Rigoletto* (conductor: Richard Bonynge) and Janáček's *Jenůfa* (conductor: Georg Tintner), accompanied by NZSO. Radio New Zealand blames NZSO for 20 percent of its deficit.[3]
First Gold Discs: *The Great Classics*, recorded by Deutsche Grammophon, awarded 10 gold discs for sales of 50,000 records in eight weeks. Conductor: John Hopkins.

1977   Japanese conductor Michiyoshi Inoue appointed principal guest conductor (three years), conducts 30th anniversary concert, 12 March.
NZBC restructured to BCNZ, Broadcasting Corporation of New Zealand. NZSO becomes independent separate entity under BCNZ. Peter Nisbet is appointed general manager and artistic director and part of RNZ Music Section

GORDON G. CLARKE

amalgamates with NZSO. The Music Library is divided between Radio New Zealand and NZSO.

NZSO departs 38 The Terrace after 14 years, prior to the building's demolition.

1978	New home: Symphony House, McDonald's Building, 132 Willis Street. A 1920s, three-storey brick building, two dilapidated wooden houses, one demolished for carpark. Orchestral studio previously a billiards saloon. First Summer Pops tour, 18 concerts conducted by the British conductor and composer Ron Goodwin.
1979	First performance on a marae: Turangawaewae Marae, in the presence of Dame Te Arikinui Atairangikaahu, the Maori Queen. 'A Night in Vienna' concert, conductor: John Georgiardis, in association with Taniwharau Culture Group and its leader, Reverend Napi Waaka.

The Eighties 1980   *Concert Pitch* launched: the orchestra's first professional magazine, free to subscribers, supporters and friends of the NZSO. Initial print run 12,000 copies, later 18,000.

February-March: second overseas tour. Featured guest orchestra at Hong Kong Arts Festival. Conductors: Michiyoshi Inoue and Owain Arwel Hughes. Ten concerts, nine programmes in Hong Kong, one in Tsuen Wan, New Territories.

First collaboration with Downstage Theatre, Wellington: *E.G.B.D.F. (Every Good Boy Deserves Favour)* by Tom Stoppard and André Previn, a play for actors and orchestra. Conducted by John Hopkins, directed by Philip Mann, with two performances each in Wellington and Auckland.

NZSO arranges transport from out-of-town for Sunday matinée performances of Gustav Mahler's *Symphony No. 8*: 500 to Wellington, 400 to Auckland.

First combined Supporters Clubs activity held in conjunction with Mahler 8 matinée concert: luncheon at Symphony House, attended by 130 supporters from groups in Hawkes Bay, Dannevirke, New Plymouth, Wanganui, and Christchurch. An annual event until 1984, when it transfers to Michael Fowler Centre.

1981   First Subscription series of early evening concerts in Auckland and Hamilton.

First major sponsorship: British Airways Corporation NZSO Study Bursary.

Royal concert for Prince Charles in Christchurch, very informal compared with earlier years.

October: First concertmaster exchange (one month): Peter Schaffer, NZSO and Donald Hazelwood OBE, Sydney Symphony Orchestra.

1982   First concert at Government House: Haydn's 250th anniversary, conducted by Sir Charles Groves, at the invitation of the Governor General, Sir David Beattie.
First TVNZ/NZSO Young Musicians Competition with sponsorship from Landmark Properties, a biennial competition for young instrumentalists. First winner: pianist Katherine Austin.
National Youth Orchestra renamed New Zealand Youth Orchestra. From 1985, New Zealand Post Youth Orchestra.
First Subscription series in Hawkes Bay.

1983   Major corporate sponsorships: Shell New Zealand Holdings Shell Scholarship for orchestral trainees; IBM for special projects.
New NZSO Steinway piano, selected by Peter Frankl, launched by seven Wellington pianists.
August: Michael Fowler Centre – first concert a 'Hard hat concert'; Conductor: Thomas Sanderling.
September: Official opening concerts conducted by William Southgate and Maximiano Valdes.

1984   German conductor Franz-Paul Decker appointed principal guest conductor for a two-year term, later extended to 1989. Chief conductor 1990-1994, Conductor Laureate 1995-.
First concerts cancelled in 38 years of touring: Napier and Auckland, due to closure of Wellington Airport by bad weather and airline industrial action.
Royal Commission of Enquiry into Broadcasting begins.
Concertmaster Peter Schaffer, his wife Zoe a horn player and David Cripps, principal horn, resign over artistic differences.
John Chisholm, assistant concertmaster and member of the Gagliano Trio, dies on 23 December, aged 37.
Combined Supporters Club and NZ Choral Federation luncheon for 400 at Michael Fowler Centre, in conjunction with NZSO Sunday Matinée Concert.
First tour with Royal New Zealand Ballet, *Swan Lake*, conductor: John Matheson, 14 performances in main centres.
World first performance of World Philharmonic Orchestra, Stockholm, conductor: Carlo Maria Giulini. NZSO is represented by Stephen Managh, violin.
First concerts to combine all major national youth music groups for Year of Youth: New Zealand Post Youth Orchestra, National Youth Band, National Youth Choir and Yamaha National Youth and College Jazz Band – 250 participants in three performances in the Wellington area.

1986	First New Zealand International Festival of the Arts, Wellington. NZSO with Joan Sutherland and Richard Bonynge. First Australasian performance of *Requiem*, by Andrew Lloyd Webber. Seen by 5000 people in four performances. New Subscription series: Tauranga, Dunedin (reinstated). American Isidor Saslav appointed fourth concertmaster. Pianist Lili Kraus dies, after 33 years relationship with New Zealand. NZSO's 40th anniversary celebrated with lunchtime concert in Wellington Town Hall. Conductor: John Hopkins, in presence of Governor General, Sir Paul Reeves. Also celebrated the Schola Musica's 25th Anniversary. Anniversary book, *The New Zealand Symphony Orchestra: The First Forty Years* (Reed Methuen), launched by Vincent Aspey.
1987	January: Donald Armstrong (NZ) appointed first associate concertmaster. NZSO performs additional Ron Goodwin Summer Pops concert as a benefit concert for the Bay of Plenty Earthquake Appeal, raising $30,000. May: Debut of New Zealand String Quartet, leader Wilma Smith, funded by Music Federation of New Zealand. August: The first orchestral exchange: cello players Vivien Chisholm, NZSO/ Hermann Backes, Düsseldorfer Symphoniker, for 12 months.
1988	Gyorgy Lehel appointed chief conductor. First job-sharing in orchestra: John and Judy Hyatt, cello players, for a five-year period. NZ Post National Youth Orchestra Australian tour, including Brisbane Expo; conductor Michael Vinten, leader Lisa Egen (first recipient of the John Chisholm Award for leader of the NZ Youth Orchestra). Soloists Michael Houstoun (piano) and Mark Te Tane Hohaia (pukaea and koauau), with Te Rangatahi Maori Group. Former Schola Musica orchestral trainee violinist Sam Konise is a finalist in TVNZ/NZSO Young Musicians Competition (and the winner in 1990). He is the first trainee from the Pacific Islands; member of Turnovsky Trio chamber group. First NZSO player granted leave to study in New Zealand: Susan-Jane Higgs, with Canterbury University-based Polish violinist Jan Tawroszewicz. Royal Commission into Broadcasting recommends disbanding Broadcasting Corporation of New Zealand. 1 December, BCNZ dissolved. NZSO becomes a Crown-Owned Entity as a limited liability company, and loses access to radio stations, financial, legal and other administrative support services.

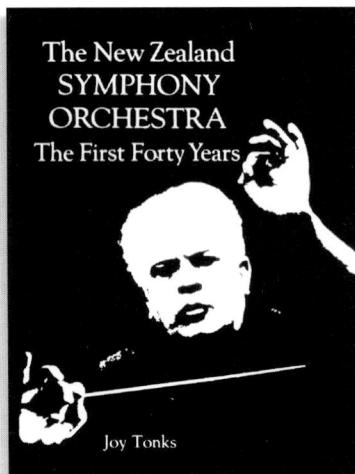

1989 February. First meeting of five-member Board of Directors appointed by Government under the chairmanship of Professor Athol Mann, Victoria University. Other members Hylton LeGrice, Rick Christie, Elizabeth Kerr and Iola Shelley. First cultural exchange, New Zealand and Finland: Finnish conductor and composer Leif Segerstam for seven concerts with NZSO, in exchange for the visit by William Southgate to Finland in 1986, 10 concerts with seven orchestras. March-October: Exchange of second oboe players: Stephen Popperwell (NZSO) and Carol Hellmers (Sydney Symphony).

September: Gyorgy Lehel, chief conductor, dies six weeks after completing his last tour with NZSO.

NZSO's first CD, works by Samuel Barber, conductor Andrew Schenck, is released early 1989; goes straight into American *Billboard* charts, and is nominated for an international award.

The orchestral training scheme Schola Musica is dis-established in its 29th year.

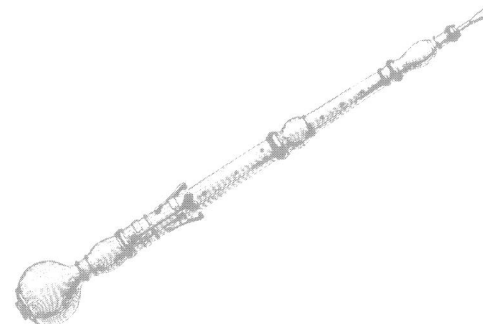

1990 Dame Kiri Te Kanawa's Homecoming Concerts, the first of the big outdoor concerts, are conducted by John Hopkins and attended by 140,000 (Auckland) and 70,000 (Wellington).

Opera at Michael Fowler Centre, third New Zealand International Festival of the Arts: *Die Meistersinger* by Wagner, NZSO conducted by Heinz Wallberg, soloist Donald McIntyre.

June-July: First Pacific Music Festival, in Sapporo, Japan, under the direction of Leonard Bernstein and Michael Tilson Thomas, with the LSO. Three young players from NZSO selected, violinists Lisa Egen and Sharon Tongs (now Callaghan) and Michael Steer, double bass.

Introduction of new assistant sub-principal positions (third chair), in second violins, violas, cellos and double bass sections.

Mini Finnish Festival (part of cultural exchange): World Premiere of symphonic work by Aulis Sallinen for New Zealand's 150th anniversary, conducted by Finnish conductor Okko Kamu.

Auckland's Aotea Centre opens: first Subscription concert in April, official opening with Dame Kiri Te Kanawa in September.

The Nineties

1991 July. Broadcasting Licence Fee phased out as a source of funding for NZSO. Direct government funding starts. Budget cut by $1.14m (15.3 percent), one month into new financial year. Drastic measures include: axing of *Concert Pitch* magazine after 36 issues in 12 years. Concerts also cancelled.

28 November: Concert to celebrate new home for NZSO, Beethoven *9* with

1er Vorstellung im vierten Abonnement.

Königlich Sächsisches Hoftheater.

Montag, den 2. Januar 1843.
Zum ersten Male:

Der fliegende Holländer.

Romantische Oper in drei Akten, von Richard Wagner.

Personen:

Daland, norwegischer Seefahrer.	Herr Risse.
Senta, seine Tochter.	Mad. Schröder-Devrient.
Erik, ein Jäger.	Herr Reinhold.
Mary, Haushälterin Dalands.	Mad. Wächter.
Der Steuermann Dalands.	Herr Bielezizky.
Der Holländer.	Herr Wächter.

Matrosen des Norwegers. Die Mannschaft des fliegenden Holländers. Mädchen.
Scene: Die norwegische Küste.

Textbücher sind an der Kasse das Exemplar für 2½ Neugroschen zu haben.

Kapell: Herr Dettmer.

Varujan Kojian, Dame Malvina Major, Heather Begg, Chris Doig, Rodney McCann and Orpheus Choir, followed by orchestra's first auction sale.

1992   January. Government purchases NZSO's first permanent home, for $1.8m: 15-year-old building, 69 Tory Street. Refurbished with assistance from NZ Lottery Grants Board.

March: general manager Peter Nisbet retires.

Graham Coxhead appointed interim general manager. New contracts negotiated under Employment Contracts Act, and first redundancies in administration and management staff.

June. NZSO's third tour, to Seville with assistance from NZ Lotteries Commission and Expo '92 organisers. Concert at Teatro de la Maestranza, conductor Franz-Paul Decker, soloist Kiri Te Kanawa. Also outdoor concert in the Plaza de San Francisco.

October: Mark Keyworth appointed first chief executive officer.

First Open Day at Symphony House attended by 3000 visitors over six hours (including short rehearsals by orchestra, guided tour of building with talks on specific areas, a display of orchestra memorabilia and the Van Lines truck).

October: A Symphony Friends group starts in Auckland.

First performance with Auckland Opera, now Opera New Zealand: *The Flying Dutchman*, Donald McIntyre.

Concertmaster Isidor Saslav completes term and returns to United States.

1993   First outdoor concerts in vineyards: Mission Estate, Hawkes Bay and Brancott Estate, Marlborough.

Wilma Smith appointed fifth concertmaster, first woman to hold the position.

Kenneth Young, NZSO principal tuba, appointed first conductor-in-residence.

Tea and Symphony concerts commence.

NZSO has funding deficit of $19,000.

1994   NZSO self-generated income reaches $3.704m. Surplus of $29,000.

Wilma Smith finalist in Arts and Culture Awards of the new Awards of New Zealand.

First performance with Wellington City Opera: Puccini's *Turandot*.

Sept: NZSO appears on the Internet (authored by Dale Gold, principal double bass), the first symphony orchestra in the world to have its own home page.

1995   Eduardo Mata appointed new principal guest conductor on 1 January, killed in plane crash 4 January.

Cancellation of NZSO tour to BBC Proms/Europe in 1996. Cancellation of tour to Hong Kong Summer Festival in 1995.

Dr Franz-Paul Decker appointed NZSO's first Conductor Laureate.

July: New Zealand Music Panel set up for New Zealand compositions.

August: NZSO Foundation launched with Corporate Concert.

November: NZSO performs at Commonwealth Heads of Government Meeting (CHOGM) in Auckland.

1996   NZSO 50th anniversary of the establishment of the National Orchestra of New Zealand on 24 October 1946.

March: debut of NZ Soloists in New Zealand International Festival of the Arts; NZSO principals with Michael Houstoun: Edward Allen, David Chickering, Dale Gold, Alexa Still, Marina Sturm, Lawrence Tilson, John Snow and Wilma Smith.

March/April: ENZSO concerts, Wellington, Christchurch, Auckland: NZSO under Peter Scholes with NZ National Youth Choir and former 'Enz' members perform the music of Split Enz; billed as 'an unprecedented fusion of NZ's premier musical talent'.

18 April: Launch of 50th anniversary season and *Bravo! The NZSO At 50*.

Pacific Entertainment in association with the NZSO and the Aotea Centre present

ENZSO

THE NEW ZEALAND SYMPHONY ORCHESTRA

Conducted by Peter Scholes

perform the Music of SPLIT ENZ

featuring

TIM NEIL DAVE SAM ANNIE
FINN FINN DOBBYN HUNT CRUMMER

EDDIE RAYNER and NOEL CROMBIE

Also featuring The New Zealand National Youth Choir

A YEAR AND A HALF IN THE PLANNING!!
OVER 100 OF OUR FINEST ARTISTS ON STAGE!!

AN UNPRECEDENTED FUSION OF NZ's PREMIER MUSICAL TALENT

NATIONAL ORCHESTRA

FIRST OFFICIAL PHOTOGRAPH, WELLINGTON TOWN HALL, 18 FEBRUARY 1947

Prelude

"I was completely overawed by the occasion... It was quite a frightening experience for a very inexperienced young player."

— *Frank Gurr, foundation clarinet player, later Principal Emeritus.*

IT is 8pm, Wednesday 6 March 1947, and the 65 members of the National Symphony Orchestra of New Zealand are assembled on stage at Wellington Town Hall with their leader Vincent Aspey, awaiting the arrival of their conductor and musical director Andersen (Andy) Tyrer.

Musicians look out onto a packed Town Hall, with an audience that includes Prime Minister Peter Fraser, who has taken a personal interest in setting up the orchestra. He is accompanied by members of his Cabinet, the Diplomatic Corps and Wellington City Council with other prominent leaders of the community. The few empty chairs are among the 200 held back for door sales at the decree of Peter Fraser, that tickets for each performance by the National Orchestra will be kept available for any citizen wishing to attend on the night.

This is a formal occasion and most concert-goers have dressed accordingly; there have been very few opportunities to do so since the war in Europe started, and the war in the Pacific is only recently ended. The programme sellers too, are formally dressed in long evening gowns, selling large grey covered programmes with a stylish coat of arms designed by Professor James Shelley, Director of Broadcasting, who has long shared the Prime Minister's dream of a permanent National Orchestra.

Anticipation is high as everyone waits for the concert to begin, their appetite whetted by the memory of the successful Centennial Orchestra seven years ago, disbanded at the start of World War II. Andersen Tyrer, conductor of that orchestra, ascends the rostrum, turns and bows profusely before launching into the National Anthem *God Save The King;* rarely has it sounded so stirring. The audience stands to attention at the first chords, then they settle back into the hard, curved-back, bentwood chairs in eager anticipation of the evening's music.

Orchestral players share their enthusiasm. This is their inaugural performance, 20 weeks after that first rehearsal on 24 October 1946. They have come a long way since that day. Two weeks of intensive rehearsal together was followed by three months apart, divided into four separate groups and dispersed to play in studio orchestras in the four main centres, to counter criticism that the National Orchestra had taken all the best local players. In February the orchestra was reunited in Wellington for another two weeks of concentrated rehearsals, culminating in this evening's concert. This has been a frustrating time for the more experienced players, but for the others, including many who have never played in an orchestra before, there has been a tremendous amount of repertoire to be learnt.

The Governor-General, returned war hero Sir Bernard Freyberg, is the only dignitary missing tonight. Disappointed at the first rehearsal because the orchestra was not ready to play publicly, and again being unable to attend tonight's concert, he was given his own private preview performance at the dress rehearsal a few days earlier, where, clearly delighted, he had stood up to return Andersen Tyrer's formal bow after each item.

The same long programme is to be performed tonight, with no soloists, and will take almost three hours. It begins with Dvořák's *Carnival Overture* and Brahms' *Symphony No. 2*, and continues after interval with Butterworth's *A Shropshire Lad*; the *Romanian Rhapsody No. 1* by Enesco; the Prelude and Liebestod from *Tristan and Isolde* by Wagner, and the Richard Strauss tone poem *Till Eulenspiegel*. This is followed by three encores, one composition each

(Above) Review by Professor J.C. Beaglehole, New Zealand Listener, 21 March 1947. (Right) Souvenir programme of the first concert, with letter from Governor General Sir Bernard Freyberg, an enthusiastic supporter of the new orchestra.

NATIONAL ORCHESTRA
OF THE NEW ZEALAND
BROADCASTING SERVICE

ONWARD

FIRST SEASON . . . 1947

WELLINGTON INAUGURAL CONCERT

TOWN HALL

Thursday, March 6th

SOUVENIR PROGRAMME   Price SIXPENCE

WELLINGTON.

24th February, 1947.

The formation of a National Orchestra is important step forward in our cultural progress which will be greatly appreciated by the music-loving section of the community.

The venture - one in which I have been personally interested for some time past - is a timely recognition of the place of music in the life of the country. It will serve to develop a greater love of music among the people as a whole, while at the same time providing a stimulus for the attainment of a higher standard of music throughout the Dominion.   I wish the Orchestra every success.

Bernard Freyberg

Governor-General.

by Johann Strauss and Percy Grainger, concluding with Weinberger's *Schwanda the Bagpiper*.

The mixed group of amateur and professional musicians who came together for the first time only five months earlier have achieved their first success, one that will be repeated throughout the country in coming months. The applause is loud and long, in an atmosphere that will be recaptured in the enthusiastic and lengthy reviews in tomorrow's newspapers.

Other reviews, namely by Professor J.C. Beaglehole in the *New Zealand Listener*, will be more critical of the programme, the playing and of conductor Andersen Tyrer, whose appointment by Government has been the cause of major complaints and controversy since its announcement nine months earlier.

*   *   *   *   *

Tonight's concert is Tyrer's reply to critics who consider him unworthy: now Beaglehole and his self-indulgent review are targets for criticism. A professional New Zealand orchestra is a reality and for audiences and radio listeners, new doors have opened.

It took a shared vision and determination to create the orchestra and to provide a secure environment, through Broadcasting, for it to grow and develop. There have always been critics as there are for any art form. Inevitably there will always be controversy, mainly concerning costs, but the orchestra survived and flourished for four decades. It was in its fifth that everything changed.

(Below Left) The first performance of the National Symphony Orchestra of New Zealand, conductor Andersen Tyrer, leader Vincent Aspey, Wellington Town Hall, 6 March 1947. (Below) An enthusiastic review from next day's Evening Post.

NZSO COLLECTION

The principal number performed was the Brahms Symphony. It proved to be a happy choice by reason of its great tonal beauty, warmth, and colour and the mystical serenity incidental to the adagio, or second movement; and the whole work was brought to a magnificent close. In the performance of this particular work the orchestra distinguished itself by display of its sound musicianship, and especially so when calls were made upon individual players, as, for instance, violin, 'cello, flute, oboe, horn as the need arose.

Following the imposing Brahms music, came "A Shropshire Lad" as something essentially English in character (as it is). Simple music, but meaningful, evoked by the lyrical spirit of the poetry to which it seemed perfectly mated.

The Enesco Rhapsody, remarkable for its beauty of form, orchestral texture and wild rhythm captivated the audience. In this, at times, frenzied music the orchestra deserved well of its moulder and conductor. The applause following the Rhapsody was unusually demonstrative and resulted in Johann Strauss's "Moto Perpetuo" being played to restore quiet. The Prelude and Liebestod from "Tristan and Isolde" was remarkable not only for its own beauty but also for the fine artistry displayed in its performance. Richard Strauss's "Till Eulenspiegel" brought the programme to its official end, but its audacious dissonances, its merry and noisy humour so affected the audience at large that it declined to move. It was successful in its demands for more when the orchestra had played Percy Grainger's "Handel in the Strand" (orchestrated by the late Sir Henry Wood) and "Schwander the Bagpiper" (Weinberger).

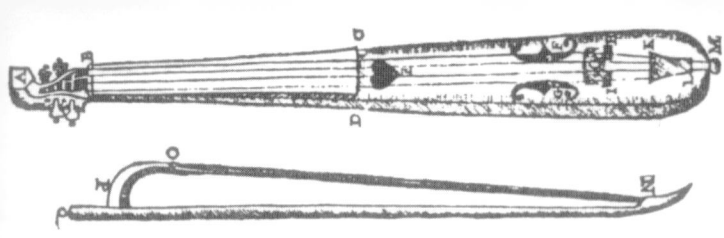

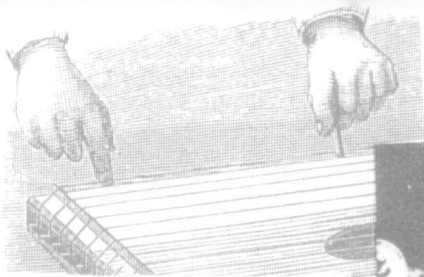

The Players

"Facing an orchestra is like facing lions." – Juan Matteucci, former resident conductor.

Mike Gibbs (left) and Albert (Fuzzy) MacKinnon warming up backstage.

TOURS were longer, travel more casual and hotels 'grotty' when John Dodds first joined the National Orchestra in 1955. Going south then meant "overnighting on the ferry, trying to find breakfast at Christchurch railway station, then wandering down to find the cheapest pub in town. The daily allowance was so meagre, just to try and survive you had to find the cheapest – and some were pretty grotty. Then rehearsal at the old Civic Theatre; it was so cold you had to sit with your coat around your legs to try and keep the circulation going."

Travelling has always played a big role in the life of NZSO musicians, once called 'the world's most travelled orchestra'. Large chunks of a musician's life were spent not making music but travelling. It is not so long ago that retiring players at their farewell party would quote the amount of time they had spent on tour with the orchestra. For Peter Glen, principal horn for 36 years, it was nine years. Jet travel in the early 1960s and funding cuts in the 1990s have reduced that time considerably.

John Dodds, principal second violin, is typical of the more varied background of players in previous years. He was a qualified joiner before the orchestra employed him in 1955, opting out after three years for a more varied lifestyle – working as a service station manager, a sales supervisor in office machinery, a coach driver and joiner. All were jobs he could combine with music, leading the John Ritchie Strings, or playing as a casual for the National and Concert orchestras until returning permanently in 1967.

John says he retains that sense of a wider world out there, which gives him a much broader experience of life than many of his colleagues, who have worked all their lives in music.

TOM SHANAHAN

TOM SHANAHAN

Backstage, Wellington Town Hall, before Vincent Aspey's (Left) last concert with the orchestra. Also shown: Gordon Skinner, Vincent Aspey Jr, Ted Pople John Dodds and Luigi Ferletti.

Even by the 1950s conditions on tour were not ideal, John recalls: "Footing it down the street to find a fish and chip shop; hotels where the bathrooms were always at the other end of the building; and being woken up at 6:00am with the rattle of tea cups; the door would burst open, with a cup of tea and a wine biscuit thrust at you. If you asked for no milk or sugar, they'd say 'Well don't stir it!'"

The real pioneers were the foundation players in the 1940s. Recruited from broadcasting studio orchestras, dance bands, brass and military bands, they were viewed like visitors from another planet when on tour in smaller centres. They had to conceal evening suits and formal dresses under coats, with their violin cases, as they ate their pies on street corners after the concert – because nothing else was open.[23]

It took two days to get from Wellington to Dunedin or Invercargill. Across Cook Strait by ferry, then a 12-hour journey on a coal-fired train; playing cards, knitting, trying to read or catch up on last night's broken sleep and waking up with nose, and eyes and ears full of cinders. But there was always Timaru, a gastronomic highlight – everyone knew it had the best pies.

One tour of the South Island took nine weeks; most took six, with a few concerts and interminable rehearsals in between. It was a great adventure, with great spirit among players and an entirely new experience: giving concerts where none had been heard before, for audiences that queued to buy tickets as soon as bookings opened.

There were few professionals; most had 'proper' jobs outside of music because there were few inside: musicians needed a second string, so to speak. They had all taken a risk, thrown away regular jobs to join an orchestra that might not last, as so many others had failed. The older string players gave it six months, maybe twelve and then they expected to be back teaching and playing in studio orchestras again. But this orchestra was here to stay.

Now

Today's players may still feel conspicuous, walking down Queen Street in tails after a concert, but otherwise few similarities remain. Most are fully professional musicians who have entered the orchestra from conservatories, universities or music schools, with training stretching back to early childhood and little or no experience of any other work except making music.

This orchestra is younger, though the age span is almost 40 years, from the mid-20s to early 60s. One third of players are women, more than in some European orchestras, and now there are two section principals, Alexa Still (flute) and Marina Sturm (clarinet), leading all-women sections. The first woman principal in a non-string section was Heather Anderson, as co-principal horn in 1981. She resigned in 1983, rejoining the section in 1995.

The NZSO has a range of nationalities, and a wealth of experience from around the world yet it remains distinctly a New Zealand orchestra. Both concertmasters, and two-thirds of musicians come from cities and towns throughout the country; Christchurch, with its tradition of high quality children's music and tuition, can claim the most.

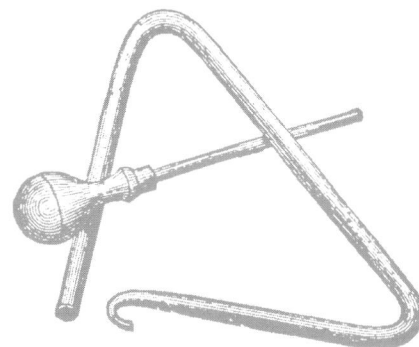

Ex-pats

The enormous turnover in personnel was what struck violist Lyndsay Mountfort when he returned after four years away and found one quarter of players were newcomers. He also noticed how much younger his NZSO colleagues looked, compared with their contemporaries in London orchestras, without the hardness and cynicism he had found over there. "I'd look at players I knew were 50-60 and they looked 10 years younger." Not only in looks either, but in their attitude to all aspects of musical life: to colleagues, conductors and music.

A trainee for three years, then an NZSO member for four, Lyndsay left in late 1986, returning in 1991. "I enjoyed my four years in London. Freelancing is always a little bit stressful; you never know what is coming next, but the quality and quantity of work was improving steadily. In the end I think London's a good place to visit but it's no place for human beings to live."

Lyndsay is one of a significant number of NZSO musicians who have spent years overseas, studying and working in other orchestras, often establishing successful careers. In the highly competitive world of music 'OE' (overseas experience) is still relevant for young players, who will benefit from the exposure to standards that are hard to find in a small, isolated country. Whether they have been away one year or twenty, the time always seems to come when the urge to return home becomes irresistible.

Invercargill violinist Michael Monaghan, who lived in Germany for 17 years, knows the feeling. He joined the NZBCSO after two years as a trainee, then in 1971 began studies at

Michael Monaghan, first violins: returning to play with the NZSO was "100 percent the right decision."

STEPHEN LA PLANT

the West German Music Academy in Detmold, with a scholarship for students from 'culturally undeveloped countries'. He returned briefly to play in the NZSO in 1975, then took up subsequent appointments with the South West German Chamber Orchestra, the West German Radio Orchestra, and for the next eight years, the Deutsche Oper am Rhein/Düsseldorfer Symphoniker, where, as its president, he represented the orchestra on the city's Cultural Board.

In 1986 Michael and the family returned home on holiday. He worked as a casual in the NZSO and found it "comparable to any good orchestra in Europe". Two years later they came home to stay. "I am a New Zealander and I came back for my children. They grew up in Germany and I wanted them to have an idea of what New Zealand was like." The conditions here could not compare with those in the 130-piece orchestra he had left, and he would miss the cultural assets of Europe, but Mike had no doubts it was the right decision: "The older you get the more compromises you have to make, and you learn how to do this and decide what is more important to you as a human being. It was 100 percent the right decision."

Violinist Rebecca Jackson left home at 18 to study in London, and stayed on to freelance in English orchestras. She had been away nine years and was about to accept a job in Scotland

(Above) Trumpeters Yoram Levy, John Taber (principal) and Marc Taddei (principal trombone), with principal horn Ed Allen, at Christmas in the Park, Auckland Domain, 1994. (Right) NZSO cricket team with cheerleaders after a friendly game against The Royal New Zealand Ballet, Kilbirnie Park, Wellington, 1995.

when she decided to come home. She auditioned and was accepted by the NZSO, where she knew no one.

"Absolutely not one person! I came from Nelson, went straight overseas; I was in the Youth Orchestra but was 14 or 15, so young I did not socialise. In London people did not believe I was a New Zealander because they would ask if I knew so-and-so and I did not know anyone!"

All three agree that auditioning for the NZSO was a daunting experience. Having made the decision to come home, she felt much was at stake. "It was horrible!" says Rebecca, who recorded her audition tape in a church. "I started this recording, it was the Mozart A major, that lovely little slow bit, and there was this almighty roar of a jet taking off from Heathrow. There was this continual noise for three hours. It was a disaster, very stressful."

In Germany Mike hired an expensive recording studio, and the piano was half a tone flat, "so I had to abandon the piano but I couldn't get another time. I had about half an hour to whip through it just trying to finish before the time ran out. Totally unsatisfactory! Tape auditions are dreadful; you can't put any of your personality across."

Lyndsay came home for his audition. But auditioning live was just as traumatic. "It was

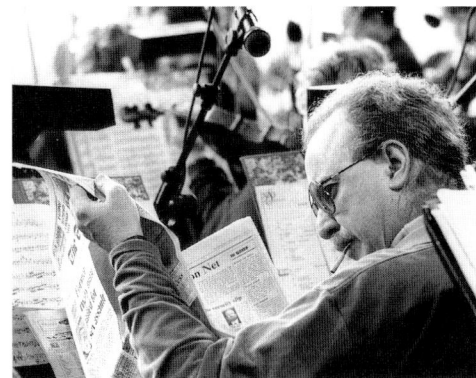

(*Above*) *Stephen Popperwell, second oboe and chairman of the Players Committee, at Opera at the Basin rehearsal, 1994. (Left) Mark Carter warming up in basement of Wellington Town Hall.*

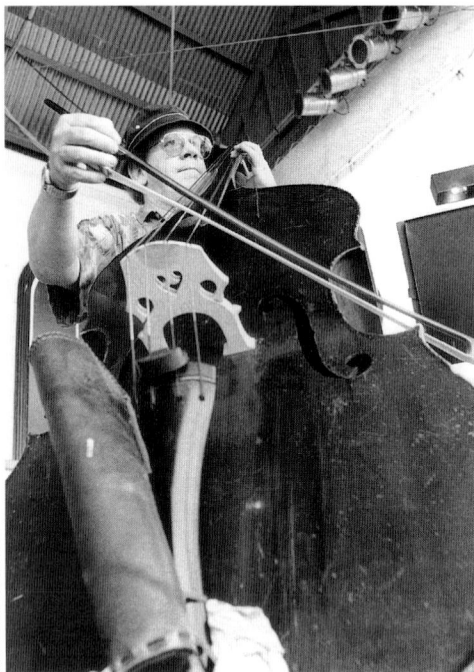

Barry Johnstone, double bass.

the worst audition experience I had ever had, and I had done a lot of them in Britain. Even big name orchestras are nothing in comparison. If you mess it up, even in London, you can walk out and do another for someone else next week. There isn't anyone else to audition for here."

Rebecca remembers it as a difficult time: "This is why it was stressful – it was the end of the line, you were coming home."

High profile principal flute Alexa Still did her audition tape "for the experience". She was in the United States, part-way through her doctorate at the State University at Stony Brook, New York, when she heard of Richard Giese's retirement. She did not expect to get the job because she was a woman and there were so few in principal chairs. She still believed this even when offered a trial, but thought: "Good. A free trip home!" Alexa was 23, the NZSO's youngest, and only woman principal, when she took up the job in July 1987. Knowing that her predecessor had held the chair for 24 years, she accepted. "If I didn't, someone else would get it and it wouldn't come up again!"

Since her return to New Zealand with her American husband, bass player Bob Adair, Alexa has successfully combined her NZSO work with a growing reputation as a solo performer, receiving acclaim for her recent recordings, three of which in 1994 received separate nominations for a Grammy Award.

Former Orchestral Trainees/ Schola Musica

The NZSO's former orchestral training scheme, known latterly as the Schola Musica, has been the greatest single source of players for the orchestra. Thirty-five years after it was formed, almost one third of the current NZSO are ex-trainees, either having graduated into the orchestra immediately after training, or after further study overseas.

String players are in the majority but two players remain still from the years when other instruments were included in the scheme: Barry Johnstone, a trainee trombonist for two years, joined the NZSO as a double bass player briefly in 1970, and then continuously since 1974. Irish horn player Bill Ryan came to New Zealand with his family, joined the trainees in 1968 and the orchestra in 1969.

Jane Freed, second violins, was in the first intake of nine trainees in 1961, and says: "It was great, really fantastic. A very exciting time and we knew we were very lucky: being paid to practise and be taught! We learnt all the Tchaikovsky, all the Brahms, and Beethoven first and second violin parts and John Hopkins would test us; we worked hard to impress him."

Jane completed a second trainee year, then spent 10 years overseas in the Bournemouth Symphony, Welsh National Opera, freelancing with London orchestras, the Royal Ballet, Covent Garden and Hamburg Orchestra. She returned home in the 70s, was leader of the Wellington Regional Orchestra, and joined the NZSO in 1983.

Lisa Egen was in one of the Schola Musica's last intakes, from 1986-87. By her last year she was playing 50 percent of her time as a temporary in the orchestra. This continued for several months until on her third audition she was accepted for a permanent position. Lisa was leader of the New Zealand Post Youth Orchestra at Brisbane Expo 1988, and was first recipient of the John Chisholm Award. She was selected for the Pacific Rim Youth Orchestra in Japan and played under conductors Michael Tilson Thomas and Leonard Bernstein. While there she became interested in the viola, studied it in London for eight months and, following a successful audition, has transferred to the viola section.

There is a big difference between the Schola Musica, she says, "and doing a music degree at university where you concentrate on concertos, sonatas and scales. The Schola taught you how to play the repertoire, how to play in a section, how to listen to each other and how to follow the conductor. Young players auditioning now often cannot play with what's going on around them, they can't listen. If I feel I missed out on anything it was the training for life, going straight from school to Schola to the orchestra when I was only 19, the youngest member for six, almost seven years."

The argument about foreign players taking jobs "that should be held by New Zealanders" goes back to the early days of the National Orchestra. It was the proud boast of first conductor Andersen Tyrer that he had filled all positions for the National Orchestra from within New Zealand. And he had: four out of every five were born here. But the orchestra had its share

Players from Overseas

André Malashenko, former principal timpanist from Canada, rehearsing at Auckland Domain, 1994.

GRAEME BROWNE

of overseas players even then, émigrés from Europe. John Dronke, a former judge, Eve Christeller, Erica Schorss and Greta Ostova had had the benefit of training and musical experience unimaginable in the New Zealand of the 1940s, where the majority of 'Nat Orch' players had no experience of professional orchestras.

Tyrer's initial success in keeping recruitment within New Zealand could not be repeated as standards rose and the inevitable gaps occurred. Few musicians met the required standard. Of those who did, not all wanted to take on the demanding lifestyle of a professional orchestral musician, with the travel involved at that time.

In 1947, only one year after the orchestra was set up, Andersen Tyrer with Government approval set out for Britain to audition players. Even the Musicians Union agreed that no replacements were available in New Zealand, so Tyrer personally recruited the first overseas players: four violins, two flutes and one french horn.

This was the start of a steady stream of British players, recruited for all positions, over the next two decades. Various systems were developed to screen and audition them with the assistance of the New Zealand High Commission and the BBC's Head of Music. Former resident conductor James Robertson played a valuable role in assessing prospective players until the late 1970s.

The Russian Connection

In July 1950 the first of four highly trained Russian musicians, viola player Ivan Federoff, joined the orchestra. As an outstanding boy soprano, soloist in the St Petersburg Imperial Capella, the best in Russia, Ivan Federoff was awarded an engraved gold watch from the last Tsar of Russia. Trained at the Imperial Conservatory of Music in St Petersburg, he played for three years in the Moscow Symphony Orchestra directed and conducted by Serge Koussevitsky. He was first violinist and sometimes soloist with the Imperial Orchestra of St Petersburg for four years, spending five years in Tomsk, Siberia, during the Revolution – where he taught in the Conservatoire and conducted opera.

Interned as a White Russian for almost five months, he was released because he was a musician, then returned to Leningrad (St Petersburg) where he was engaged as a violinist and soloist with the Academic Philharmonic. After leaving Russia he taught music for five years in Shanghai, then moved to Java where he taught and played in orchestras for 21 years. He joined the Radio Symphony in Jakarta in 1935, and was conductor of that orchestra from 1939-49. He was interned again, as a naturalised Dutchman, in a concentration camp in Java during the war.

Ivan Federoff conducted many first performances of now standard works, including a studio performance of the *1812 Overture* in June 1952.

Vladimir Gerasimuck too, escaped from Russia into China and then to Indonesia. "He was a very wonderful trumpet player," conductor James Robertson told me, "very distinguished,

not too noisy, lovely, lovely playing." Ten years after joining the orchestra his career was cut short when he was hit by a truck on a pedestrian crossing while on tour in Auckland. He never fully recovered from his injuries.

Vladimir Latyshew, a bass player, and his son Victor, a violinist, arrived via Australia where Victor had been playing. Vladimir was born in Moscow, trained at the Academy of Music and played in symphony and chamber orchestras in Kiev and Odessa, then spent the next 22 years in Bucharest as a member of the Romanian Symphony Orchestra. He played opera in Katowitz in Poland during the war, and from 1946-49 was first principal bass of the International Symphony Orchestra in Munich – in which Victor, who was born in Romania, was second concertmaster. Victor left the National Orchestra after three years while Vladimir stayed on long after retirement age, as principal bass for the last five years.

The classical training of these four musicians and their extensive orchestral experience was appreciated by former resident conductors James Robertson and John Hopkins, who credit them with helping to raise standards in the National Orchestra.

In 1985 another Russian joined the orchestra. Yury Gezentsvey was in Venezuela when pianist Monique Duphill told him about the concertmaster's job that was advertised. Of New Zealand he knew nothing, but he had seen a publication: "The only photo I saw was of running

Cellos, basses, woodwinds and brass in rehearsal, Tower Beethoven Festival, November 1995.

GRAEME BROWNE

people, green surroundings and many, many people running. And when I was telling some people I was going to New Zealand I had some difficulties to explain exactly where, because one of the TV channels had a map of the world behind the news reader, and they did not have anything there in the corner of Australia. There was Australia and there was nothing else. So [people were] asking, "Why are you going there? There is nothing there!" Bravely he set out for this unknown country, to taste his first memory of New Zealand, "clean air and delicious apples".

Concert Orchestra

Principal harp Carolyn Mills arrived from the United States in 1989.

The ill-fated Concert Orchestra (1962-64) set up to accompany the New Zealand Opera, and the New Zealand Ballet was a voracious devourer of musicians. Constant touring combined with unsatisfactory pay and working conditions led to player dissatisfaction and quickly exhausted limited local musical resources. Overseas musicians filled the gaps but the turnover was high. A few of these itinerant musicians – including some recommended by 'friendly' overseas management – had drinking and behavioural problems.

On the other hand several imported players later became highly respected members of the NZSO. Principal violist Vyvyan Yendoll, who arrived in 1962, is the last of the British imports from the 1960s, who included principal bass clarinet Walter Hamer, who died in 1994, and principal clarinet Alan Gold (not a Chamber Orchestra member), who retired in 1993.

As a young player, recently graduated from the Royal Academy of Music in London, Vyvyan jumped at the opportunity to travel to New Zealand, seeing the Concert Orchestra as a training ground for orchestral playing and the experience of working in a different country. The conditions were not the best but he remembers the time with nostalgia:

"A kaleidoscope of operas, ballet, concerts in the smallest towns with filthy orchestral pits, dressing rooms smelling of sweat and grease paint, makeshift orchestral unpacking areas – one a coal-room; long bus rides, even longer tours, many different conductors and a very high turnover of players."

When the orchestra was disbanded many of its remaining members joined the Symphony Orchestra, swelling its numbers to over 100 players.

The Americans

By the mid-1960s the United States with its bottomless pool of orchestral players was replacing Britain as the most effective source for orchestral recruitment, often with assistance from the National Orchestra Association. Former principal flute Richard Giese was the first American musician to arrive in 1962, and former principal trumpet John Taber, from Boston, arrived two years later, aged 23. It was a different New Zealand then and a very different orchestra, according to John:

"It was quite a culture shock, being so much influenced by Britain and British philosophies in those days... The orchestra was a great bunch of people, very different from today and we had a lot more fun. Of course the technical standard was not so good but I do think the concerts had far more heart and spirit in them than they do today. I learned a lot from John Hopkins, because we played so much repertoire and it was marvellous, a lot of 20th century music I have not played since."

John served in the President's Band in Washington and held principal positions with the Montreal Symphony, under Franz-Paul Decker; the Hague Philharmonic; and the Orchestre National Bordeaux-Aquitaine, before returning to New Zealand in 1992 for the Seville Expo tour under Franz-Paul Decker.

Percussionist Bud Jones had one of the most unusual reasons for coming to New Zealand. He knew the country from *National Geographic* magazines and visited in 1965 with a jazz band as part of a Far East and South Pacific tour.

Bud, as a teacher with a degree, and as a student working on a post-graduate degree in Public School Administration, had both a teachers' and student deferment when the build-up for Vietnam began – until that day in 1966 when all deferments were dropped. He was 23. The first call-up was for those aged 22 years and nine months, and it was not long before a certain letter arrived:

"Greetings from the President of the United States," it said. "Congratulations on becoming a member of the United States Armed Forces" – and told him to report to a certain government building.

"So that was it, I was out of there," says Bud. "I got in my car, drove hell for leather to San Francisco and caught the *Oriana* to New Zealand. I had my ticket, my drum case and a suitcase when I landed in Auckland and six £10 notes when I changed my U.S. money – plus one American dollar I couldn't change, that I carry with me today."

He became a music teacher at Hamilton Boys' High School and joined the National Orchestra under Juan Matteucci soon afterwards. Bud still remembers that first day in the orchestra. "I was scared to death. I had not played much symphony stuff for three or four years, and had been playing drums in a jazz band – so I arrived early. Nothing was set up, the whole thing was in disarray, nothing seemed organised and I thought 'Oh no! what am I going to play?' They were all just standing around smoking, very friendly but I was ready to start work. I didn't think I was going to survive the first day! But we started and played and they said 'Just bang on the cymbal here and there' and it all seemed to come together. It was quite relaxed and completely disorganised! It's something maybe I've come to appreciate, a kinda Kiwi way, that it will all come together and there's no great hassle. It wasn't very good but we didn't get fired and on concert night the orchestra played its damnedest. There was a terrific spirit then."

The FBI kept tabs on Bud for years until Uncle Sam, in the guise of President Nixon, forgave him and he could return to the States. By then New Zealand had become home.

Bud Jones, rehearsing for the 1995 BP Summer Pops Tour.

STEPHEN HARKER

Bud retained his American citizenship, unlike principal horn Ed Allen who joined the NZSO after 19 years with the Utah Symphony and became a New Zealander in 1992. It used to be quite a culture shock for some overseas players accustomed to living in big cities, with restaurants and a night life. Dale Gold, principal double bass, came here in the 1970s, having grown up in Chicago, trained at the Curtis Institute and played in the Atlanta Symphony and Philadelphia Orchestra.

"Twenty years ago they used to say: 'New Zealand is like California twenty years ago' – now New Zealand has more of its own personality and things have caught up." We now have almost as many benefits (and problems) as those large American cities, plus airfares have dropped so it is easy to return to the States for the long orchestral summer break.

The Inca Invasion

Back in 1965, resident conductor Juan Matteucci and Broadcasting's Head of Music Malcolm Rickard embarked on the orchestra's most adventurous recruitment campaign, for players in North, South and Central America and Europe. The result was 'The Inca Invasion'. Violinist Ron Jara is the last remaining member of that small group from Latin America, who arrived in New Zealand speaking very little English and with some exaggerated ideas about what they were coming to.

Juan Matteucci was the linking factor. Although they knew next to nothing about New Zealand, which had no embassy in Chile or direct transport link, they knew maestro Matteucci as the former resident conductor of the Chile Philharmonic Orchestra. Together with other recruits, four members of that orchestra were accepted and made the long journey to New Zealand via the United States. They were in for a shock, Ron remembers:

"New Zealand was very quiet. The bars closed at 6:00pm and there was very little to do after that. There was no coffee, only three kinds of cheese and no drinkable wine. Language was an enormous problem and the cost of living was very high. They called us the Spanish Armada – because everyone left after three months!"

From the start there were misunderstandings about conditions, some as a result of the language barrier, others because they had not received the assistance they expected. All found it difficult to adjust to life here. One by one these players left New Zealand but Ron Jara stayed on and later married American Nancy Luther, principal piccolo, who arrived in April 1973.

Recruitment

From the mid-1960s onwards rank and file vacancies, mainly strings, were filled by orchestral trainees, young New Zealand musicians – the best possible source, so it was no longer necessary to import players. The orchestra was becoming more stable, as conditions improved with two large pay increases during the 1970s providing a professional salary scale. Vacancies dropped and the average annual turnover was four players.

During the 1980s overseas recruitment began to increase again at principal or occasionally sub-principal level. A flurry of early retirements had followed changes to the superannuation scheme, providing optional retirement for those aged 50, instead of 65 years. It proved irresistible to many orchestral members and long-held chairs began to change hands, sometimes after 30 years or more.

The Government recruitment policy at that time permitted overseas appointments, provided no New Zealander was suitable. There was a list of preferred immigrants and musicians were not on it. The result was a very lengthy recruitment process: local auditions were held first, then if no appointment was made, the position was re-advertised locally and overseas for a further round of auditions. Approval of entry for an overseas player was far from certain even at this point and once here they were not made to feel welcome. It was not possible to make an appointment, so professional players had to leave rehearsals to wait hours in a queue at the local immigration office. That procedure changed with the introduction of the points system in the 1990s.

Violinist Mabel Wong and violist Philip Rose from the New Orleans Symphony Orchestra were the first NZSO players to benefit from this change. They had loved it here on holiday in 1992 and the points system, based on age, health, qualifications and work experience,

Double bass players (from left): Robert Adair, Barry Johnstone, Vicki Jones (sub-principal) and Dale Gold (principal).

GRAEME BROWNE

Principal trombone Marc Taddei, who arrived in New Zealand in 1987 from New Jersey, says: "It's good to see positions being filled by New Zealanders. It's testimony that there are some good teachers in New Zealand now and good programmes up and running."

Downside: Occupational Health Issues

enabled them to return "on a flyer" without jobs. It was then or never, before points were lost because of age. They came prepared to do any work until orchestral jobs turned up and as luck would have it, auditions had been scheduled. Philip was appointed in February 1994 and Mabel engaged for contract work.

The orchestra impressed them "as a group that enjoys being together and feels like an extended family, where foreigners could fit in because so many players had studied overseas. Although isolated geographically, there was a very cosmopolitan outlook on orchestral playing, and the NZSO seemed so much more part of the world in its awareness of the orchestral scene". Concert attendances were higher than they had seen anywhere else – but so too was the work load: 25 hours per week (at times, five concerts in four days under three conductors) compared with 20 hours in the States.

Today overseas musicians make up one third of the orchestra, including Satomi (Suzuki) Badley from Japan who came to New Zealand with her husband Alan whom she met while studying in Vienna. Satomi joined the NZSO in 1989, 20 years after principal oboe Hironao Kuwashima, the NZSO's first musician from Japan, who was killed in a car crash on the way to a Wanganui concert in 1971. Violist imports include Norbert Heuser from Germany, Sandro Costantino (who resigned in 1995) from the Dominican Republic, and Jenaro Garita from Costa Rica. Violinist Janet Armstrong is from Zimbabwe.

The early retirement of double bass player Michael Steer during 1995, after two years on ACC leave, highlights the problem of OOS (Occupational Overuse Syndrome, formerly known as RSI) in the NZSO and its effect on musicians whose work involves a repetitive action.

A trainee for three years, Michael trained at the prestigious Curtis Institute before joining the NZSO in 1986. In his case the condition built up slowly, becoming a serious medical problem as he prepared for an audition in autumn 1993. He pushed on for some considerable time, when he should have stopped playing completely.

"I suffered most over the last two years from the anxiety of ill-defined disability. To lose one's job in the orchestra is perhaps manageable; to lose one's ability to play altogether can be devastating. When one has difficulty holding a pen or tying one's shoelaces life has to take on a new meaning."

Still in his early thirties, he is developing a new career as a dealer in modern and post-war collectables. "With careful management I can perform an ever-increasing range of activity within the limits of my OOS. I have not given up hope of being able to return to some sort of playing again in the future."

NZSO members cannot help but feel affected by what has happened to colleagues like Michael Steer. Violinist Katherine Rowe: "I didn't worry about things like OOS, when I joined. I could just pick up the violin and play. Now, approaching my 30s, I have to be more careful. There's a lot more responsibility in the orchestra towards things like warm-up classes before work; people wear earplugs; they used to think it looked stupid. People are more aware now."

Some injuries are sustained far from the concert stage. Former principal timpanist Gary Brain was on an overseas flight in 1989 when a steel case fell out of an overhead locker onto his wrist. Two years and eight operations later he faced the fact that his days of orchestral playing and giving school concerts were over. He was then in his forties with no other training. The award of a fellowship from the French Foreign Affairs Ministry enabled him to train as a conductor in Paris, from where he is now building an international career.

Ed White used his physics training to design the NZSO's travelling bass cases in the 1970s. In the 1980s he developed sound deflectors – perspex screens on a music stand base, to place between sections. These have helped, but did not solve the problem investigated for ACC by retired broadcaster Ray Morrison.

Hearing tests on players began under the auspices of the Department of Health in the old Symphony House and continue under NZSO. In the past decade several players have had to retire due to hearing loss.

This continues to be a serious problem for the NZSO, according to Robert Ibell, chairperson of the NZSO's Health and Safety Committee, despite five major investigations by specialists between 1980-1995, with follow-up action taken as a result. "Now legislative and financial constraints, (ACC and levies), have put further pressure on the Company, to force it to take additional action to reduce sound levels to safe limits for all players.

"We are also exploring other avenues: large shield prototypes are being constructed and tested and we have been lent electronic earmuffs to try – but they are not suitable in their current form. Perhaps nothing will succeed in reducing sound levels to within safe limits. The studio may just be too small – and it's not cost-effective to increase its size. Most other orchestras in the world rehearse in [their own] performing venue; the NZSO does not and already the search for another new home has begun."

"It's happening everywhere," says Roger Lloyd, former artistic manager and clarinettist, of hearing loss and tinnitus, the scourge of musicians worldwide. "People have been playing in orchestras for three centuries, in big orchestras for the last century; how is it we are going deaf?" His belief is that instruments are getting louder: particularly the brass in the last 50-60 years, and "woodwind are constructed so that they are powerful and penetrating – they have got to be to get through all this racket. You are sitting there with a 250-year-old violin; you can't make that louder so you have to have more people". It does not help if the conductor too is going deaf – and demands "Louder please!".

Hearing

Bassoon section (from left) Lawrence Tilson (principal), David Angus, Wendy Cooper.

GRAEME BROWNE

Trumpet player Gil Evans suffered a hearing problem after 32 years as an NZSO member, 52 years after he began playing as a seven-year-old. In those days no one had any idea that playing the trumpet could be a health hazard. Teeth and mouth are traditional problem areas for brass players, Gil says, but "the last thing you expect is for your hearing to go".

But something did go, and he actually heard it, in the pit playing for the ballet *Cinderella*. There may have been a build-up, he thinks: the Summer Pops Tour, recording sessions and then the ballet. "We had done the rehearsals and at the first matinée, at the end of the second act where there is a big climax with wood blocks and all sorts of things – all of a sudden, snap!" He felt it at the back of the head but did not think too much about it then, although it was sore, until it happened again at the evening performance – and in the same place. This time it was severe tinnitus and pain, but without hearing loss.

In the 10 months that followed, Gil field-tested earplugs for the first time ("It's like retraining") and kept trying to go back to work. "I had been short-blowing to keep my chops in, but after awhile I found that when I got to the top of the stave then everything went berserk inside my head again. I was starting to get nauseous and off-balance and still cannot get up to the top of the stave to keep it going consistently, without it hurting."

Gil Evans does not know if it will improve, as he has been told each case is individual. Now he is learning to be a house-husband for Sharyn, his wife in the second violins, and says,

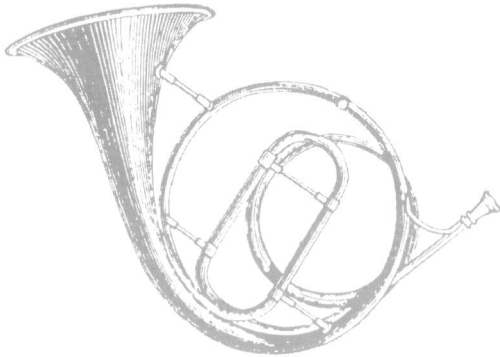

Peter Sharman and Ed Allen (principal horn) in rehearsal.

GRAEME BROWNE

"Even if I've finished playing, I have had a marvellous time. I wish I could do it all over again."

In the past few years the costs of health problems like these have been devastating, both in human terms and for the NZSO. It's not only big health issues like OOS and hearing. Fingers and hands are precious tools for a musician, the kitchen and garden a danger zone. Even a minor skirmish with a potato peeler can mean a major disaster for a string or wind player. Roger Lloyd: "The silliest things make it impossible to do your job, a little nick off your finger means you can't actually cover the hole and stop the air coming out – therefore you can't play".

The smallest injury can mean weeks off work and a replacement engaged. Often once the injury is better, the unrehearsed musician may have the frustration of waiting for a programme change before returning to work, requiring the casual player to stay on.

Feuds between desk-partners are not unusual in orchestras. Overseas one hears horrendous stories of musicians who share a stand but have not spoken for years, or do so only through their lawyers. Players could face a life-sentence sharing a desk with an incompatible partner, like two former cellists who used to jealously measure the space between chairs. New players could wait several years for a more senior colleague to leave before they could move up in their section.

Rotation

All that changed with the introduction of a rotation system for NZSO string sections, introduced by former concertmaster Isidor Saslav. Now players change seats with each new conductor, moving one back down the inside desks, round the corner and up towards the front again, each section administering its own complicated rotation roster.

"It's very refreshing, you get to know everybody and therefore become more tolerant and more adaptable – and more amused," says violinist Jane Freed.

The majority of players seem to agree but some, like cellist Christopher Salmon, fear that it adversely affects orchestral discipline: "A newcomer can join the orchestra and instead of starting at the back and working their way up, they can find themselves sitting in the second or third desk within weeks. They no longer have respect for the position, nor for the other players in the section."

There is a real advantage in being able to sit closer to the front, where all the action is. It is good musically and for the personal development of the individual, and also ensures that boredom and lethargy (the why-bother-no-one-can-hear-me-back-here syndrome) have no chance to set in.

Players may still find themselves seated beside a disagreeable colleague, but for probably no longer than a month, and with any luck the new conductor's tour will be a short one – and then it will be time to change partners again.

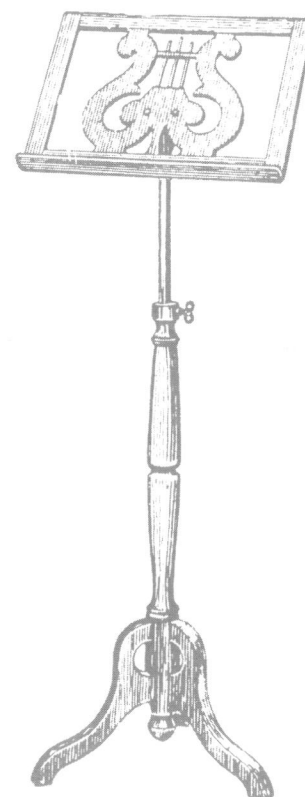

The Study Bursary

For over 30 years the orchestra has recognised the need for young players and those in mid-career to extend their musical horizons. The orchestral study bursary began in 1963, a scheme possibly without precedent in other orchestras, the envy of orchestral musicians everywhere. It acknowledges New Zealand's unique isolation, and the importance of maintaining standards. Since it began, 35 NZSO players have benefited from the opportunity to travel overseas, undertake approved advance study in their instrument, experience as much music-making as they can fit in and observe trends in orchestra playing.

Violinist Katherine Rowe joined the NZSO straight from Canterbury University and did not have the money for overseas study. The bursary gave her that opportunity when she was selected in 1993. "It's a wonderful scheme," she says. "People were amazed that I could travel there on pay to study without having to worry about money."

Katherine spent her six months based in London, where she studied with Majiee Rakovsky, former leader of the English Chamber Orchestra, now Professor of Violin at the Royal Northern College of Music.

Section colleague Robin Perks received his bursary in 1989, enabling him to return to Vienna for study with Dora Schwartzburg, to listen to a lot of rehearsals and attend concerts in Vienna, Berlin and Salzburg. It is a part of the world that he knows well. He spent seven years studying and working there, mainly in Germany and Austria because, he says, "I revere the great German composers".

The bursary is held annually, finance permitting, and prospective bursars must present a proposed plan of their studies, to a panel including the chief executive, artistic manager and concertmaster. There is no restriction on location, and some assistance with lesson fees is provided. The six-month period may even be split between teachers, or, as Kenneth Young did in 1983/84 in different countries and continents: in studies with John Fletcher of the LSO in London, Paul Humempel of the Berlin Philharmonic and Ron Bishop of the Cleveland Orchestra.

In 1995/96 there were two bursars to carry on the tradition. Sub-principal first violinist Ursula Evans was planning to return to Germany where she had studied and worked previously. Awarded the bursary in 1994, she was unable to take it up because of OOS, and has had to postpone it again for the same reason.

The 1995/96 recipient is Bruce McKinnon, principal percussion, now studying with Graham Johns from Christchurch, longtime principal of the Royal Liverpool Philharmonic Orchestra, who played as an extra in the NZSO's Seville concert. Bruce plans also to check out other orchestras' percussion sections, and how they run their budgets, visit some instrument manufacturers and take lessons with Chris

Principal percussion Bruce McKinnon, the Lexus Study Bursar 1995/6.

PHOTOGRAPH: GAEL KERBAOL

Lamb in New York. "It's 20 years since I finished university," he says (with Victoria's first B.Mus as a percussion major). "It seemed a good time to take the Lexus Bursary."

For the same reasons that the orchestral bursary is so valuable, rare opportunities to participate in international ensembles should be embraced with enthusiasm. The value of this experience to players and ultimately the orchestra, cannot be over-estimated.

The first time that the NZSO was invited to take part in an orchestra such as this was in 1971, when former principal clarinet Frank Gurr was a member of the World Symphony Orchestra. Two performances were given in New York and Washington under the baton of Arthur Fiedler, with a commercial recording of the occasion issued later.

It was to be 14 years until a similar event was staged. In 1985 the first World Philharmonic Orchestra was assembled in Stockholm with the theme of 'Music and Peace' in association with the Nobel Peace Prize.

Maestro Carlo Maria Giulini conducted 92 players from 56 countries in a performance of Bruckner's *8th Symphony*, with proceeds going to UNICEF. The New Zealand Symphony Orchestra was represented on this occasion by violinist Stephen Managh, who subsequently travelled to Rome to take up his 1985/86 Study Bursary. "Nothing could surpass the feeling

International Orchestras

(Left) Rehearsing for Tower Beethoven Festival, November 1995. Janos Fürst, conductor; Michael Houstoun, soloist. (Overleaf) Members of The New Zealand Symphony Orchestra, March 1996.

GRAEME BROWNE

Barry Johnstone

John Jones

Mabel Way

Jane & Fred

Diana Cochrane-de Peña

Norbert Heuser

Stephanie O'Rahilly

Micky Prost

Neil Ch760

Wilma Small

Diane Cooper

Peter A Thomas

Gregory L.M.

Katherine Rowe

Michael Cucanno

Muriel Maughan

Peter Van Drimmelen

Ronald Armstrong

Nancy Luther Tata

Dan Gold

Graeme Sutherland Browne

Tom

Matthew Ross

Christopher Kane

Robert Orr

Peter Barber

of goodwill and satisfaction of taking part in the [World] orchestra," he commented.

Brian Shillito, sub-principal viola, was NZSO representative in Rio in 1986, where 106 musicians from 57 countries performed Beethoven's *7th* for Maestro Lorin Maazel. It proved to Brian that "the music world is small, close-knit, with networks of friends that extend to just about everywhere that musicians work. The WPO experience proved that."[25]

In 1987 John Dodds, principal second violin, was selected for the honour, this time in Tokyo under Giuseppe Sinopoli. By now the orchestra had risen to 110 players from 58 countries. The performance of Ravel's *Daphnis and Chloe Suite* and Mahler's *Symphony No. 1,* were emotional experiences: "People were in tears and one could feel the warmth and support everywhere. It was wonderful how colleagues from every nationality and race could come together in a common cause to produce such a magnificent concert."[26]

Dale Gold in 1988 was the last to take part in this event. In Montreal the orchestra of 60 nations was conducted by French composer/conductor Francois Legrand, one of its two founders, in a performance of Beethoven's *9th* that linked choirs in 20 countries.

Moscow was planned as the next venue in 1989, but amidst fears for musicians' safety at that time of unrest, it was cancelled and principal cello Farquhar Wilkinson missed out. After that there was silence, but if the orchestra is ever reinstated, the NZSO should be part of it.

Exchanges

Peter Barber departed for Tokyo in 1982, the recipient of the first Japan Foundation Scholarship. In what was to have been an exchange set up by conductor Michiyoshi Inoue, between the NZSO and the NHK Orchestra, Peter spent over four months with NHK although no player from Japan came to New Zealand.

The only foreigner in the 140-piece orchestra, Peter says he "learned a lot about dedication and the best ensemble playing I've ever heard in my life – or likely to hear. It was only four months but it felt like four years!"

The language was a constant trial, despite a course before he left home, and one in Tokyo, but he received "unanimous praise"[27] from NHK colleagues for his attempts. Japan was an interesting experience but not what he wanted. A year's study in Germany with Professor Reiner Moog at the Köln Music Academy three years later, proved more valuable. He returned there for a second year, this time with a Deutsche Academic Scholarship, and accompanied by his wife Mary and their first child Jacqueline.

Vivien Chisholm, NZSO/Hermann Backes, Düsseldorfer Symphoniker
"We swapped houses, cars, jobs, salaries and were going to swap cellos, but I decided to take mine and loaned Hermann my second one," says cellist Vivien Chisholm. "This was a complete exchange in every sense of the word."

Language and repertoire could have been a problem, so Vivien took German lessons before leaving home. The Düsseldorfer Symphoniker divides equally between opera and symphony, and although the opera repertoire was new, and "therefore a challenge" she was familiar with "a much wider repertoire on the symphony side [and] didn't feel out of my depth in that way. Also our orchestra [NZSO] is very quick working and I think my sight-reading skills and survival techniques were pretty good by comparison."

NZSO colleague and friend Michael Monaghan, then a member of the Düsseldorfer Symphoniker, spent two years setting up the exchange and cutting through a lot of complicated red tape at the German end. From the NZSO end the 12-month exchange went very smoothly, with Hermann Backes (who brought his family), a respected and well-liked temporary member of the Orchestra.

"The exchange was an exciting and valuable idea," Vivien says. "Musicians' jobs are almost identical, whichever country they come from and whatever language they speak. I still hope that other members will try and create their own exchange."[28]

Stephen Popperwell, NZSO/Carol Hellmers, Sydney Symphony

There were no language problems when Stephen and Carol exchanged chairs as second oboes for six months in 1989. Inspired by Vivien Chisholm's successful venture, and with the co-operation of both managements, the two swapped houses for six months, with each paying their own expenses.

The result? Stephen played in the SSO under former NZSO principal oboe Guy Henderson in the Sydney Opera House and Town Hall; while Carol, who had toured out of state twice in nine years in Sydney, was amazed by the travel she did around New Zealand with the NZSO. Both musicians found the exchange "beneficial and stimulating".

"It's a lifelong process refining the artistry of a musician," says Peter Barber. "All the experience you can put into people helps them grow and the orchestra is the sum of each individual really – so the better you can make the individual, the better the orchestra."

The sorry state of the New Zealand Symphony ( )
Kiri Te Kanawa at Expo 92 in Seville.

Orchestral maneuvres in the dark

Financial spotligh[t] hits our orchestra

WHEN Arts Minister Doug Graham expressed concern about the 15.2 per cent Budget cut to the New Zealand Symphony Orchestra's funding he knew what he was talking about.

The removal of $1.3 million from the funding of the orchestra threatens its existence in a way not paralleled by any other decision since its creation in 1946.

In justifying such a big cut, the Government pointed to recent capital grants made to the orchestra as being compensation. But these grants, for the purchase and refurbishment of a

The players volunteered a $30 cut to their $75 a day touring allowance and substantial reductions to clothing, instrument and other allowances. They also agreed to put 7 per cent of their pay into a trust with the money available on loan to the orchestra, which doesn't provide savings but helps the cash flow.

THE NEW Zealand Symphony Orchestra is racked by boardroom

Orchestra's future hits a sour note

— 'No orchestra of international standing is part-time, particularly one cleaning dunnies at night'

,000. y
ys there
week be-
ved and it
the pro-
rchestra
be pos-
item till

al mana-
greed to
ward by
bet has
for 2:
it ha
andards
a new
ive with
relations
ra man-

orchestra can overcome the financial obstacles "that would be beneficial and provide greater long term security".

But the orchestra is still at the mercy of the Government, and Mr Graham's lack of finesse is stalling urgently needed reform.

The fear is that the Ord

The Government promised "the orchestra's present level of funding will be guaranteed. Nothing must be allowed to compromise the standards or professionalism of this, New Zealand's largest and best established corps of performing artists".

The words proved to be yet another piece of empty rhetoric.

wall for the state-funded orchestra since Labour introduced
ideology in
criticism th
failed to se
t itself in t
society an
portunities
owever it
ntage of in
orchestra
nt in the last three years.
the sudden shock of Mr

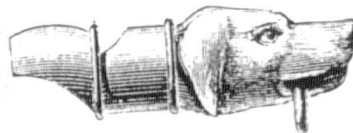

cations have
ed to four and a top
overseas candidate, who ha
marketing and orchestra ma
uge.
ted
ear.
nove
ctur
ruct
hes
ble
ll t

are doing is re
ernment of its commitment. To

e Gov- such as the QEII Arts Council,
where some could be siphoned

nt salary cut. Apart
philh

Day of reckoning

board and Chris
Diabe chief executive of his Col
ies it killed the comp y within de

Mr Graham's new
should dilute the

No Strings Attached?

"[The orchestra] is an organism, imperilled as a tree might be by transportation or even by having its customary shelter stripped away... [It is] an instrument which cannot be whittled down or economised on and still play the music written for it, the tradition is that orchestras are subsidised by the cities or countries fortunate to have them." – Adam Report, 1973.[8]

THE orchestra's fifth decade was off to a good start. Celebrations for its 40th anniversary year began in 1986, continued throughout 1987 with a gala season and concluded with a 'Farewell to 40' concert on 28 November 1987, 13 months later. The long-awaited new concertmaster Isidor Saslav had arrived and New Zealander Donald Armstrong, the orchestra's first associate concertmaster, was due to start in the New Year.

But events outside NZSO's control were already in motion and were destined to have a huge impact on its future. These began in September 1983, with another public enquiry into Broadcasting.

There had been so many of these, and 12 previous restructurings had left it battle-scarred and weary from encounters with politicians of both parties, who seemed unable to leave it alone. Like the BBC on which the BCNZ was modelled, soon itself to be under review, it could be said that "The urge for radical change came neither from the broadcasters nor the listeners but from politicians and civil servants".[9]

The architect of the last and most determined restructuring, Roger Douglas, Minister of Broadcasting in the 1973 Labour Government, was by 1984 back in government as Minister of Finance. In the 11 years in between, the drawn-and-quartered NZBC had been reassembled as BCNZ under National, with four separate entities reunited under one chairman and one Board.

With that restructuring, and the subsequent 1983 Commission of Enquiry barely completed, Labour returned to office and almost immediately announced a Royal Commission on Broadcasting and Related Telecommunications in New Zealand. The chairman, Professor Robert Chapman, was a member of the Adam Committee which in 1973 was given four months to investigate and develop its plan for New Zealand Broadcasting. That report had been perceptive about the effect on Broadcasting of "being subjected to a series of enquiries", which had inevitably reduced productivity, and its vulnerability to "short-term judgements". It expressed the hope that theirs "would be the last such enquiry for some time to come..."[10]

These two enquiries and the inevitable restructuring that followed took five years to reach what was termed 'The Appointed Day'. Although Broadcasting kept the NZSO fully informed of the various enquiries and transitional arrangements for distributing assets, it featured so rarely in the information generated that it all seemed somewhat remote.

The old NZBC/BCNZ had operated rather like a family business, with wealthier fee-earning members like television, commercial radio and the *New Zealand Listener* subsidising those unable to support themselves: the YA and YC radio networks (later the national and concert programmes) and Symphony Orchestra. No government or taxpayer money ever came direct to the orchestra; it went to Broadcasting and was redistributed, as the Adam Report acknowledged: "As part of a big organisation there was no need to 'disentangle' the costs nor to state precise debits and credits for services ..." Had these hidden costs been revealed it is unlikely the orchestra would have survived for so long. Few politicians seem to grasp the concept that no symphony orchestra in the world can pay its own way unless kept "forever in rehearsal".[11]

"The Broadcasting Fee was the way in which consecutive Governments restrained Broadcasting in those days," says Tony Lenton, former NZSO accountant, who was then chief accountant, BCNZ. Although it was one of the lowest in world, they refused any increase in the Broadcasting Fee for over 12 years, while also limiting income by a "very strict control on television advertising and the ban on alcohol advertising".

Restrictions and restructurings had achieved a wedge between the Broadcasting family. BCNZ was by then dispirited and financially crippled. With RNZ and TVNZ already reluctant to continue shouldering the burden of the non-profit-making divisions, and committed, as new State Owned Enterprises, to making a profit, neither wanted the responsibility of "a drain like the orchestra". There was little resistance to the new plans.

New Zealand Symphony Orchestra Limited

The Appointed Day finally arrived on 1 December 1988, and this time there would be no going back. The Broadcasting pie had been well and truly carved up this time. TVNZ and RNZ were now independent State Owned Enterprises; the *Listener*, a subsidiary of both, was later sold to publishers Wilson and Horton; while Broadcasting Services, TVNZ's engineering and technical wing, became Broadcast Communications Limited (BCL) in May 1989. Corporate Services disappeared altogether.

The New Zealand Symphony Orchestra Limited became the world's first limited liability orchestral company, answerable to three shareholding ministers of the Crown: Arts,

Commerce and Broadcasting, later reduced to two, Cultural Affairs and Communications.

General Manager Peter Nisbet had always feared it might happen. Almost overnight the protective umbrella of the Broadcasting infrastructure, that had maintained the orchestra for 42 years, was gone, "its customary shelter stripped away".[13]

NZSO was left without access to financial, legal and industrial services, a new payroll system had to be set up, and the vital lifeline of Radio New Zealand stations throughout the country was lost. Even with their own staff numbers seriously reduced in latter years, these local stations had provided essential backstage and front-of-house services, back-up support and invaluable local knowledge since touring began in 1947 – thus enabling the orchestra to tour 100 or more players with only two staff members.

NZSO staff had noticed changes even before the final split. "Little by little around the country our support was going," says Joy Aberdein, public relations manager and editor of *Symphony Quarterly*. "Those broadcasting people were not there any more, or if they were they were not so interested in helping us. Their jobs had changed; they were under pressure to bring income into their own areas. Unless they were particularly enamoured of the orchestra like Warren Cooper in Napier or Peter Boyd in Auckland. We were increasingly on our own. We had to monitor the papers and the advertising; front-of-house became an increasingly big load."

As part of Broadcasting, the New Zealand Symphony Orchestra had access to studios for its advertising, Joy says, "but whereas Radio was always very good, Television was more difficult, playing NZSO advertisements, as it was bound to, late at night or early afternoon when there were few viewers. After the change-over we had to buy television time and it was exorbitantly expensive."

In March 1989, three months after the demise of BCNZ, the Broadcasting Licence Fee at last was raised, from $71.50 to $108. Under the new arrangements the NZSO's funding from this source would be phased out in three years, and thereafter come direct from Government – a prospect which would strike fear into the heart of any arts organisation.

"The direction of the restructuring was completely diverted," says Tony Lenton, "by the Maori Council and Wellington Maori Language Board claim that the Crown had not met its Treaty of Waitangi obligations to the Maori language through State Broadcasting." Assets were frozen for three years and former BCNZ Chairman Hugh Rennie blamed Treasury and the Commerce Ministry for a bungle that meant the new SOEs started out with no money in the bank and no assets they could sell.[14]

The NZSO was assigned neither capital nor capital assets under the terms of the restructuring operations, its only assets being those in operational use, "some musical instruments, music library, desks and chairs with a net book value of $300,000 but an estimated resale value of not more than $100,000".[15]

The main barrier to any privatisation moves is the scheduled October 29 Appeal Court hearing on a Treaty of Waitangi claim. The Maori Council and the Wellington Maori Language Board say the Crown has not met its treaty obligations to the Maori language through state broadcasting. The claim has blocked the transfer of former Broadcasting Corporation assets to RNZ and TVNZ for nearly three years.

Mark Keyworth, who was general manager of The Royal New Zealand Ballet at that time, has a story that illustrates what he sees as the lack of thought that went into setting up the orchestra. The two companies were then touring *Romeo and Juliet*: "I received a rather pleading phone call from Peter Nisbet asking if I could help them out of a problem. They had been cut loose from Broadcasting but no one had set them up a bank account so the Ballet, which was always fraught with financial struggles, had to lend the orchestra enough money for the week's wages. I think that's quite a paradox!"

Tony Lenton comments: "To some extent the focus on some of the slightly less significant issues was taken away by the Maori claim, and a lot of detailed administration of the change-over was left for the last minute. When I arrived in June I had one month to the end of the budget year to tidy up loose ends – one of these being that the NZSO was entitled to claim payment for staff accumulated annual leave, something no one else realised. "That eventually brought a cheque for three-quarters of a million dollars."

NZSO Board

From February 1989 the NZSO Ltd had its own Board of Directors to guide it through future minefields. All five members had some experience of, and interest in, music. Professor Athol Mann, Dean of the Faculty of Commerce and Administration at Victoria University, was a longtime subscriber, as was Dr Hylton LeGrice from Auckland, an ophthalmologist and company director (awarded an OBE in 1995), whose wife Angela, widow of Alex Lindsay, is a former long-serving NZSO first violinist. Wellington musician Elizabeth Kerr was then music manager of the QE II Arts Council and wrote music reviews for the *Listener*, and is now general manager of Concert FM; Iola Shelley, musical co-ordinator of the Christchurch Symphony Orchestra, and Rick Christie of Cable Price Downer, now of Tradenz, was a former president of Music Federation of New Zealand.

Orchestra members were disappointed, says Ed White, former fourth horn and chairman of the Players Committee. They had made "many, many applications to have a representative on the Board, but that was rejected almost unanimously and continuously." Although there were some meetings between Board and Players Committee members in the early days, these lapsed for several years until reinstated in 1995.

The new Board, concerned solely with the NZSO, was in marked contrast to the Broadcasting Board, to which Peter Nisbet and other BCNZ chief executives had answered. It was a standing joke that the orchestra was always the last item on that Board's agenda, and inevitably time would be running out, says Murray Alford, former music executive. "They would say 'Ah yes, the report on the NZSO. Everybody read it? Good. Shall we accept it? Yes!' bang, bang, bang – and everything went through."

It came as no surprise to Dr LeGrice, now chairman, that he was invited to join the NZSO Board. He had felt for some time that the orchestra would benefit from direction from its

> The central issue is that while the Government has told the orchestra to reduce its dependency on the state, it has not given it the structure to do that.
>
> The board sent the plan to Mr Graham on November 5 last year, and was told he would get back in a week. Five months later he still hasn't done anything decisive.
>
> A copy of the report was also sent to the Treasury, which has made its own response.

own Board, he says, and had suggested that to his friend Hugh Rennie, two years earlier.

Dr LeGrice knew the NZSO very well from an artistic point of view. He had followed it almost all of his life and, from his experience in living overseas for seven years, could measure it against the world's best orchestras. Yet he was "quite shocked", he says, by the impression he had that it was administered as a "sort of cosseted government department where things happened without rhyme or reason, with very little accountability in terms of having a finite amount of funding".

As a national asset it was undersold and not well marketed, in his opinion. The challenge was how to increase its market awareness and yet ensure its survival in its present form, on a very tight budget. Also it needed complete restructuring:

"The parameters were not thought out and the orchestra came across from Broadcasting with... a very inadequate balance sheet as a reward for 42 years of its playing history... Nobody took into account the total infrastructure that this company had to set up. That was hugely expensive in terms of money but also a big culture shock."

There was another shock at the end of 1989, the axing of the Schola Musica in its 29th year. The orchestral training scheme was set up by John Hopkins in 1961, and Ashley Heenan was its musical director until 1984. The axing was a big disappointment for Michael Vinten, who took over its direction in 1985. "I consciously tried to broaden our scope of activities but we were not given time to fully settle on a 'new look' before the NZSO Board abandoned it," he says. "There was not enough time to put my mark on the scheme and get it moving in a direction relevant to the time we were in."

Response to the closure was surprisingly muted, although the financial reasons given were hard to argue with. A final concert held at St Andrews on The Terrace, where the Schola had played so often over the years, was low-key and there was little public recognition of the achievements of what was an important musical institution.

Its legacy lives on in the present orchestra, with Donald Armstrong as associate concert-master and 21 other former trainees; plus an estimated 70 to 80 percent of its young musicians for whom it made a music career possible.

Under the new funding arrangements the orchestra in its first year, 1989-90, received, as expected, 67 percent from the Broadcasting Licence Fee and 33 percent from Internal Affairs. In the second year, 1990-91, this was reversed with 33 percent from the Licence Fee and 67 percent from Government through the new Ministry of Cultural Affairs (MoCA). In the third year, 1991-92, MoCA would pick up the tab completely.

That was the scenario but things did not go as expected. In July 1991, Ruth Richardson, delivering her first 'Mother of all Budgets' as Minister of Finance, announced a figure of $6.4 million for the Orchestra, $1.3 million less than in 1990. The NZSO was already three

Funding Crisis 1991

months into its new financial year, with the current season's concerts, artists and programmes advertised since the previous year, and forward planning, including several signed contracts to 1993, well advanced for the next three years. It was devastating.

Peter Nisbet recalls that there was no encouragement from Doug Graham, the Minister of Cultural Affairs, when they went to see him. "'The old age pensioners have been cut, the domestic purposes benefit and the students, how could we expect to leave the orchestra alone?' he said."

In Peter Nisbet's view, the original mistake was separating the orchestra from Broadcasting. "It had always been my concern that once exposed to political whim, the orchestra would suffer financially. After all, when the present Government was elected in 1990 it was with a printed policy statement of maintaining the orchestra at its current level. And the first budget, what did they do? They cut it back 15.3 percent and said nothing beforehand."

The urgency of the situation called for unprecedented action for what was regarded as a fight for survival. A special taskforce was set up one weekend under facilitator Allan Roberts, with a united group made up of Peter Nisbet and representatives from Board, management and players.

Oboist Stephen Popperwell was a taskforce member: "We had a brief to brainstorm the whole deal and try to work out how funding could be best streamlined."

"We had to see how we could live with a lower level of allocation from Government," says Brian Morris, office manager, another member.

Everything that could be done, was done; concert ticket prices were raised and publication of the orchestral magazine, *Concert Pitch,* ceased after 12 successful years and 36 issues. Some decisions were regretted later. The cancellation of the two concerts for Nelson's 150th Anniversary, at less than two weeks' notice, was one of these, but indicative of the desperation of the time. To the people of Nelson however, who had not seen the orchestra for three years, it must have seemed unforgivable, no matter what the circumstances; a newspaper leader suggested it was "designed to stir provincial public opinion and encourage the Government to give back the money".[16] Whatever the reason or intention, although it saved $22,000, it was at the cost of alienating an entire community celebrating a most significant anniversary.

Many orchestral players would have preferred a main centre concert cancelled instead. "They were very concerned about protecting concerts in individual areas like Dunedin and Napier," Ed White remembers, "and they gave an extraordinary demonstration of their support. [The orchestra] simply did not have enough money to carry out activities to the end of the concert season, so we took a reduction in our dress allowance and per diem (daily allowance on tour), for a limited period of time and went to the effort of raising an interest-free loan for the company, as a five to seven percent deduction from salary. Rob Morrison of

The management's first efforts at cost-cutting backfired. Two concerts in Nelson were immediately cancelled to save money. That brought justifiable howls of outrage from a city that hasn't seen the symphony for three years. More cuts in the touring schedule were rumoured but the management has since settled down to find more creative ways to meet the shortfall.

Ord Minnett Securities set up a special trust fund and we collected over $100,000 and were on target for raising $250,000. It was returned six to nine months later, but I think we demonstrated to the Board and management the players' commitment for the concept of the orchestra working not only in main centres, but also in provincial areas."

To address the more fundamental problems of funding, a further approach was made to Ord Minnett, which, with marketing and artistic consultants Leon Grice and Dr Allan Badley (now NZSO) produced a report outlining a financial, marketing and artistic strategy designed to protect the orchestra's long term future, says Ed. "Although the recommendations were not implemented, many of the changes to the NZSO over the past few years reflect some of the underlying philosophy."

Treasury had its own cunning plan for the orchestra, as *The Dominion* discovered.[17] Treasury papers obtained under the Official Secrets Act, recommended turning the orchestra "into a part-time band, either by cutting concerts from 94 to 47 a year, saving an estimated $3.7 million, or by reducing the orchestra to a regional one, saving $5.3 million".

"The idea is a disaster," said Board Chairman Athol Mann. "Immediately the fulltime professionals of the calibre we have would seek positions elsewhere out of New Zealand. It's reversing 45 years of developing an orchestra to international standard."[18]

As usual at such times, the rumour mill was hard at work. There was talk of a commissioner being brought in to run the orchestra, of its transfer to the QE II Arts Council, and conspiracies at top levels. An understandable reaction with people's lives and livelihoods at stake: the disbanding of the New Zealand Opera Company was not forgotten.

in May Doug Kidd's razor gang asked for more.
Papers obtained under the Official Information Act show that officials, working under the Treasury, came up with a bizarre recommendation to turn the orchestra into a part-time band, either by cutting performances from 94 to 47, saving an estimated $3.7 million, or by reducing the orchestra to a regional one, saving $5.3 million.

A Permanent Home at Last

The funding cut was the bad news that followed hard on the heels of good news, that the orchestra, which for 44 years, according to Peter Nisbet, had lived "like a hermit crab, occupying someone else's shell", was to have a permanent home at last.

There had been many disappointments in the past, and a list of the orchestra's previous homes is well summed up as: "temporary, rented and largely unsuitable".[20] Former concert manager Peter Averi (later artistic administrator, Wellington City Opera) liked to trace the downward spiral of the orchestra's housing, from its beginnings in 1946 at the Broadcasting Studios in Waring Taylor Street, once a gentleman's club. Five years later, in 1951, it moved to the St Paul's Cathedral Sunday School room in Sydney Street East and, for 13 years from 1964-77, it was housed in the Broadcasting Studios at 38 The Terrace, a former Masonic Lodge and Temple. With that building due for demolition, the Orchestra moved in 1978 to the first Symphony House in Willis Street, the 1920 brick McDonald's building, previously home to a Chinese restaurant and furrier, that shook with every passing truck, and a studio, originally a billiards saloon, that was prone to flooding without notice. This was an unsuitable home for 14 years. Toilet facilities were inadequate, the orchestral common room was far

NZSO COLLECTION

(Above) St Pauls Cathedral Sunday School room in Sydney Street East, home of the National Orchestra 1951-1963. (Right) Old Symphony House in Willis Street, the orchestra's home from 1978 to 1991, where the front of the building shook with every passing truck, and the studio at the back was prone to flooding.

NIGEL MORRIS

too small for 100 players, there were no practice rooms, the studio acoustic defied all efforts at improvement and access for the truck was appallingly difficult in Willis Street.

Over the years many other possible homes were investigated, of which the Wellington Town Hall would have been the best had it been available, but since its refurbishment and the increased demands on it, this became unlikely. The net covered venues in Wellington and the Hutt Valley and included factories, cinemas, theatres such as the St James and two wharf sheds, with the Embassy Theatre, Studio 11 at Avalon, National Film Unit and Shed 7 on Wellington waterfront considered the most viable options.

Shed 7 was the ultimate choice. It offered the best facilities with in excess of 4000 square metres of rehearsal space, large enough to allow for audiences at rehearsals, and available for public use outside NZSO requirements. This was indeed an exciting prospect, as part of Wellington's new major waterfront redevelopment of Lambton Harbour, it would have other national and cultural neighbours, like the Museum of New Zealand. Circa Theatre was a probable partner in the building.

The total cost to earthquake-strengthen and refit Shed 7 was $5.5 million, but with valuable assistance promised by the New Zealand Lottery Grants Board and Lambton Harbour Management, only $4 million was required. The out-going Labour Government gave its approval at one of its last Cabinet meetings. The incoming new National Government Minister of Arts and Culture, Doug Graham, told *The New Zealand Herald* the orchestra was outstanding and respected worldwide. "It deserves a decent home and I am keen to see they get it," he said. "More spending is currently under review, but I will be going into bat for the orchestra."[21]

That was December 1990. In January 1991 the NZSO received a phone call, Peter Nisbet remembers: "'Shed 7 is too expensive. There are plenty of cheaper buildings around and you had better start looking for one.'" Another disappointment, and not only for the orchestra but for Circa Theatre too, which had to revise its plans for a new home. But if you had to go shopping for a building it was a good time to do so: real estate prices were still low and there was plenty to choose from. The 15-year-old, two-storey Rank Xerox office building and warehouse was the NZSO's choice, and this time Government agreed.

A few months later came the Budget and it was difficult not to see a link between the two. In the opinion of reviewer John Button, the funding cut was a direct threat to the orchestra's existence "in a way not paralleled by any decision since its creation... Capital grants made... for the purchase and refurbishment of a desperately needed new home have nothing to do with operating costs," he said. They belatedly honoured "a guarantee to provide adequate housing when the orchestra was split from Radio New Zealand... With an annual cost of $8 million dollars [the orchestra] is one of the most cost-effective orchestras of its kind in the world."[22]

Peter Nisbet, increasingly under pressure to 'do something', scheduled a benefit concert,

The eye-catching mural by David Waterman on the old house once used for storage by the NZSO.

the orchestra's first. It was later renamed a Celebration Concert, to celebrate the purchase of a new home, and to avoid sounding ungrateful, or any suggestion that it was under-funded. Four of the country's top singers, Malvina Major, Heather Begg (who flew back from Sydney), Chris Doig and Rodney McCann, needed no persuading to support the orchestra by singing without fee, in a performance of Beethoven's *9th Symphony* in which the Orpheus Choir and conductor Varujan Kojian, without prompting, also donated their services.

After the concert, local radio personality Lindsay Yeo auctioned off a combination of NZSO family treasures and donations including Sir John Barbirolli's baton, a bust of Beethoven, and a new Weinbach piano. Violinist Nigel Kennedy donated a signed football and photograph; conductor William Southgate (who bought the Barbirolli baton) a signed Folio Edition of his own *2nd Symphony*; and Michael Houstoun a signed score of Beethoven's *Emperor Concerto*. Auction and concert proceeds raised a healthy sum towards the new home.

By the end of 1991 only Dr Hylton LeGrice remained of the five original Board members, the others having been replaced by Wellington businessmen Sir Roderick Weir and Terry Fitzgerald, with Fletcher Challenge executive David Andrews from Auckland becoming the chairman. The fifth position remained vacant meanwhile, later filled by Felicity Price from Christchurch.

In January 1992 the NZSO moved into its new home, with the move project-managed by by then-administration manager NZSO, Alwyn Palmer. The refurbishment was completed thanks to the New Zealand Lottery Grants Board but with nothing left over for extras. Bright blue carpet left behind by Rank Xerox was patched together to cover the ground floor, with a second-hand job-lot of seaweed green carpet purchased for the top floor. The generally detested 1960s, orange vinyl-covered chairs and square yellow Formica coffee tables which had furnished players' common rooms for almost 30 years, now adorned the small, inside common room of a third orchestral building, the new Symphony House in Tory Street.

Several changes had been made to the original refurbishment plan and the final result was not completely successful. Compared with the previous Symphony House however, it seems a palace. It has a reception area, a music library almost three times the size, some light and roomy offices, ample storage and equipment space, five practice rooms, a spare room for table tennis, a large carpark for the players adjacent to the studio with a loading bay for the truck, and a small basement below for management cars.

It was the studio, the most important area, that proved inadequate. A large concrete warehouse 27x17 metres, it was almost double the size of the Willis Street studio, and almost half as high again. Hopes that the high noise levels experienced in that building would vanish here were dashed when the retrofit was completed and it became evident that there were very serious problems.

Since then "a variety of methods have been tried in order to improve the acoustics", says cellist Robert Ibell, chair of the orchestra's Health and Safety Committee. "A special ceiling has been installed and acoustic curtaining has been hung; carpet was laid but that was later rejected. New risers, shields, and absorbent panels to reduce reverberation in a particular frequency range have been purchased and the distance between certain rows of players increased."

Although these measures have met with some success, Robert says that noise levels still exceed legal limits for some players, depending on where they sit. "We have all been issued free musicians' earplugs but some people are unable to use them or feel they cannot play satisfactorily with them." The search for a solution goes on.

During the turmoil created by the funding crisis, Peter Nisbet gave notice he intended to retire in December 1991. Consequently his job was widely advertised, here and overseas, but it was clear that any appointment was a long way off. At the Board's request he agreed to delay his departure for some months to allow them time to process all the applicants.

Three months later no appointment had been made, nor looked likely, and Peter Nisbet was not prepared to wait any longer. His new home was built and waiting in Paihia, the Wellington home sold, so although the recruitment consultants had by then gone back to the drawing board, he retired on 31 March 1992.

The retirement party was low-key, reflecting the mood of the time, but no price could be

Peter Nisbet Retires

The NZSO's first permanent home, Symphony House, 69 Tory Street, Wellington.

STEPHEN HARKER

on the gift he received from the orchestra. On his last day he was taken to the studio on a pretext, where the orchestra played the first movement of Schubert's *Unfinished Symphony* for him. It remains a special memory. "It was an honour," he told me simply.

"That was the most poignant sight of my working life," says Tony Lenton. "People tend to celebrate some leaders of the orchestra but in my view Peter Nisbet was the difference between its surviving or not. He will never get the recognition he deserves. I will never forget him sitting in front of the band while they played one of his favourite pieces. He had some difficulty in controlling himself, but it was the only way the orchestra could say what it needed to say. It was an extraordinary thing and quite a beautiful thing."

Peter Nisbet controlled the orchestra for 22 years, first as head of music for radio, and then NZSO general manager/artistic director from 1977. The most important thing in running an orchestra he says "is the planning of its artistic development and its artistic enterprise. If you don't get the artistic things right you won't have an orchestra. I know you need money but alongside indefinable things in the artistic undertaking, money is a breeze."

Interim Management

There could be no greater contrast in personality to Peter Nisbet than interim manager Graham Coxhead, who was appointed by the Board to replace him. As an engineer with no previous experience in the arts or music, his challenge was to try to bring an artistic organisation into the late 20th century.

The first change was a small one: staff tea breaks were not encouraged, although the orchestra retained theirs. It has never been quite the same in the new building. The old tearoom in Willis Street was famous, and remembered with nostalgia by those who left. The room was an afterthought, small and narrow like a tramcar, so colleagues had to step over one anothers' feet to get in, and once in they had only a 50/50 chance to sit as it held only eight or nine chairs. Conductors, soloists, players and trainees sometimes joined in and staff were expected to try and make the effort to attend what was in effect an informal staff meeting, a constant interchange of information that kept everyone in touch with what was happening. It had the spin-off effect of engendering an atmosphere former music executive Murray Alford remembers as like "being in the middle of a huge, very close family. There was a very definite family feeling about the administration of the orchestra".

Tea breaks were included in the old Broadcasting agreement, which was the next to go. New individual contracts would replace collective agreements and the intention was for players too to have similar contracts under the newly introduced Employment Contracts Act.

The annual negotiations over the Orchestral Agreement had undergone a change in recent years. Originally this had tended to be a rather gladiatorial, formal arrangement with a team of orchestral players, spearheaded by a negotiator from the PSA, facing Broadcasting

ILLUSTRATION OPPOSITE INCLUDES PHOTOGRAPHS BY GRAEME BROWNE (CENTRE LEFT) & STEPHEN LA PLANT (LOWER).

We are the music makers,
We are
the dreamers
of dreams

(Above) A phenomenon of the 1990s: music draws the multitudes to the Auckland Domain for Coca-Cola Christmas in the Park, December 1993. (Right) Wellington generated as much enthusiasm, though on a smaller scale, for the NZSO with Montana Opera at the Basin the following year.

MARGARET GOULD

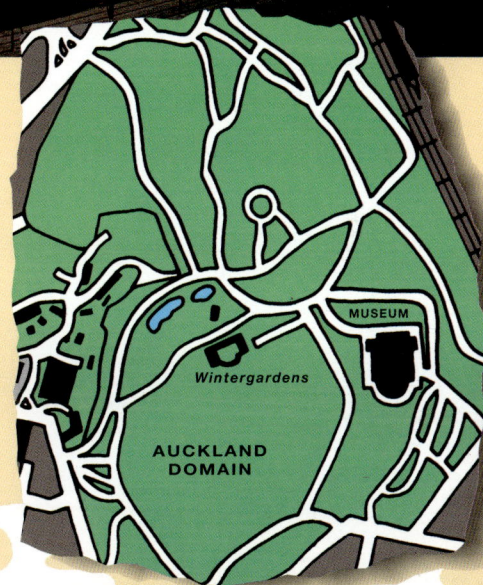

MUSEUM

Wintergardens

AUCKLAND
DOMAIN

(Left) Michael Gibbs celebrating 40 years with the
orchestra, in June 1993. Shown here with colleagues
including Donald Armstrong, William Southgate and
Graeme Browne.

THE DOMINION

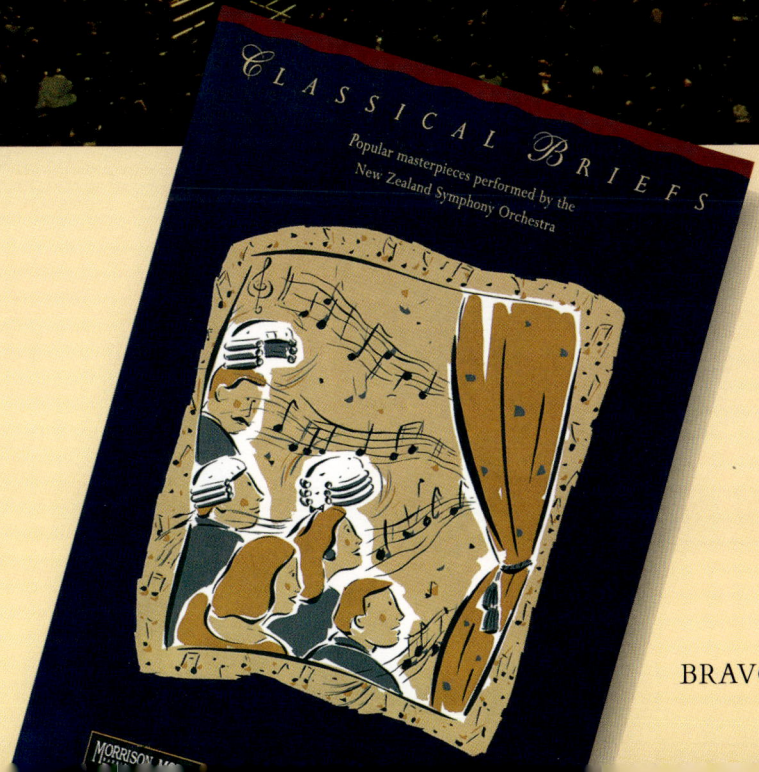

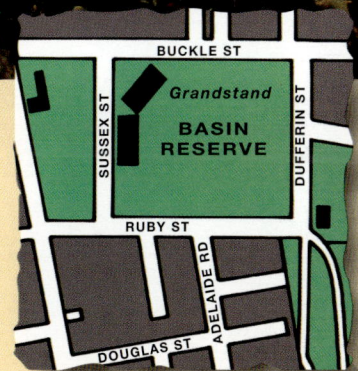

CLASSICAL BRIEFS

Popular masterpieces performed by the
New Zealand Symphony Orchestra

BUCKLE ST
SUSSEX ST
Grandstand
BASIN RESERVE
DUFFERIN ST
RUBY ST
ADELAIDE RD
DOUGLAS ST

(Above) Exciting finale to Lotto Twilight Opera at the Basin, Wellington, December 1995. (Opposite page) Montana Opera at the Basin, December 1994.

BRAVO! *69*

MORRISON

PHOTOGRAPHS: NEW ZEALAND LISTENER

Scenes from first rehearsal of the National Orchestra of New Zealand, 24 October 1946, include (Top Left) Lady Freyberg with conductor Andersen Tyrer.

PHOTOGRAPHS: BCNZ

PHOTOGRAPHS: NEW ZEALAND LISTENER

The performance was broadcast in its entirety. By means of radio many in New Zealand who are sufficiently interested have opportunity for becoming acquainted with great orchestral works. But listening-in may not be quite good enough nor so fully satisfying as to be in unison with the conductor and the players as hearing and seeing them in a concert hall itself. So it proved last night.

"Evening Post" March 7, 1947

*Superstar soloists appearing with the NZSO have
included Nigel Kennedy (Above) and Dame Joan
Sutherland with Richard Bonynge (Right).*

industrial negotiators with a small NZSO management team (who, like the author, probably wished they were somewhere else). A lot of grandstanding used to go on in those days from both sides, and the PSA's forcefulness was much appreciated by the orchestral team members, who still remember Tony Simpson ("superb" says Ed White) and Francis Weavers ("fantastic" says Stephen Popperwell). I have to say that the effect from the employers' side of the table was of course quite the opposite!

With the split-up, the NZSO lost BCNZ and gained the Wellington Employers Association. The PSA negotiators changed too and in a more congenial atmosphere in the last round held in the old building both sides decided to go it alone. The professionals went out the door and stayed in the background to advise when required, while management and players faced each other the way it should be. Both parties said it worked much better.

Discussions on the new contract began with consultant Rob Campbell but before long Graham Coxhead took over, sitting at one end of the long Board table, with Ed White, chair of the negotiating team, seated at the other end and the rest of the team ranged between the two. These were confrontational and exhausting meetings, 35 in all, ranging from two to six hours each. It took its toll on all committee members and when after six months Graham Coxhead's term was up, with the Agreement still not completed, it was left for the new incoming chief executive to finish off in a couple of sessions.

"These were some of the most troublesome times for the orchestra in my 20 years," recalls Stephen Popperwell, who was part of the Players negotiating team. So was cellist Allan Chisholm: "We could never understand how there could be so many meetings and why we couldn't get anywhere."

"People went home with headaches. We had to sit there and talk and talk. As long as there was another meeting we would go to it," says Ed White.

Graham Coxhead was the orchestra's first non-Broadcasting manager, experiencing an arts environment for the first time. It was difficult for either side to find common ground. Players felt strongly that some knowledge of music and musicians was essential for successful management of the orchestra. "It's not just a chocolate factory," was the comment heard.

"Graham was concerned there could be inefficiencies within the ranks of the orchestra, as in some government departments," says Ed White, "but 89 players is the bare minimum for a modern, world-class orchestra; most have 105. There were some inefficiencies that were looked at, but the amount of fat was very small."

As the months went by, players were becoming anxious that their current Agreement would expire before negotiations were completed. Their requests for this to be rolled over were refused initially, but in the end this had to happen because there was some good news on the horizon at last. The orchestra was to tour overseas once again.

Pulcinella: Scherzi

[Allegro ♩ = 104]

poco a poco accelerando

e. Stravinsky sparked a riot with his

① arco *au talon*......

Più mosso ♩ = 92

The Maestros

"One of these days we will play what these b—s conduct – and then God help them."
– Leader Vincent Aspey, quoted by contemporary colleagues.

SOME musicians say they can tell if a conductor has got what it takes 10 to 15 minutes after taking up the baton. This is a theory that NZSO players should have ample opportunity to test, when in any given year they may play under the baton of 20 or more conductors.

"It is almost like a prostitute," says Conductor Laureate Franz-Paul Decker; "every second or third week they get another guy!" There is both an upside and a downside to this. The orchestra is quick and responsive because it works with so many people, yet there is a perception that the pendulum has swung too far, and that a new approach should be considered in its Anniversary Year, 1996.

It was different in the 1940s, 50s and 60s. Resident conductors were New Zealand-based, and the first few worked their three-year contracts exclusively with the orchestra, apart from the occasional visit by a guest conductor or a conductor exchange with the ABC in Sydney. This system lasted 23 years, until 1969 when a guest conductor system was established.

It is no easy task building a new orchestra, as New Zealand's first permanent National Orchestra was in 1946. Many of its players had neither played in a professional symphony orchestra, nor heard one live before.

The Resident Conductors

Advice had come from major conductors like Sir Malcolm Sargent and Antal Dorati. "Don't fall for big names," the latter had warned. "Get a young and enthusiastic man who knows his job and grows up with the organisation."[4] Someone, although they did not say it, prepared to desert the musical life of Europe for a 'conductor's graveyard' in New Zealand.

GRAPHIC BASED ON PHOTOGRAPHS BY (CLOCKWISE FROM TOP LEFT)
TOM SHANAHAN, STEPHEN HARKER, TOM SHANAHAN, GRAEME BROWNE

NZ LISTENER

Andersen Tyrer 1946-49

First rehearsal of the National Orchestra, 24 October 1946. Andersen Tyrer, conductor; Leon de Mauny, assistant conductor/music editor and a very happy group of players.

At 53, Andersen Tyrer was enthusiastic and prepared to put in all the hours necessary to train his fledgling orchestra. He was well-known as a pianist, composer, conductor and music examiner, and received acclaim for his work as conductor of the successful Centennial Orchestra in 1940. Six years later, his appointment by Government to the unadvertised position of conductor of the National Orchestra caused a furore and the debate raged almost unabated throughout his three-year term.

Tyrer returned home to Britain in 1949 and never conducted the orchestra again. Few were prepared to give him credit for his considerable achievement in its establishment. In three years the progress made had been extraordinary: the orchestra was seen and heard not only in main centres but in provincial towns where orchestras had never been seen before. Almost all of its concerts were broadcast and thousands of children had attended its schools performances.

Under Andersen Tyrer, the orchestra had learned and performed an enormous volume of symphonic music; it had played in the pit and toured an NZBS production of Bizet's opera *Carmen*, and toured with the International Grand (Italian) Opera Company.

Michael Bowles 1950-52

Andersen Tyrer's successor was more experienced, and this time two committees, one in London and one in New Zealand, the latter with non-broadcasting representatives, recommended his appointment. Born in Ireland, Michael Bowles was a former principal conductor of the Irish Broadcasting Service, founder of the Dublin Symphony and had guest conducted the BBC Symphony and BBC Scottish. He was a composer and later wrote a book on conducting – although his own conducting was not highly regarded in New Zealand.

A firm disciplinarian, Michael Bowles put his own stamp on the orchestra. He extended its repertoire and, although several resignations resulted, terminated the group system whereby the orchestra split into four separate groups for three months a year, to perform with local studio orchestras in Wellington, Auckland, Christchurch and Dunedin, to counter criticism that the National Orchestra had taken the best players. Michael Bowles introduced the Subscription series, the Proms series, gave the first outdoor concert and he took part in the first conductor exchange with the ABC in Sydney. He also conducted the orchestra in its first filming by the National Film Unit.

Warwick Braithwaite

Chief conductor 1953-54

Warwick Braithwaite from Dunedin was not a resident conductor, although he tends to be included in that list. He became the youngest professional conductor in Britain. After completing his studies at the Royal Academy, he was principal conductor of Sadlers Wells from 1931-40, then conductor of the Scottish National Orchestra. From 1947 he was resident conductor at Covent Garden. Under Warwick Braithwaite's direction a more professional approach was made, rehearsal times were reduced and performances increased. He conducted the first 'Pops' concert, and the first Royal Concert for the inaugural Royal Tour by HRH Queen Elizabeth in 1953.

Often controversial, Warwick Braithwaite's programmes were criticised, once prompting a deputation of concert-goers to complain to the Director of Broadcasting.

James Robertson

Resident conductor National Orchestra 1954-57

Resident conductor NZBC Concert Orchestra 1962-63

A British conductor with a first class masters degree in classics and modern languages from Cambridge University, James Robertson studied conducting under Constant Lambert, worked with Glyndebourne Opera, was conductor and chorus master for the Royal Carl Rosa Opera,

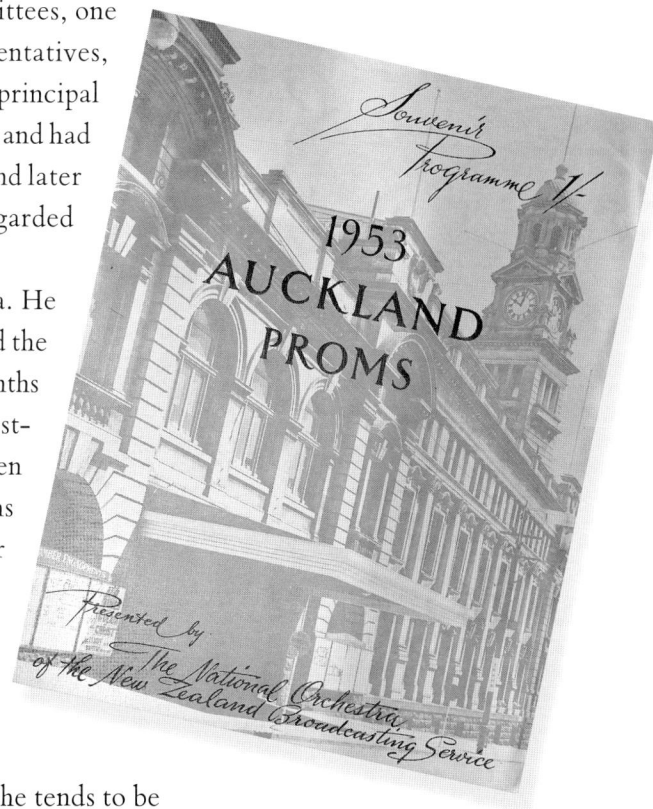

Programme cover for the first Proms concert held in Auckland.

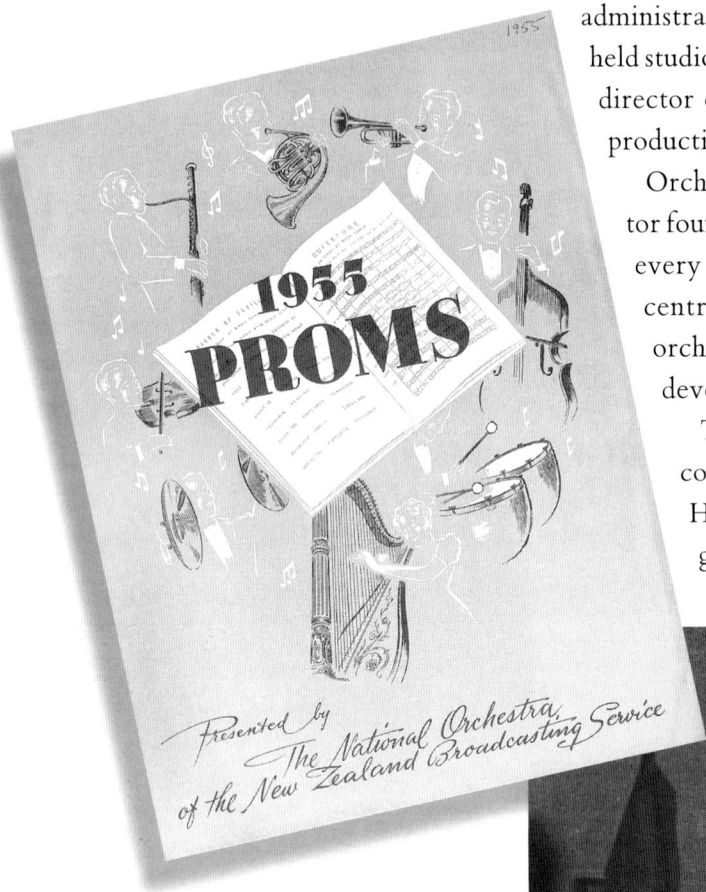

and then was appointed director and conductor of Sadler's Wells Opera for eight years.

A man of great charm, Robertson achieved public acceptance of the National Orchestra as never before, and he used every opportunity to promote it. He was a "brilliant music administrator".[5] He gave opera talks on radio, then entire operas in studio broadcasts; held studio workshops for composers, concerto players and conductors and was musical director of the New Zealand Opera Company, directing in 1957 its first full-scale production *The Consul* by Menotti.

Orchestral tours became shorter under James Robertson, who as an opera conductor found the amount of symphonic repertoire a nightmare, especially on tour where every concert was broadcast and he had to rehearse new programmes in every centre. Fewer concerts were broadcast, at his request. He re-auditioned the orchestra, an unpopular move but one which was necessary for its professional development.

The first resident conductor to be invited back, James Robertson was conductor of the doomed NZBC Concert Orchestra for two turbulent years. He returned to conduct the National Orchestra in 1969 and 1973, and in 1976 gave the first New Zealand performance in concert of Puccini's *Turandot*.

James Robertson, the orchestra's third resident conductor, takes a rehearsal in the St Paul's Sunday School room, 1957.

SPENCER DIGBY/NZBC

John Hopkins 1958-63

Each of the resident conductors made his own distinctive and unique contribution to the development of the orchestra, but none more than John Hopkins. At 24 he was the youngest-ever conductor of a major British orchestra, the BBC Northern Symphony, younger too than any of its players. He was only 29 when he came to New Zealand.

He brought enormous energy and enthusiasm to the position and a prodigious repertoire. Mahler symphonies were introduced and he broadcast all the Sibelius symphonies; the orchestra recorded its first commercial album; programme planning became more systematic, and a series of contemporary music concerts entitled 'Music in our Time' continued for three years. He was director of the New Zealand Opera Company and associated with The New Zealand Ballet.

Two major achievements stand out in his six-year era: the establishment of the National Youth Orchestra in 1959 and the Orchestral Trainees in 1961. He also re-auditioned the orchestra. John Hopkins left New Zealand in 1963 to become Director of Music at the ABC. He returns regularly to conduct the NZSO. In 1990 he conducted Dame Kiri Te Kanawa for the record-breaking outdoor 'Kiri's Homecoming' concerts, and he returns for the 50th anniversary year.

(Below Left) John Hopkins in 1995: he is one of the key figures in the orchestra's first half-century. (Below) John Hopkins in 1962 with Claudio Arrau, one of the greatest artists to perform with the NZSO.

REECE SCANELL

TOM SHANAHAN

Juan Matteucci brought Latin fire and colour to the repertoire.

Juan Matteucci 1964-69

The sixth resident conductor, Juan Matteucci was born in Italy and moved with his family to Chile. He studied mathematics and medicine at the University of Chile until on the death of his father, Juan took over his chair as principal cellist at the Symphony Orchestra of Chile. Awarded a Chilean Government Scholarship, he studied and made his debut conducting at the Verdi Conservatory in Milan. On his return he became associate conductor of the Symphony Orchestra of Chile, then permanent conductor of the new Philharmonic Orchestra. He joined the National Orchestra of New Zealand in July 1964.

After five previous British or British-trained conductors Juan Matteucci brought Latin fire and colour to the orchestra, and soon won the affection of the public with exciting concerts. During his term the orchestra increased to more than 100 players by absorbing the remaining members of the Concert Orchestra, made its first appearance on television, and became more innovative to counter the effect of this new medium. Juan Matteucci's was the longest of the resident conductorships, and the last.

Laszlo Heltay

Associate conductor 1964-66

The Hungarian conductor trained at the State Conservatoire and Franz Liszt Academy in Budapest and studied under Zoltan Kodaly. He left Hungary during the revolution in 1956. Laszlo Heltay came to New Zealand from Oxford University where he formed the Kodaly Choir and Orchestra.

Juan Matteucci was not happy about this appointment, although the two positions were advertised at the same time. When Laszlo Heltay arrived in New Zealand the Concert Orchestra was to be disbanded and his position had changed. The arrangement was never successful. After his return to Britain, Heltay became a respected choirmaster, notable for his Brighton Festival Chorus.

Chief and Principal Guest Conductors

A resident scheme was no longer feasible. The orchestra's standards had risen and it was considered unrealistic to expect a conductor of the required status to live here and work with an isolated orchestra, so far from mainstream music, with his or her own international career on hold.

The new plan was to extend the number of guest conductors and establish long-term relationships with them as principal guests or chief conductors; spending four or five months with the orchestra every year for three years, to give stylistic direction and contribute to artistic policy. A leader of the calibre of Alex Lindsay was crucial to carry the extra responsibility associated with the new title of concertmaster.

It took four years after Juan Matteucci left before a chief conductor was in place.

Brian Priestman

Chief conductor 1973-75.

The last of the British conductors, Brian Priestman twice applied to be resident conductor before making his first visit in 1972 and beginning his three-year term the following year. A former musical director of the Royal Shakespeare Company at Stratford-upon-Avon and Aldwych, he divided his time between the NZSO (three months) and the Denver Symphony Orchestra (four months). He was impatient with bureaucracy and associated with several controversies during his time in New Zealand.

Brian Priestman had a theatrical streak that was demonstrated to good effect in his family concerts, 'Magic and Spells', where he arrived in a puff of smoke, swirling a long black cape. He had some triumphs with the complete *Pulcinella* (Stravinsky), *Romeo and Juliet* (Berlioz), *Hiketides* (Xennakis) and Shostakovich's *10th Symphony*, but his work on the important first Australian tour in 1974 was criticised. When his three-year contract ended it was not renewed and Brian Priestman has not conducted the orchestra since.

Michiyoshi Inoue

Principal guest conductor 1977-80.

This tall young Japanese conducted the NZSO first in 1975. Energetic and balletic on the podium, he was one of two who conducted the NZSO at the Hong Kong Arts Festival in 1980. Michiyoshi Inoue introduced Japanese music to the NZSO's repertoire and has returned on several occasions.

Franz-Paul Decker

Principal guest conductor 1984-88.

Chief conductor 1990-94.

Conductor Laureate 1995-

Born in Cologne, where he made his conducting debut at 22 with the Cologne Opera, Franz-Paul Decker has conducted some of the world's finest orchestras, and divides his time between Cologne, Barcelona, Montreal, Ottawa and New Zealand.

Dr Decker says he has had a "love affair" with the NZSO since he first conducted it in 1966, when he was "very positively surprised [by its] highly professional musicians. It is the longest relationship I have had with any orchestra in the world."

Violinist Robin Perks remembers the impression made by Dr Decker on his first visit as "awe inspiring. He was more demanding in those days. He required string players to play desk by desk a difficult passage and this really frightened many of us, but the results in concerts were probably the best achieved to this point."

Under his baton the NZSO has scaled new heights, most notably in works by Richard

Michiyoshi Inoue studied under Celibidache in Italy and made his debut at La Scala as winner of the Milan Guido Cantelli Competition. In 1983 he succeeded Seiji Ozawa as Musical Director of the New Japan Philharmonic.

A "love affair" with the NZSO: Dr Franz-Paul Decker, Conductor Laureate 1995-.

Strauss, Mahler, Bruckner and Wagner, and he has given several outstanding first performances, in keeping with his aim to extend the NZSO's repertoire. These include Bruckner's *9th* (1976), Strauss's *An Alpine Symphony* (1987), and Schoenberg's *Pelleas and Melisande* (1990).

Franz-Paul Decker took up the post of chief conductor in 1990. In 1992 he conducted the orchestra in two concerts in Seville for Expo '92: at Teatro de la Maestranza, with Dame Kiri Te Kanawa and outdoors in the Plaza de San Francisco, a thank you concert for the people of Seville.

Franz-Paul Decker's outstanding creative achievement and on-going commitment to the NZSO was given significant recognition when he was named the orchestra's first Conductor Laureate.

Gyorgy Lehel

Chief conductor 1988-89

Musical director and chief conductor of the Budapest Radio and Television Orchestra, Gyorgy Lehel first visited New Zealand in 1983 and returned in 1986. He was named chief conductor in 1988, but was unable to appear that year, having undergone major surgery. In 1989 Lehel honoured his commitment and returned despite his failing health and that of his wife Susan.

The last concert was in Dunedin and finished with the Saint Saens *3rd Symphony*. It had been the first piece Susan had heard him conduct, and now it would be the last. He knew he was dying and she had brain cancer. "He was so ill he could hardly stand up," says Peter Nisbet, "but he was determined to do that work for her. I've never seen so many of the orchestra in tears as there were that night, on stage and in the dressing room afterwards. It was very hard, very emotional. He did the slow movement of that symphony, and it was absolutely heart-wrenching. He said 'I have done my duty' when he left, and he only lasted another six weeks."

Gyorgy Lehel died on 25 September 1989, aged 61 and was given a state funeral in Hungary. Susan died 18 months later.

Eduardo Mata

Principal guest conductor designate 1995-97

The highly respected Mexican conductor was killed on 4 January 1995, four days into his three-year term as principal guest conductor of the NZSO, 18 months before the NZSO's planned tour to Europe in 1996. So much had been hoped for from the new partnership with Eduardo Mata, who was musical director for 16 years, and later Conductor Emeritus for Life of the Dallas Symphony, and principal guest conductor of the Pittsburgh Symphony Orchestra. His NZSO concerts had made such an enormous impact then, that the need for a more permanent relationship was obvious.

Gyorgy Lehel on his second visit to New Zealand, 1986, shown with Marian Tache and Richard Panting (first violins).

TOM SHANAHAN

(Above) Eduardo Mata, 1993: "first and foremost a musician". (Below) Kenneth Young, 1995: principal tuba, composer and conductor-in-residence.

"I was lucky to have him as my conductor in Brahms 1 when I started my trial [for concert-master]," Wilma Smith recalls. "It was a terrific musical experience. Although he was not an outgoing or effusive chap, we had very good talks at a level that was genuine. He was first and foremost a musician and was seriously interested in the orchestra and communicating information with me about what he thought it needed. It was a good working relationship already. I was personally shattered when he died... I was so looking forward to that relationship continuing."

Eduardo Mata was killed piloting his own plane in Mexico. He had flown a hired aircraft around the North Island on his visit here in 1993, and had planned further flying on his return in 1995.

Kenneth Young

Conductor-in-residence 1993-95

Kenneth Young holds a unique position in the NZSO. Principal tuba since 1976, he is a New Zealand composer whose works include his first symphony, performed by the NZSO and overseas. In 1993 he became the orchestra's first conductor-in-residence.

The family interest in brass bands started Young off on cornet, which led to the euphonium and then tuba. He took up composing in his last year at school, and was principal percussion and tuba player in the Christchurch Symphony. In 1975 he played in the National Youth Orchestra's acclaimed world tour. He joined the NZSO in 1976, and was granted leave for advanced tuba study in the United States.

Kenneth Young is seen most often conducting the highly successful 'Tea and Symphony' Concerts, and also Children and Family concerts. He first conducted the orchestra in 1985, with a studio recording of a piece he wrote for the late John Chisholm. Soon afterwards he had to step in to conduct a James Galway concert at short notice when the visiting conductor Hans-Hubert Schönzeler became ill. He did the same again when Piero Gamba suffered a reaction to a severe wasp sting. More recently he replaced Vernon Handley who had contracted the 'flu on arrival, conducting Elgar's *Enigma Variations* for the first time, with one day's notice.

He says his most satisfying concert was in 1989, conducting his first NZSO Subscription series concert with a programme of Béla Bartók's *Concerto for Orchestra* and Mozart's *Symphony No. 39*.

Kenneth Young does not like conducting his own work. In his view "composers make very, very poor interpreters of their own music. A conductor looks at a score from a completely different perspective than a composer," he says. "There's too much emotional involvement conducting one's own works and it makes it very hard to concentrate on the objective nature of conducting."

The NZSO has played host to some very distinguished guests in its 50 years. The most important of these was a small, bent and fragile-looking man in his late 70s, who telephoned one day out of the blue, to ask if he could visit and conduct: someone had told him there was a "rather good orchestra" down here and he had decided to come and see for himself. This was the great composer Igor Stravinsky, whose two performances in Wellington and Auckland will never be forgotten.

Robert Craft, Stravinsky's assistant and later biographer, conducted the first half of each performance, the *Pulcinella Suite* and *Symphony in Three Movements*; Stravinsky the second, *Apollo Musagetes* and the *Lullaby* and *Finale* from the *Firebird*.

"It was quite magical," John Hopkins, then resident conductor, remembers. "A very, very special occasion. The orchestra was literally on the edges of their chairs. He was very pleased with them and I was told in Australia... that he spoke very warmly there about the orchestra. The ABC people said he was extremely happy in New Zealand."

Such momentous happenings occur only rarely in orchestral life in a country so isolated from the great music capitals. A highly regarded artist may arrive at the tail-end of a brilliant career and disappoint, or the vital chemistry between orchestra and conductor fails to ignite, as with Rafael Fruhbek de Burgos. At other times conductors who are not so well known can arrive without fanfare, and make an enormous impression.

British composer Sir William Walton, who toured in 1964, was an unassuming man, yet

Maestro Superstars

PHOTOGRAPHS: TOM SHANAHAN

(*Above*) *Igor Stravinsky in rehearsal during his 1961 visit.* (*Left*) *Receiving a standing ovation from an enthralled audience in the Wellington Town Hall.*

developed a special rapport with players who performed under his baton in seven concerts of his works: the first and second symphonies, the violin concerto and *Belshazzar's Feast* with the combined Royal Christchurch Musical Society and the Christchurch Harmonic Society.

Margaret (Sicely) Tibbles remembers *Belshazzar's Feast*: "I thought it was the most marvellous music I had ever heard... the hairs stood up on the back of my neck."[6]

Juan Jose Castro, a conductor/composer from Argentina, was one whose only visit in 1952 is still talked about. A last-minute replacement, and despite limited English, he elicited a wonderful response from the orchestra.

Conductors Antal Dorati in 1973, Josef Krips in 1959 and Kurt Sanderling in 1981, who each toured just once, are others whose visits are highly regarded. The latter two were quite elderly when they came here but others of their family continued the tradition, when they themselves could not return. Henry Krips, younger brother of Josef, followed in 1962, and Kurt Sanderling's son Thomas performed in New Zealand in 1983 and 1986.

Two Czech conductors made an impact: Karl Ancerl, principal conductor of the Czech Philharmonic, which toured in 1959, returned to conduct the National Orchestra in 1961, and Vaclav Smetacek in 1965 and 1975. In 1969 Russian conductor Anatole Fistoulari visited.

Occasionally a brilliant first visit is unfortunately overshadowed by a lacklustre return, the magic lost. The 'second tour syndrome' seems to have no obvious cause, and there are varied views and explanations as to why this happens. Principal viola Vyvyan Yendoll suggests that a conductor works that much harder the first time, but "on finding the orchestra so good and responsive does not try so hard next time" – and that's a fatal mistake.

On Alceo Galliera's first visit in 1963 players were moved by his performances. Four years later, it was a different story. His wife had died, he had become morose and it was the players who suffered from his mood swings.

In this case the reason seemed clear, and in others it can be traced quite simply to deteriorating health, personal or specific circumstances. Hans Hubert Schönzeler from Leipzig, a respected Bruckner conductor, had suffered a severe illness, unknown to the NZSO, before his arrival in 1983. He tried bravely to honour his commitment by conducting when he was ill. His concerts featured major international artists James Galway (flute), Julian Bream (guitar) and Julian Lloyd Webber (cello), whose performance was on the brink of disaster, with the orchestra unable to follow Schönzeler's directions and desperately following the concertmaster. With five concerts still to go, the SOS went out and conductors Michiyoshi Inoue, Nicholas Braithwaite and Kenneth Young saved later performances.

Special Friends   With some conductors the NZSO has had long-standing special relationships without the formal title of principal guest or chief conductor. Another Czechoslovakian conductor, Walter Susskind, was one of these. Short-listed to follow Andersen Tyrer as resident

Superstar flutist James Galway of Ireland.

conductor in 1949, he withdrew because of other commitments, but later visited regularly as guest conductor every two or three years from 1967 until his untimely death, aged 56, in 1980. A fine musician whose colourful idiosyncracies kept players amused, he had a special interest in this orchestra. Had he lived, a more significant relationship was planned.

Susskind's death left a vacuum but he is remembered for some fine performances, among them an extraordinary *Sing Along Messiah.*

Sir Charles Groves, too, had a special affection for the NZSO. He made his first tour in 1976, and his fifth in 1987. The Conductor Laureate of the Royal Liverpool Philharmonic, he had had long-term relationships with the Royal Philharmonic in London, the Los Angeles Philharmonic and was musical director for both the English and Welsh National Operas. A wish to spend his later years here, where he would have been a tower of strength to the NZSO, was sadly never realised. He died in 1992 aged 77.

"He wasn't an audience man," Farquhar Wilkinson, former principal cello, remembers. "He didn't have extravagant gestures but he was always in control of what was going on, and I felt he really used the orchestra as an instrument. He knew what players were capable of doing and I loved playing for him."

Around the same time, the NZSO experienced a run of unexpected deaths of several of its most favoured conductors, including two who had conducted performances of the NZSO and Royal New Zealand Ballet, and were scheduled to do so again.

New Zealander Ashley Lawrence, a respected international ballet conductor of the Royal Ballet at Covent Garden, had conducted the NZSO in a very successful *Romeo and Juliet* with the Royal New Zealand Ballet in 1988 and was to return for *Cinderella* in 1991, but died suddenly, aged 52. The engaging Russian conductor Varujan Kojian, who had conducted the orchestra in its New Zealand Festival of the Arts performances with Rudolf Nureyev in 1988 and several other concerts since, including *An Evening of Opera* with soprano Alessandra Marc, was Ashley Lawrence's replacement. Such was his success that he was invited back for the next ballet, *Petrouchka,* in 1993 but he too died suddenly the same year aged only 50, soon after his last visit.

American conductor Andrew Schenck was the third to die. Best known for his critically acclaimed recordings with the NZSO of the music of Samuel Barber, for the Koch label, he had also recorded CDs of music by Respighi and Randall Thompson. Aged 51, his death on 19 February 1992, of a rare cancer, came soon after his successful debut with the prestigious Boston Symphony Orchestra, nine months before he was due to conduct the NZSO in concert.

Conducting was once thought to be the profession to ensure long life. So many of the old school seemed to reach their 70s, 80s and upwards with the energy of men half their age. In the past decade that has changed, if the New Zealand figures are an indicator.

The pace of life has increased for all international artists, says orchestra manager David

Pawsey. "The old troupers started off travelling to New Zealand by ship and never really got used to flying. They needed a couple of days off to get over their traumatic flight and their jet lag. The new breed are jet-setters. They arrive at maybe 4 o'clock of an afternoon and are rehearsing with us the following morning at 9.30. They bring their laptop computers and are into e-mail and sending faxes everywhere. It's rush, rush, rush. The moment the concert is finished, it's bang onto the next place."

The Pop Conductors

Another of the NZSO's special conductors, Ron Goodwin, who turned 70 in 1995, is much more relaxed. He has celebrated several birthdays on stage with balloons and birthday cake during his nine visits, spanning the years 1975-1993. Eight of these were Summer Pops tours, with a Christmas Party Concert in 1993. Three albums have been recorded in that time; one received a Platinum Disc Award, the other is due for release in 1996.

Ron Goodwin has often been quoted as saying that he thinks of this country as his second home and it is clear that his many loyal followers think of him as part of the family. His

The orchestra played and the audience sang Happy Birthday to conductor Ron Goodwin at the Hastings Summer Pops in 1984, with Mrs Heather Goodwin and Hastings City Councillor Ron Churchill.

RUSSELL ORR STUDIOS

88 BRAVO!

generosity in mounting benefit concerts when natural disasters have occurred during his tours (the Southland Floods Appeal in 1984, and the Bay of Plenty Earthquake Disaster Appeal, which raised $30,000 in 1987), will long be remembered.

"I fell in love with New Zealand on my very first visit," he says. "Working with the orchestra has always been a great pleasure, partly because of their musicianship, partly because of the warmth of the audiences and partly because I have made so many good friends among the players."

He says they co-operate with the outlandish things he asks of them, but knowing "musicians' mad sense of humour", the potential is there for things to get out of hand.

"We were doing the *The Stripper* as an encore and I heard on the grapevine that for the final concert some of the musicians had actually hired a professional stripper to come out of the audience and take her clothes off on stage. Well, you couldn't let that happen at a family concert, and everyone would have thought it was my idea anyway!

"At the last minute I asked the concertmaster to tell the orchestra we would not be playing *The Stripper* that night; we would play the other encore. And when I opened the score on stage, someone had pinned three white feathers in it!"

Not all conductors are successful in the Summer Pops slot, and the mix can be elusive with some big names failing to attract. British conductor Stanley Black was popular on his first visit in 1972 but less successful two years later – while Andre Kostelanetz, a big name then, made two visits for the 'Mini-Proms' in 1970, and the Proms proper in 1976.

Arthur Fiedler was the biggest drawcard in the Pops concerts, known as much for being the former conductor of the Boston Pops as for his well-known penchant for fire engines. He was 71 when he came first in 1966, still with energy and charisma to burn.

Playing pop music and Beatles numbers with a full symphony orchestra was new then and there were long ticket queues for the Fiedler concerts, with even the enormous Dunedin Town Hall turning people away from his four concerts on the second tour in 1968.

John Dankworth, conductor of the LSO's Summer Pops, is known as a composer of jazz, classical and film music, an arranger and a jazz musician. He has made two very successful tours with the NZSO in the BP Summer Pops in 1991 and 1994, on the last occasion with his daughter Jacqueline. John and his wife Cleo Laine founded and direct the Wavendon Allmusic Plan, which aims to organise courses to break down the barriers between various spheres of music: jazz, classical and pop.

British-American conductor Skitch Henderson made his first visit in the 1996 Summer Pops slot. Founder and director of the New York Pops at Carnegie Hall, he has conducted most major orchestras in the USA, and performed widely in Canada, Europe and Australia. After studies under Fritz Reiner and theory with Arnold Schoenberg, his career has encompassed work with MGM and showbiz greats Judy Garland, Bing Crosby and Frank Sinatra.

NELSON MAIL

Skitch Henderson: from Schoenberg to Sinatra to Summer Pops.

Sir William Southgate, 1995: "We have a national treasure in the New Zealand Symphony Orchestra."

New Zealand conductor/composer Sir William Southgate puts his own individual stamp on the Summer Pops concerts which he conducts with big symphonic pop arrangements.

Sir William says he is largely self-taught in this, and when asked to do arrangements for the Michael Moores television shows in the 1970s he had to "invent the style and everything else, in the same way I invented my own style when it came to composing". Knowing the NZSO players as he does, he could write with them specifically in mind, annotating his score accordingly: "Get your fluegel out Mike!" for former NZSO trumpeter Michael Gibbs, whose playing in *Don't Cry For Me Argentina* is "one of the most wonderful performances I've ever heard".

Sir William first worked with the NZSO as a casual horn in the *War Requiem* under John Hopkins in the 60s. The next time was in 1975, soon after returning to live in New Zealand, when he conducted some studio recordings. In the 20 years since, he has conducted the orchestra almost every year, across a broad spectrum of repertoire and for a variety of events; including the Commonwealth Heads of Government Meeting in November 1995.

His most moving experience occurred when the NZSO performed his second symphony in 1988. "At the end of the last rehearsal I said thank you ladies and gentlemen and they gave me a huge round of applause. It was more than gratifying, it went right to the heart. The marvellous thing about [them is that] they are good about any kind of music. Wonderful. They not only play all the repertoire extremely well, they can play difficult new music – and they can swing as well."

The New Zealand-Finland Cultural Exchange in 1986/89 was the watershed for William Southgate's breakthrough as an international conductor, while remaining based in Wellington. Sir William was knighted in the 1995 New Year Honours List, the first New Zealand conductor to be so honoured.

John Matheson too did most of his training in London. He lived in Europe for 30 years, working with Sadlers Wells and the Royal Opera and first conducted the NZSO in Berlioz's *Damnation of Faust* with Kiri Te Kanawa in 1972. He conducted the Matheson Proms and the recording *Donald McIntyre Sings Wagner* in 1975, an all-New Zealand performance of the Verdi *Requiem* in 1982 and *Swan Lake* with The Royal New Zealand Ballet in 1985.

Andrew Sewell, a young New Zealand conductor who has been living and working in the United States, will be conducting the orchestra in its 50th anniversary. Other New Zealand conductors in the last decade include respected choral conductor Peter Godfrey and Peter Scholes.

Nicholas Braithwaite does not qualify as a New Zealander, having been born in England, but as the son of former resident conductor Warwick Braithwaite, his ties with the country are strong. He conducted the NZSO for the first time in 1977, exactly 30 years after his father conducted the National Orchestra for the first time in 1947, its inaugural year. Since

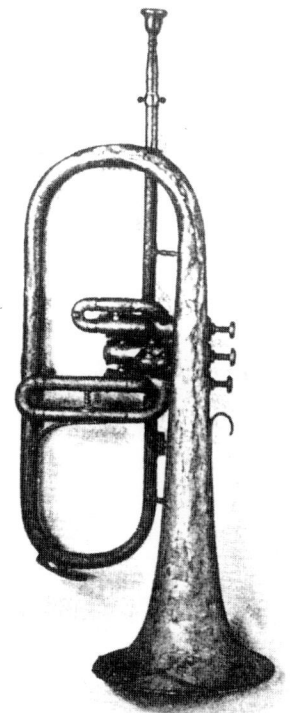

then he has been a regular visitor, most recently conducting the NZSO for the acclaimed *Peter Grimes* with Wellington City Opera.

Women Conductors   Prior to the last decade only one woman had conducted the NZSO. New Zealander Dorothea Franchi, who also played harp in the orchestra, conducted her own work, *Do-Wack-A-Do Ballet Suite* in the 1965 Proms and again in 1975, for a concert commemorating the Golden Jubilee of Radio Broadcasting in New Zealand.

Since then there has been Dalia Atlas in 1989, the recipient of several important international awards and founder, director and conductor of the Pro-Musica Orchestra and Technion Symphony in Haifa, Israel. There have also been visits from Paris-born Catherine Comet, music director of the American Symphony Orchestra in 1991; Jane Glover in 1993, former artistic director of the London Mozart Players and closely associated with Covent Garden; and two visits from Cuban-born Odaline de la Martinez, who studied at the Royal Academy and Royal College of Music in London. She was the first woman to conduct the BBC Proms in 1984 and later set up the European Women's Orchestra. Odaline de la Martinez made her first visit here for the Asia Pacific Festival in 1992, and returned in 1995 when she also conducted at the Women Composers Festival.

Conductor/composers   Since Harry Luscombe conducted his *Fantasia and Fugue* in 1949 there has been a regular queue of New Zealanders to conduct the orchestra in their own work, including Sir William Southgate, Ashley Heenan OBE, Larry Pruden, Kenneth Young and Edwin Carr, but not it seems, Douglas Lilburn.

Overseas composer/conductors like Igor Stravinsky and William Walton conducted theirs in the 1960s, Polish composer Krzyztof Penderecki was to have come in 1983, and then in 1989 there was Leif Segerstam, part of the Finnish Exchange.

Looking rather like a young Santa Claus, he made a greater impact on NZSO players than anyone could have imagined. English was not of course his first language, but the uses he applied it to were creative in the extreme. Dale Gold, principal double bass: "I have always written down when the conductor says something funny about the music and with Segerstam we found people were already doing this all over the orchestra so we compiled a list, *The Quotations of Leif Segerstam*, with almost a hundred quotes..."

"Something is satelliting out of control of the beated music!"
"Whatever bumble thing... a small dog noise... almost a gorilla sound ..."
"There is a slight worm to be executed very much together."
"Please compose the six rests that are missing."
"Don't make it sound as brutal as my left hand, please."

"You don't need to count here. You won't get lost because at the end, I will turn around and look at you stoppingly!"

"I want the music more traumatised."

"Like an old time Western locomotive we can get the organity of the puffing."

"Keep an irony rhythm."

"Three centimetres of wavy lines, then you play the music."

"It is very beautiful what you played, but you are forgetting one thing that makes it tomorrow too loud."

"Who would sacrifice a violin?"

"You could really be princessy pochissimo."

"The gravity is on the beat composed."

"The string section without the basses is a plasmatic living cluster."

"Just play in your box until you come to the climax... so that we hear the clappering."

"The quintuplet should be freshly and rudely the same as the triplet."

"Could I have something which is close to that which is underneath the pencil?"

"Hypnotic and destiny-filled."

"Tonnmeister, are you heavy enough in the glockenbox?"

"Listen to these gorilla players." (in reference to the cello section)

"More grease in the pianissimo."

"The non-metric pulsator on the podium."

"Use parabolic crescendi... they are more animalic."

"My left hand will look at you."

"I have words for everything that can be expressed: coincidentimently; embryomalic; electrific-ally; fiveishness; flimmer; inexclickable; Fenugrish five things; I am fluxating in 8; it is a Valsefy."

(Above) Leif Segerstam. (Below) Odaline de la Martinez.

Through Dale Gold's efforts, the NZSO became the first orchestra to appear on the Internet (see page 215). Forty more followed soon after, but he says it is still regarded "as the best and most innovative, containing everything from our schedule... to viola jokes".[7]

"The Segerstam list was circulated around the world. Mathew Ross [violin] was in Scandinavia and saw it on a wall, and I got a note from a guy in a Swedish orchestra who said he gave it to Segerstam [who] very proudly said, 'I didn't really say all those things!'"

In the decade to 1996 some longtime friends returned, including choral conductor Sir David Willcocks, French conductor Louis Fremaux and pianist Stephen Bishop-Kovacevich, as both conductor and soloist. Stanislaw Skrowaczewski conducted the orchestra in 1988, as did Maxim Shostakovich in that year's International Festival, returning in 1993; Heinz Wallberg conducted Die Meistersinger in the 1990 Festival and the NZSO again in 1991; American Andrew Litton and Lucas Vis made first visits here in 1993 and the latter returns in 1996.

New Friends

The five years to 1995 saw many new faces on the NZSO conductor's podium. Some recent newcomers to New Zealand have long been respected, the most distinguished being Sir Neville Marriner, founder and artistic director of the important Academy of St Martin-in-the-Fields. Sir Neville conducted the NZSO for the International Festival of the Arts in 1992, and returns in 1996.

David Shallon, music director of the Jerusalem Symphony Orchestra, was previously chief conductor of the Düsseldorf Symphony Orchestra from 1987-93. Born in Tel Aviv, he studied in Vienna and worked as first assistant to Leonard Bernstein in concerts throughout Europe. He made his debut with the Vienna Symphony Orchestra in 1980 and the Berlin Philharmonic in 1986, and has conducted many other major orchestras and opera houses in Europe. David Shallon made his first visit to New Zealand in 1991, returning in 1995 and 1996.

Yan Pascal Tortelier, son of the late cellist Paul, is a young French conductor whose musical career began as violinist. Now principal conductor of the BBC Philharmonic, he was previously principal conductor and artistic director of the Ulster Orchestra. His concerts with the NZSO in 1994 were among the highlights of that year.

Janos Fürst, born in Hungary, has long been a friend of the NZSO. Since his first visit in 1983 he has returned regularly to conduct the orchestra, frequently in Central European repertoire. In 1995 as conductor of the hugely successful Tower Beethoven Festival in Wellington and Christchurch he gained new friends, as summed up by a Christchurch reviewer: "the feeling of cohesion and purpose [between Fürst and the NZSO] was electrifying".

Polish conductor Jerzy Maksymiuk proved an exciting addition to the NZSO's 1995 Subscription series with his October concerts with the Prokofiev *No. 1*, Rachmaninov *No. 3* and Cesar Franck's *Symphony in D Minor*. The founder and former conductor of the Polish Chamber Orchestra was here in 1984; he is currently Conductor Laureate, formerly chief conductor, of the BBC Scottish Symphony Orchestra.

The Russian conductor Alexander Lazarev made a sensation when he conducted the NZSO in the 1994 New Zealand International Festival of the Arts. As chief conductor and artistic director of the Bolshoi Theatre, one of the most important posts in Russia, the NZSO would have benefited enormously with him as replacement conductor of its cancelled European tour. Alexander Lazarev, who conducted the Shostakovich *Symphony No. 8* on his last visit, returns to conduct *No. 10* (and also Mahler *5*) in 1996.

The search for a principal guest conductor continued into early 1996. It's a challenge to find the right person, says Wilma Smith: "The orchestra has had some good relationships with conductors, but it's so elusive. Good conductors and great ones are certainly very few in the world, so when you find one [like Eduardo Mata] you go 'Hallelujah!'"

Janos Fürst conducted Tower Beethoven Festival concerts, 1995: the feeling was electrifying.

Effervescent Polish conductor Jerzy Maksymiuk visited for the NZSO Subscription series, 1995.

PHOTOGRAPHS: STEPHEN HARKER

TEATRO DE LA MAESTRANZA

Aotearoa, Obertura

Douglas Lilburn (1915)

La música de Douglas Lilburn [...]
landesa, en su sonido y en las [...]
suscita en aquellos que la oyen [...]
se debe que Nueva Zelanda [...]
musical, y su influencia h[...]
para los compositores que [...]

METRO
0481
SENCILLO

UTILIZACION
SEGUN TARIFAS
CONSERVESE
HASTA LA SALIDA

653 4

PROHIBIDO FUMAR
EXCEPTO ZONA
RESERVADA PARA ELLO

Seville and other Musical Journeys

"Night of Magic at the Maestranza Theatre."

– Spanish review of NZSO concert, Expo 92, Seville.

THE NZSO's brief history is littered with its cancelled overseas tours. Together they represent years of detailed planning and costing work: choosing an itinerary, programmes, conductors and soloists, arranging flights, surface travel, transportation of the instruments, booking accommodation, trying to find finance.

As early as 1965 the National Orchestra was planning its first overseas tour, to Australia, South-East Asia, the West Coast of the United States, Canada, and Honolulu, to celebrate its 21st birthday in 1968. The Prime Minister Sir Keith Holyoake had expressed 'interest'.

One year later the plan was for a five-country, 15-concert tour in 1969-70, including Hong Kong, Japan and Alaska. A combined tour with Sir Malcolm Sargent and the Christchurch Harmonic Society to the 1970 Expo World Fair in Osaka was considered, and that too had Government 'interest'. Then the South-East Asia tour resurfaced, but in 1968 when the BCNZ requested a 'joint venture' Government seemed to have lost interest. "Not in the present economic circumstances," it was told.

Australian Tour

In fact none of the NZSO's three overseas tours resulted from its own initiatives. The first, in 1974, was a surprise invitation from the ABC to replace the Sydney Symphony in its subscription concerts during the SSO's first tour to Europe – the SSO's negotiations for the LSO or LPO to substitute having fallen through.

Brian Priestman, then chief conductor, chose a very demanding set of programmes to showcase the orchestra in its nine concerts. Only two of these were repeats, and some of the music, because it had not been performed for two years, required extra rehearsal, at a time

NZSO PLAYERS PHOTOGRAPH: NEW ZEALAND HERALD

when Brian Priestman was busy working with his other orchestra, the Denver Symphony.

Works by New Zealand composers Edwin Carr, Douglas Lilburn, John Rimmer and Anthony Watson featured in the seven different programmes. Soloist Kiri Te Kanawa sang Mozart and Puccini arias, and Richard Strauss's *Four Last Songs*, and Michael Houstoun played Prokofiev's *Piano Concerto No. 3*. Principals Vyvyan Yendoll (viola) and Wilfred Simenauer (cello) were two "splendid" orchestral soloists in another Strauss work, *Don Quixote*.[29]

"The NZBCSO endeared itself to Sydney audiences during a gruelling whirlwind visit... in which it gave seven concerts in eight days with five changes of programme," said *The Australian*. "At its best it was quite thrilling."[30]

After its Sydney performances at the Town Hall and the newly opened Opera House, the tour continued to Canberra and concluded in Adelaide, where it enjoyed its greatest success, "20 minutes of applause, and a standing cheering ovation".[31]

The concerts drew surprised praise from the Australian critics, who had not expected such a high calibre orchestra. "It is not a minor league unit," said the *Sydney Morning Herald*,[32] which mentioned "several outstanding achievements in its concerts". The choice of works like Vaughan Williams' *4th Symphony* and *Don Quixote*, was much praised. "It was not only

The NZBC Symphony Orchestra on stage at the Sydney Opera House, November 1974, with Kiri Te Kanawa, soprano; Brian Priestman, conductor; Margaret (Sicely) Tibbles; Alex Lindsay, concertmaster; and John Chisholm, assistant concertmaster. (Opposite page, Top) The Australian tour was the orchestra's first taste of international performing. (Opposite page, Lower) The NZSO was the featured orchestra at the Hong Kong Arts Festival in February-March 1980.

GORDON G. CLARKE

first class but gave a far more interesting programme than many from our own orchestra," Sydney's *Daily Mirror* commented.[33] Canberra too was very appreciative: "A fine body, well disciplined... this was a particularly fine concert, and the NZBCSO made an excellent impression... May they come back again soon."[34]

Subscriber resistance in Sydney, which left many seats empty, was disappointing for players. It is a consolation to imagine that those unadventurous Sydney subscribers, reading the rapturous reviews next day, lived to regret missing Kiri Te Kanawa, the sensation of the tour, in her outstanding Australian professional debut performances.

Within months of this success two more tours, one to North America, the other to the Australian Music Forum, were mooted. Neither eventuated, but there was optimism about a third, more ambitious proposal, a 44-day world tour first planned for 1979-80, then 1981. For the first time Government intended adding a cultural dimension to its trade and political interests, linking New Zealand's butter exports with orchestral concerts in Washington, San Francisco, London, Paris, Bonn, Brussels, Amsterdam, Copenhagen, Leningrad and Moscow. It was agreed to in principal by Cabinet in July 1978, but rejected in August 1979. Prime Minister Robert Muldoon said it was "not viable".

Hong Kong Tour

The invitation to perform as the featured orchestra at the Hong Kong Arts Festival in 1980 arrived before the European tour was cancelled, and helped to lessen that disappointment.

There were no qualms about accepting this all-expenses paid tour but as planning progressed over 18 months, NZSO management was frustrated by its lack of control over the important factors of repertoire, conductors and soloists. The workload was heavy again, like Australia, but probably less satisfying musically. In three weeks the orchestra performed 10 concerts with nine different programmes. Eight concerts were in Hong Kong City Hall, the other two at Tsuen Wan in the New Territories.

Concerts were divided between two conductors: Michi Inoue, who was the logical choice as NZSO principal guest conductor, and Welshman Owain Arwel Hughes, who had never conducted the NZSO before, nor since. Violinist Ruggiero Ricci and Swedish baritone Hakan Hagegard apart, the overseas soloists were not those which NZSO would have chosen, and any New Zealand content in the tour was hard won, with local music represented by composers Douglas Lilburn, David Farquhar and John Rimmer.

Pianist Michael Houstoun, brought in to replace a cancelled Festival soloist, joined NZSO soloists to perform Schubert's *Trout Quintet,* one of two chamber works presented as a means of showcasing New Zealand artists in the tour. This was something that "did not sit too well as part of an orchestral concert" as Michael remembers it, and "musically it wasn't a great experience".

Players found that despite very comfortable conditions in Hong Kong, they had to

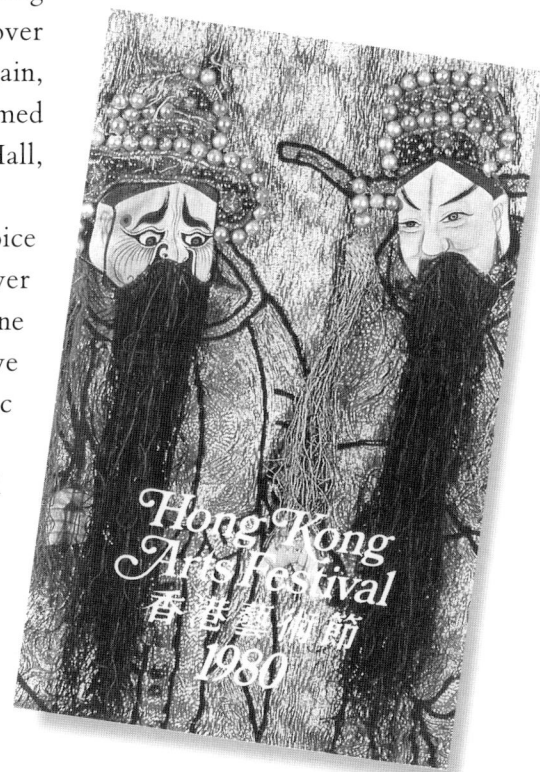

contend with two competing conductors, various health problems and poor reviews. Unwittingly the NZSO found itself caught up in the crossfire of a long-running dispute between the Hong Kong Philharmonic Orchestra and Festival organisers. Audiences loved the concerts, and displayed genuine enthusiasm which our group of NZSO Supporters observed night after night at those concerts – but this was never reflected in any reviews in Hong Kong papers, nor in the very critical article that pre-judged the orchestra before its arrival, written by someone who had neither heard nor seen it before.

Seville

Now the orchestra had another opportunity to tour. The suggestion came from Ian Fraser, commissioner general of the New Zealand Pavilion at Expo '92, Seville, who thought the NZSO should perform there on New Zealand Day.

A musician himself, and a long-time supporter of the orchestra, Fraser argued that as other countries were sending their orchestras for National Day celebrations, this country should do the same. It would have the added value of convincing Europeans that New Zealand had more to offer than just dairy products and All Blacks.

From the NZSO's point of view this was the long-awaited chance to launch itself into the international arena, with the Expo concert the centrepiece of a major orchestral tour. Although a campaign was quickly mounted, the initial response was not promising so orchestra manager David Pawsey set off overseas to check out the options first-hand.

In London during discussions with Ian Fraser he discovered that the one performer the World Expo organisers had not been able to attract was Dame Kiri Te Kanawa. As a personal friend, David contacted her to suggest she join the NZSO in Seville.

At their first meeting with the Expo committee in Seville, David and Ian were in no doubt that the NZSO lacked sufficient status to replace an opera performance scheduled for that date at the Teatro de la Maestranza.

That was until the New Zealanders mentioned the strong possibility that Dame Kiri Te Kanawa would be with them. "The mood of the meeting changed immediately," says David. "The opera was cancelled to enable the NZSO performance to go ahead on 26 June, the eve of New Zealand's National Day at Expo."

For the rest of the tour, timing was not perfect. It was summer, the concert season in Europe had come to an end, and music festivals were the only possibility. Painstakingly a tour began to take shape to include Montreal, Hamburg and other European cities, with Perth, Australia, on the way home.

Like so many more before it, the tour eventually fell apart, leaving only the one secure date, the Seville Expo concert. The NZSO Board was "very uneasy" says Dr Hylton LeGrice, "because it took the liability of having the orchestra's shortfall" and coming so soon after the recent debacle over funding, it seemed irresponsible to spend so much money to go

overseas for just the one concert. Reluctantly, the Board then proceeded to cancel the tour.

The April announcement brought an adverse response from the media, with charges of mismanagement. Five days later the tour was on again. The New Zealand Lottery Grants Board announced it would underwrite the additional funds needed, $400,000, to get the NZSO to Spain, while on the same day the Government tabled a supplementary grant of $762,000, to cover the orchestra's immediate deficit.

Newspapers critical of the tour's cancellation, now did an about-face. It was criticised for going ahead, quoting the Board's original stance that it was irresponsible to travel so far for one concert; the manner in which it was cancelled and then reinstated was badly handled. It was disappointing to hear a respected entertainer like Sir Howard Morrison – who later appeared on stage with the NZSO in Seville – speaking out against the tour.

Sceptics who questioned if the cancellation was genuine would have been convinced had they seen former NZSO travel manager Rex Collins in action. His was the nightmare job to try and make new bookings for all those cancelled arrangements for an orchestral party of over 108-strong, including a supporters party of family and friends, for eight flights on three

The eve of the great adventure: Franz-Paul Decker and NZSO members assembled for an Auckland Subscription concert before flying off to Seville next day.

NEW ZEALAND HERALD

airlines from Auckland to Sydney, to Bangkok, Frankfurt and Seville, then back again to Wellington as well as with accommodation in Seville. All of this to be obtained at the right price and in the middle of the busiest travel season.

The tour came in the midst of the NZSO's own Subscription season. Two concerts had to be performed in Auckland on the Friday and Saturday evenings before setting out on the 36-hour journey to Europe on Sunday morning. Two other concerts scheduled for that time were cancelled and replaced with recitals by veteran pianist Shura Cherkassky.

Stage manager Grant Gilbert packed out the instruments after the Auckland concert, loaded them into the aircraft at 2:00am and flew to Sydney at 5:00am. He had five hours to oversee the Australian work crew transfer 30 cubic metres of equipment to the orchestral flight, and repack a 10-metre pallet, but their slowness meant he only just made it.

The rest of the travellers, including conductor Dr Franz-Paul Decker, left Auckland on a cold winter's day with the temperature in single digits, and flew halfway round the world to a spot almost exactly geographically opposite: Seville, where summer temperatures in the upper-40s were the norm.

It was a concern that players would have to contend with this very long flight, followed by jet-lag and a dramatic temperature change, with only one day to recover before rehearsals started. But their own resilience won out, plus a 'cold snap' that had not only sent temperatures plummeting to a more comfortable 25°C before their arrival, but also helped them to acclimatise as temperatures rose again.

'Stalag de Gines'

Accommodation was stretched to capacity in Seville, so as New Zealand Expo staff recommended, the NZSO stayed at the Villas de Gines, seven kilometres from the city. This had been built to cater for an expected influx of less affluent Expo tourists, which had not eventuated. The small, self-contained units were clean but with walls so thin that David Pawsey answered the question "What time is it?" before realising it was asked by someone two cabins away.

It was apparent the complex had been constructed in haste and not properly finished. At least two of the orchestral party suffered potentially serious accidents: one received an electric shock and was catapulted across the room after stepping out of the shower and touching the wall; another shut her door and was hit on the head by a piece of ornamental brick surround from the roof.

These long tin sheds were renamed 'Stalag de Gines', but they had some advantages that were not immediately obvious. Security was not the problem that it was in the city, where, as Ian Fraser had warned, Expo was attracting less desirable tourists. Hylton and Angela LeGrice experienced this for themselves, when Angela was robbed of all her personal jewellery as well as their precious irreplaceable concert tickets. An unsuspecting couple who bought

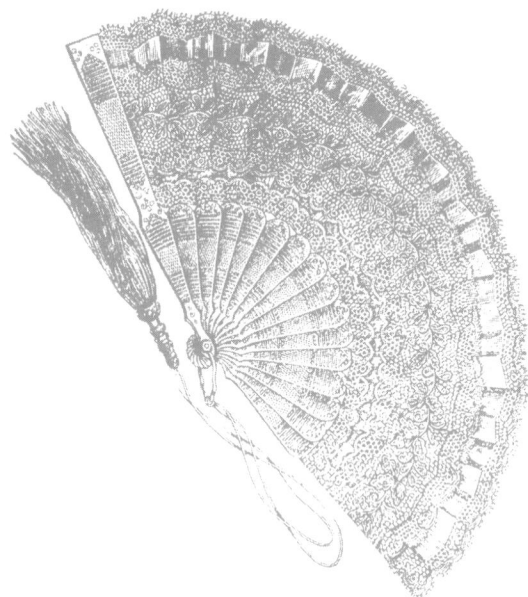

the tickets on the black market were swooped on by officials almost the moment they were seated in the theatre that night.

The other advantage was the opportunity to experience something of local life, as it was only a short walk to the small Andalucian village of Gines. Players were soon at home with the people, and some, like the late Charlie Mountfort, helped out behind the bar at Manuel's, one of several small restaurants. New Zealand Expo staff members and Maori performers lived in the same area, as did entertainment co-ordinator Max Cryer, whose new townhouse burnt out due to faulty wiring and left him, on the eve of New Zealand Day, with only the clothes he stood up in.

Rehearsals took place at the Salo Apollo, home of the newly-formed Seville Symphony Orchestra. Security was strictly enforced here, as elsewhere in Seville and Expo, and it was necessary to personally endorse every NZSO player who came through the door. It was noticeable too, that on the day Dame Kiri was to join the orchestra in rehearsal, many of the young international musicians from the Seville Symphony just happened to drop in.

It was there too, that the extra players joined the group, all three ex-pat New Zealanders living in Europe. Their participation represented a big saving in not having to take casual players from New Zealand to play in the two works for which they were required. London-based clarinet Rachel Nicholson (now NZSO principal bass clarinet), interrupted her honeymoon and brought her husband Ian with her; second harp Helen Webby had been studying in Holland, while Graham Johns, principal percussion with the Royal Liverpool Philharmonic, had not long returned after performing at Expo with his own orchestra.

Seville's Teatro de la Maestranza was built for Expo '92. It was the scene of one of the NZSO's greatest performances.

JOY TONKS

Teatro de la Maestranza

As the concert date got closer it seemed strange that no tickets went on sale until a couple of days before the performance. We need not have worried. When bookings opened all tickets sold out in a matter of hours, with another thousand requests that could not be met. Originally available for NZ$100, they were rumoured to have been resold on the black market, only hours later, at a price between four to seven times higher – the ratio depending on who you spoke to. We were frequently stopped in the street by people begging for tickets.

The Teatro de la Maestranza, Seville's new opera house built for Expo at the end of 1991, was already a venue for some of the world's greatest orchestras and performers, against which the NZSO would be judged. Three weeks after the NZSO's performance it was the scene of a tragic accident when part of the roof caved in after stage machinery for the opera *Otello* collapsed onto the stage, killing a member of the Paris Opera chorus and wounding 20 others. A memorial concert in Paris was conducted by former NZSO timpanist, Gary Brain.

There was a high degree of nervous anticipation on either side of the stage at 9:00pm on Friday 26 June, for the orchestra and the New Zealand party seated with Dr Decker's family, in the well-dressed audience. The Maestranza's gently sloping auditorium with excellent acoustics and sight-lines, held 1700 people, with not an empty seat in sight.

Conductor Franz-Paul Decker raised his baton and the programme began with a Spanish offering, Manuel de Falla's *El Amor Brujo (Love the Magician)*, and followed with one from New Zealand, Douglas Lilburn's *Aotearoa*, one very well-known to the audience, the other completely unknown, though from the warm reception this was not obvious. Then Dame Kiri entered, stunning in an off-the-shoulder gown of black and silver, to sing Mozart's *Exsultate Jubilate* to rapturous applause.

At interval we promenaded in the surprisingly small foyer and returned to hear an even more exhilarating second half, which began with the orchestra and Franz-Paul Decker in a once-in-a-lifetime performance of *Der Rosenkavalier Suite* by Richard Strauss. "While keeping the tightest control they went over the top," wrote Lindis Taylor of the *Evening Post,* one of two music critics in our party, "and all its madness, its kaleidoscopic shifts in tempo, colour, dynamics had the audience gasping. They broke into a rhythmic clapping in triple time, a style unique in Andalucia and reserved for exceptional performances."[35]

Peter Shaw, critic for *Metro* magazine: "The sweep and grandeur... had the audience shouting its approval – which only goes to show that the NZSO under its chief conductor is indeed a world class instrument."[36]

Dame Kiri's return to sing Strauss's magnificent *Four Last Songs*, concluded the main part of the concert with tumultuous applause and the entire audience on its feet. The curtain calls went on and on and on, 11 of them in over 20 minutes. Dame Kiri returned to sing two further Strauss songs as encores, *Zueignung* and *Cäcille*, but the audience was still not satisfied. Finally she returned and sang *Pokarekareana* unaccompanied. It was an incredibly moving and

"Danza del terror" from *El amor brujo*

Allegro ritmico

unforgettable performance even for the international audience, but for the New Zealanders it was a highly charged, emotional experience that left many in tears.

Though the audience would have stayed all night, Dame Kiri signalled that there were no more encores. She took concertmaster Isidor Saslav by the arm and they left the stage together. The orchestral players followed.

No one on that stage or in that audience will ever forget that performance. "It was an unbelievable triumph," Lindis Taylor wrote. "The atmosphere after was one of stunned exhilaration and triumph among New Zealanders present. We knew the adventure had paid off. Dame Kiri was the essential ingredient of course but clearly this great orchestra had given for Decker the performance of a lifetime."

For Franz-Paul Decker, whose hopes of a full overseas tour for the orchestra had been disappointed, it was nevertheless a highlight. "I was extremely happy to have the chance to

The moment of triumph at Teatro de la Maestranza, Seville. Dame Kiri Te Kanawa, maestro Franz-Paul Decker and members of the NZSO: back row, Walter Hamer, Ed Allen, Peter Sharman, André Malashenko, Michael Gibbs. Middle row: Felicity Bunt, Nancy Luther-Jara, Mary Scott, Carole Hohauser, Alan Gold, Alexa Still. Front: Lisa Egen, Emma Brewerton, John Dodds, Janet Armstrong, Jane Freed, Vyvyan Yendoll.

NEW ZEALAND HERALD

take them there. It was a huge success and people still speak about that concert. We could not have been [from] further away and that helped to have such an impact."

Conductor-in-residence Kenneth Young: "It was just stunning! It was fantastic, just fantastic! It was world-class and it would have been impossible to think of that kind of standard of performance, 10 years ago, even five years ago."

Prime Minister Jim Bolger and Mrs Joan Bolger were in the audience, and could not help but be caught up in all the excitement. Afterwards they joined the celebratory party in one of the vine-covered outdoor village restaurants nearby, where a special entertainment had been arranged: one of the most successful flamenco dancers in Andalucia, a woman originally from Palmerston North.

New Zealand Pavilion, Expo

The next day was New Zealand Day and players were expected to join in the celebrations at Expo. The coaches arrived early but found access through the gate barred, probably for security reasons. The drivers tried another; same problem. Finally two Spanish-speaking members of the orchestra, Ron Jara and Dale Gold, managed to convince guards to let us in to the wrong end of the huge complex. Musicians ran to catch up the New Zealand parade as it left our pavilion, collecting small New Zealand flags to wave as the procession led through the wide avenues between pavilions under a canopy of living plants. It stopped at the Palenque, an outdoor concert area, for the New Zealand entertainment and the official speeches by Prime Minister Jim Bolger, the Spanish Minister of Industry, Trade and Tourism, and Emilio Cassinello, Expo's commissioner general.[37]

The New Zealand pavilion, credited as being one of the five top attractions of over 100 international pavilions in the 538 acre Expo park, was a reconstruction of the craggy cliff face of Young Nicks Head in Gisborne, complete with waterfalls and mechanical gannets that perched, stretched their necks, flapped their wings and squawked. Every hour on the hour the music of the Maori entertainers brought people running to the outdoor stage, the only pavilion with entertainment outside the site, to hear what Spanish media termed "the earthquake from the Antipodes".[38]

Inside, people queued for an hour for its three theatres, in one of which the Auckland Philharmonia mimed on-screen music recorded by the NZSO, making some players uncomfortable. At the end of the presentation sightseers found themselves cunningly conveyed to the food hall which was stocked with high quality New Zealand products.

Orchestra players attended various receptions in the Pavilion Lounge. The New Zealand Chamber Orchestra, led by Donald Armstrong, performed at two, with one of these occasions featuring Douglas Lilburn's *Landfall in Unknown Seas*, with Ian Fraser reading the poem by guest of honour Dr Allen Curnow. On New Zealand Day a luncheon and an evening reception was given for the Prime Minister Mr Jim Bolger and Mrs Bolger.

LINDIS TAYLOR

The reception drew many international and distinguished visitors. It soon turned into a Kiwi party when the New Zealand men, including the Prime Minister, took off their jackets and, encouraged by Sir Howard, joined in a spirited version of the haka. Later in the evening, further encouragement had the PM at the microphone to sing a solo *Danny Boy*. The invited guests were impressed. A British businessman told me, "I can't imagine John Major doing that".

New Zealand's thank you to the people of Seville, delivered on a tiny stage in the magic setting of the Plaza de San Francisco. Concertmaster Isidor Saslav (left) with conductor Franz-Paul Decker.

Two days after its success at the Maestranza, the NZSO gave its final performance, a free outdoor concert in Seville. Graham Coxhead, determined the orchestra should do more than just one performance, suggested a charity concert. This found no favour with city officials, so it became a 'Thank you' concert from the people of New Zealand to the people of Seville.

The venue was the Plaza de San Francisco, one of the largest and most beautiful squares in the city, where an eight metre square stage had been set up for Corpus Christi the previous week. David Pawsey and Grant Gilbert saw at once that it was totally inadequate for 100 orchestra players and their instruments and an extension to double the size was promised. David recalls: "We turned up with the truck and gear and there was nothing. No one knew anything. It was Sunday, siesta, and no one wanted to know!"

Two hours before the concert was due to start they were told the extension was not coming. Only Kiwi ingenuity could save the day. They fitted everything they could on stage then borrowed the risers for the PA system from the sound engineer, used trestle tables for the

Concert in Plaza de San Francisco

Poster advertising the free concert in the Plaza de San Francisco, Seville, 28 June 1992.

percussion, and placed the harp, celeste and timpani on the ground, Grant remembers. "I think André [Malashenko, timpani] couldn't see and couldn't hear either, so he just played along with the odd glimpse of the conductor's baton every now and then. Diane [Cooper] behind the celeste, hadn't a chance and Carolyn [Mills] on harp was like André, and played whenever she saw the baton."

Without the promised guard rail, which also failed to turn up, there was real concern that someone might fall off the stage.

Once on stage Franz-Paul Decker had to stay there, unable to go off between items because there was no way he could get past the tightly packed musicians. As conductor of the Orquesta Civat de Barcelona for 10 years he is very much at home in Spain, and frequently addressed the audience in Spanish. He was presented with a special medal of honour from the Mayor of Seville as the city's thanks for the concert.

'Los Maoríes' were already famous in Seville as 'the stars of Expo' and led by Sir Howard Morrison they provided a popular start to the concert, performing on that tiny stage in front of the seated orchestra.

The setting was quite magical and as the sky began to darken, people crowded into the tree-lined square of 17th and 18th century buildings, a white canopy fluttering overhead. Official seating provided for a thousand was quickly filled with another three to four thousand people crowding in right up to the edge of the stage: family groups, parents and children, grandparents, and a few tourists.

They were a wonderful audience, totally silent and attentive during the concert, but clapping enthusiastically as each work ended.

For this programme Dr Decker had chosen shorter orchestral works by Manuel de Falla, Bernstein, Tchaikovsky, Prokofiev and Shostakovich, with *España* by Chabrier a very popular choice, accompanied by calls of "Olé!" and the distinctive rhythmic clapping heard previously at the Maestranza concert.

One of the encores, *Sevilla* by Albéniz, was especially appreciated and brought loud shouts of pleasure from the Sevillian audience. When it was over and the last encore played, they continued to stand and clap, surging forward as the players began to file off stage to make a corridor for them, still clapping enthusiastically and shaking musicians' hands, then following them along the street to the Old Town Hall, which was being used as dressing rooms. It was the most extraordinary and emotionally-charged scene. Players were visibly overcome by the warmth and generosity of this response to their playing, with many of them in tears.

"I was one of the last off the stage," says Nancy Luther-Jara, principal piccolo. "I was packing instruments, and they were still there, clapping every single person as they came off. I was just dumbfounded!"

Next day the orchestra returned to Frankfurt and went their separate ways, some returning home, the majority spending their five days leave on a brief holiday in other European cities.

For years Franz-Paul Decker had called the NZSO "the world's best-kept secret". The Seville tour, short though it was, had helped to let more people in on that secret. Certainly its success was far beyond that which could have been anticipated. That Dame Kiri would receive accolades was no surprise, but as an NZSO person sitting in that audience, I felt the most satisfying aspect was hearing that same enthusiasm for the orchestra (perhaps down a notch or two), especially the *Der Rosenkavalier Suite*. This was played in the 'Overtures to Seville' concert before they left home, but at the Maestranza players performed as if inspired. It was the pinnacle of their achievement.

Spanish critics were ecstatic. Two reviews were waiting when the players returned home, the first, by Ramon Maria Serrer in Seville's largest paper,[39] headed: 'Night of Magic at the Maestranza Theatre', spoke of "rarely having seen an audience more absorbed in a recital of such quality" ...the orchestra was "splendid... An extraordinary ensemble... whose quality can be likened to that of the great British orchestras..." and concluded "this was heaven".

The second review was by Francisco Melguizo, who said it was "a total success... with or without Kiri Te Kanawa it merits the most glowing tribute... The orchestra conducted by Franz-Paul Decker, was the perfect accompaniment, but its greatest merit was in the excellent orchestral performance in the remainder of the programme... It was by choosing a symphonic section of *Der Rosenkavalier* that the New Zealand Symphony Orchestra gave us the full measure of their splendid ability, interpreting very successfully the structure of the work which [is] the most celebrated of [its] composer. Conductor and conducted were worthy recipients of the acknowledgement accorded them by the audience."[40]

If there was one disappointment it was the quality of the television recording of the Maestranza concert. Filmed by a Spanish company, it did nothing to convey the sound or excitement of that performance. That apart, the whole party would agree with Lindis Taylor that "the Seville adventure has indeed exceeded the wildest expectations of its success."[41]

For principal cellist Farquhar Wilkinson, retiring after 39 years, the tour was a wonderful finale, although he had not felt so nervous before a concert for years. "The orchestra played superbly [at the Maestranza]. You can't imagine playing *Der Rosenkavalier* better than with Franz-Paul Decker. You feel you could walk off a plank for him!

"The outdoor concert was extraordinary, a tremendous atmosphere and it must create some benefit. There are other ways of communicating with other countries and cultures than by sending rugby teams and kiwifruit. In Europe music is a very big part of their culture and it is exciting to know the orchestra can go and create the impression it did; it negates the feeling that there is nothing here but mountains and sheep. That was achieved in Seville."

Orchestra shows off in great style

The New Zealand Symphony Orchestra embodies all those components which realise artistic excellence. It is of the nation and for the nation and we are humbled by our responsibility to guide it towards the 21st century.

Lost in Anguish quite despairing Heav'n alone for Virtue

GOVERNMENT FUNDING

vernment Funding for the Company's year to
erating costs is provided through *Vote: Cultural A*
e funding is remitted to the Company under
d conditions of a *Purchase of Services*
ted each year with the Ministry of Cult

5. ABNORMAL ITEMS

Abnormal items charged
comprise $74,544 of red
from restructuring of the

...eaves magic
...ip...
...orchestra

There are no extraordinary
1992 item was the costs of

te Cultural Affairs
pplementary Estimates
composer

Ron Wel
...

Clapping was out of control but the orches-

Change of Key

"The orchestra is like an instrument – give it to a star, you will have a superior performance than the same instrument in the hands of a beginner."

– Yury Gezentsvey, principal, first violins.

D URING one of the rehearsals at the Salo Apollo in Seville, interim manager Graham Coxhead made an announcement that, for once, raised cheers and not the fears of musicians. A permanent appointment had finally been made, he said. The orchestra would have a new chief executive from 1 October: Mark Keyworth.

As chief executive of the Royal New Zealand Ballet Company for the past six years, Mark Keyworth was a name well-known in the arts community, and the incomparable orchestral grapevine had picked him as a contender some time before.

This knowledge, more than any other, was an inspiration that better things lay ahead, giving players an additional incentive for their success on stage at the Maestranza the following night.

Australian Mark Keyworth, a Fellow of the Royal Society of the Arts, was deputy general manager of the Queensland Arts Council for 10 years before joining the New Zealand Ballet in 1986. The Symphony's gain was the Ballet's loss unfortunately, and caused some initial recriminations between two of the country's major arts organisations.

"Basically it was a career move," says Mark, who was first approached for the NZSO job in September 1991. "Also, I think I had done as much as I felt I could do with the Ballet and if I was to stay in New Zealand it was time to take on another challenge."

He admits under-estimating the magnitude of that challenge, with many of the problems not evident then. In his view the orchestra was a "cobwebbed old lady that wouldn't take too much to dust off and give it the shiny look of the new corporate it was expected to be".

But that old lady had a past. It had made her why she was and what she was. This made

From Tutu to Tutti

The ebullient Mark Keyworth getting down to basics on his appointment as chief executive, October 1992.

NEW ZEALAND HERALD

CHANGE OF KEY *111*

rapid change less likely to succeed than change that was more structured and slower. Mark shared the public perception of a well-funded orchestra and thought that financially, after the Ballet, it would be a breeze. So that was another shock. "It is no better off than any other arts organisation in the country, only it's on a different scale."

The NZSO and its new chief enjoyed a lengthy honeymoon period in which the mood of players and management alike lifted and a feeling of optimism prevailed. Three successful events held in the first two months were indicators of the Keyworth management style: a full Company meeting started a new tradition; an Open Day at Symphony House brought the public in their thousands; and a masked ball celebrated the orchestral year's end.

Everyone entered into the spirit of the ball; scenery was borrowed and costumes hired from the Ballet Company and a pre-ball workshop to make plaster masks was run by violinists Rebecca Jackson and Michael Monaghan. No one recognised the rather formidable looking matron in tweed skirt, wig and pearls as principal violist Vyvyan Yendoll, who had shaved off his beard for the occasion. No one could fail to recognise the stately Pope as Mark Keyworth.

"It was all part of a deliberate policy to raise morale, which was at an all-time low," Mark says. "Insufficient care had been taken in equipping both the administration and orchestra for the totally foreign environment they were entering into." Too many dramatic changes in a very short time and a lot of knee-jerk reactions had created uncertainty. "Strong direction and stability" he felt was what was needed now.

Artistic Manager   One of Mark Keyworth's most urgent requirements was the appointment of an artistic manager to fill the vacuum left by Peter Nisbet. Advertisements were already in circulation around the world, and by the time he left for New York for his usual December meeting of the International Society of Performing Arts, of which he is a Director, he had three front runners to interview.

Englishman Roger Lloyd was his choice. The former general manager of the Ulster Orchestra was in the United States studying orchestral administration for his Winston Churchill Travelling Scholarship. Two days before Christmas 1992 he was offered the job: he accepted on Christmas Day and was in Wellington by the end of January.

Roger Lloyd's career at the Ulster Orchestra began as a trial for second clarinet. He was a player for nine years, and the player's representative on the Steering Committee when the orchestra became an independent company. Three weeks later, the second clarinet became general manager, causing suspicion on the part of staff – "I was chairman of the Players Committee, and they are notoriously troublesome" – and applause from players expecting to call in the 'Old Pal's Act'.

Orchestral management he found was like playing music itself, the essential thing being detail. "This makes all the difference between average and good and excellent. The same with orchestral management, you can leave nothing to chance and say 'that will look after itself', because it can't and it won't."

The new appointment relieved the pressure on music executive Murray Alford for whom Peter Nisbet's retirement marked the 'Time of the Troubles', when he had to hold the artistic fort virtually on his own, apart from some weeks when Felicity Bunt, former second flute and general manager of the New Zealand Chamber Orchestra, worked with him in the artistic section before moving overseas.

The sudden loss of a major conductor had left Murray with a complete Subscription season to put together for 1993, and only 12 days before the information was due to be sent out. "We got it put together. It was not the greatest series, but it worked. It was, I think, the most difficult time of my life. The pressure was intense, particularly the turnover of telexes with conductors who wanted to play things which from our point of view they couldn't, because they had been done too recently – or we did not have the resources to do them. A very, very trying period indeed!"

By the time Roger Lloyd arrived the 1993 season – artists, repertoire and programmes – was in place, as too was 1994, apart from the odd gap for a soloist. Roger's 'years' were 1995 and 1996, when he could invite artists and programme works to widen the perspective of orchestral music performed by the NZSO.

The management restructuring was now complete; instigated by Peter Nisbet and prepared by his executive taskforce it first convened to initiate cost-saving measures during the 1991 funding crisis.[42]

New Vision:
Management Restructuring

The new structure replaced one in which most senior and middle management, seven to nine members, reported directly to Peter Nisbet. This rather unwieldy arrangement worked because of his extensive knowledge and interest in every aspect of the operation. Clearly it could not continue under any new regime, and even the five-stream plan devised by the taskforce was reduced further still, at his request, to artistic, finance, marketing and personnel.

Implementation of the new structure took effect under Graham Coxhead, resulting in the first redundancies in the orchestra's history. The shockwaves from this were felt not only by those staff affected, but by everyone at Symphony House.

By January 1993 Mark Keyworth's management team was complete: in March I asked for early retirement from my position as personnel manager. Former NZSO executive secretary Sally Mitchell, who is the daughter of an LSO musician and has a degree in politics, took up the challenge. She returned from a second term at Parliament, as personal assistant for Alliance Leader Jim Anderton, and in December the NZSO personnel position changed hands for the first time.

Many issues needed to be addressed. A Company Mission Statement and a Strategic Plan were formulated, and over coming months the orchestra's performing base would be broadened and extended, recording opportunities investigated and new audiences targeted. The players' contract, marketing and sponsorship were top priorities.

The myth persists that orchestral funding was excessively generous under Broadcasting. In fact funding was always tight and rose or fell, usually the latter, depending on the political pressures and constraints at the time. Outside sponsorship was unknown, neither encouraged nor sought, until into the 1980s, by which time Broadcasting was feeling the bite from reduced resources available from the Broadcasting Licence Fee. Like the move towards a more professional promotion of the orchestra, sponsorship was gained gradually, co-inciding with publication of the orchestra's first professional magazine *Concert Pitch* in 1980.

In 1981 British Airways became the orchestra's first corporate sponsor, with sponsorship of the annual NZSO Study Bursary and a subscribers competition. Landmark Properties sponsored the TVNZ/NZSO Young Musicians Competition in 1982; and in 1983 Shell New Zealand Holdings instigated a three-year Shell Scholarship for Schola Musica trainees. IBM gave $25,000 for special projects, which included a music commission for composer Jack Body and the 1984 Summer Pops Tour by Ron Goodwin.

The orchestra's first sponsored concerts began in the same Pops Tour: a car suspended above players' heads was a feature of the private concert for Toyota held at the Michael Fowler Centre. In Christchurch, the first violins dressed in red Canterbury rugby jerseys, were conducted by rugby coach 'Grizz' Wylie. Many members of the public found this unacceptable and the NZSO received surprisingly many written complaints.

Sponsorship was vital to the new company and identified by the first Board as a priority. When Gillian Vosper was appointed marketing manager, from a similiar position with Auckland's collapsed Mercury Theatre, her experience in event marketing in the arts injected a new professionalism that achieved impressive results. Together with Mark Keyworth they formed an effective team that has seen returns from sponsorship rise from around $150,000 in 1991 to over $1 million in 1995.

"It's a huge achievement," says Hylton LeGrice, "in a country that is sports-mad, has a very small population and a very tight, limited amount of sponsorship available."

The new Symphony House made it possible to entertain exclusive corporate guests 'at home' in a manner not previously contemplated by the NZSO: catered soirées, with the orchestra performing private concerts in the studio for the NZSO's major sponsors.

"Long before I came here the period was past when you could depend on corporate charity, because it just does not exist," says Mark Keyworth. "It really [is] buying a product that [is] going to build the image either of the brand or the product of the sponsor. That was the key challenge... and the one we have been hugely successful in."

Members of the NZSO were featured on the cover of Concert Pitch *magazine, January 1988. This was based on a brilliant 1987 poster devised by Joy Aberdein and Nigel Morris of the NZSO publicity department; additional artwork by music librarian Nigel Cole and photographed by Stephen La Plant. The design was admired by musicians around the world.*

Mark Keyworth believes his honeymoon with the orchestra lasted about six to eight months. Then it was time to "get down to the hard work of the marriage".

Part of that hard work involved the orchestral agreement. Bitter negotiations had gone on for six months before Mark joined the NZSO; a swift settlement was essential. Within two weeks of his arrival it was all wrapped up, with both sides able to feel reasonably satisfied with the outcome.

Later negotiations were more difficult. The existence of what he considered to be a very strong union-based collective mentality, "one that seemed to exist in many, many orchestras around the world" was one of the first things Mark discovered after the honeymoon. It was something he said he had not encountered in any other arts organisation, in 16 years of management, and he found it hard to come to terms with.

Two chairmen of the Players Committee agree they are union-minded "in the sense that I like to be part of the collective contract," says associate principal cello, former chairman Allan Chisholm, "and I like to know we have the support together."

Second oboe Stephen Popperwell, current chairman, concurs, "in terms of sticking up for terms and conditions we can be pretty union-minded".

Mark found these terms and conditions in the players' contract "archaic", and cites "the absolute fixed nature of call times and breaks. The company needs more flexibility to operate efficiently," he says, "but there is still a very stringent work-to-rule attitude that seems to have been broken down in other employment communities that has not been broken down in the orchestra."

Allan Chisholm: "Having played in orchestras all my life I just accept that rehearsals start then and end then – and that is that. It sounds like a heavy union attitude but it's just the way musicians are in a group when they have to play for a conductor. Sometimes it is someone they don't want to play for... it's not always unbelievably wonderful... so when it's 12 noon that is the end of rehearsal."

"It's a basic thing about being an orchestral musician," says Stephen Popperwell. "Your work is not just between the set hours of the rehearsals anyway. If we all just started playing those hours of the rehearsals you would have no symphony orchestra in about a week."

This is something that Ed White noticed on moving from orchestra to management after becoming travel manager in 1994. Although he spends more hours at Symphony House, eight instead of five, he says his "actual working hours have gone down significantly" now he has no necessity to practise the horn.

Some terms and conditions date from the original 13-clause NZBS/Musicians' Union Agreement of 1946. Others were added from time to time by Broadcasting or negotiation. In 1976 representation changed to the Public Service Association. A new round of negotiations will resume in 1996 prior to the expiry of the current contract.

Orchestral Agreement

STATEMENT OF OBJECTIVES

1 To maintain and develop the Company as New Zealand's premier national music resource.

2 To provide the public of New Zealand, nationwide, the opportunity to hear in person live concerts, recordings and broadcasts played to the highest international standards of artistic excellence.

3 To demonstrate excellence internationally through performances in association with soloists and conductors of the highest international repute.

4 To maintain its pivotal cultural role in New Zealand music through the provision of direct access for New Zealanders to a full range of orchestral and related repertoire, to support, for the teaching and development of young musicians, New Zealand composers and artists of the highest calibre, and in the development and support of associated small orchestra groups derived from the orchestra's fulltime strength.

5 To maintain a financially viable organisation through the management of income, overall management of resources and prudent financial policies.

6 To maximise revenue from non-State sources.

The NZSO's Statement of Objectives, as first published in 1993.

Funding

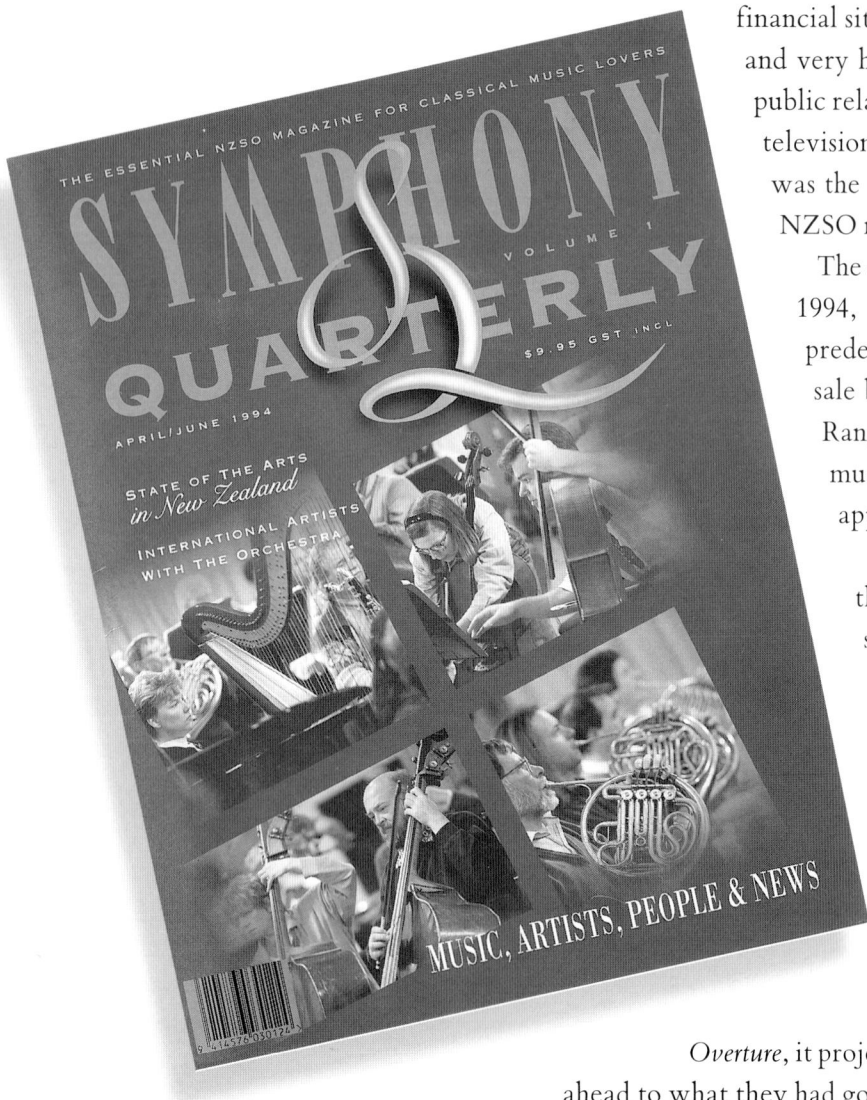

First issue of Symphony Quarterly, *the NZSO's new magazine, covered a wider range of musical interests under editor Joy Aberdein, the orchestra's longtime public relations manager.*

By the end of 1994 the NZSO, with justifiable pride, was able to announce that the $19,000 deficit of the previous year, 1992/93, had been turned around to a profit of $29,000 in the current year 1993/94. The result of "very careful management and increased sponsorship dollars".

This was a remarkable achievement considering that funding of $8.3 million in 1991 had been reduced to $7.8 million by 1994. Income generated from the NZSO's own activities, including box office returns and sponsorship funds, was at its highest ever at $3.704 million.[43] By 1995/96 it was $5.326 million.

A follow-up feature article on the orchestra had a positive headline: 'A Revitalised NZSO Faces A Bright Future'.[44] This seemed to sum up not only the NZSO's improved financial situation, attributed by Mark Keyworth to the "new strategic plan and very hard work", but also a new and brighter outlook: "On a purely public relations level the orchestra has become much more public; a snappy television campaign highlighted the faces producing what the slogan said was the 'Greatest Sound in New Zealand'. There was also a new glossy NZSO magazine, *Symphony Quarterly*.

The orchestra's new 1990s-style magazine had been launched in January 1994, its editor public relations manager Joy Aberdein. Unlike its predecessor *Concert Pitch*, a free publication, *Symphony Quarterly* was for sale by subscription, at concerts or from book and magazine outlets. Ranging over a broad spectrum of international and New Zealand musical interests, beyond the confines of NZSO artists and events, its appeal is more widely spread.

The magazine's extended programme and artist coverage made the usual printed concert programme redundant, for other than special gala performances. This was a significant change for concert-goers, some of who claimed the magazine's format was too large to carry to concerts, an argument largely countered in later issues with the inclusion of a small, attractively-presented booklet containing the programme information in a more convenient form.

The subscription campaign came later in the year, and *The Evening Post* was right when it described the promotion as 'snappy'. Fronted by a succession of 40 full-on, bright-faced NZSO players to the background music of Berlioz's *Le Corsaire Overture*, it projected an effervescent and infectious image of an orchestra looking ahead to what they had good reason to believe would be a very successful year.

Few orchestral years have started with the potential of 1995. One year before its 50th birthday the orchestra was poised to take that last step forward to realize its dream of becoming an international player on the world stage. It had a new chief conductor and a major European tour to prepare for in 1996 – the BBC Henry Wood Proms in London, Concertgebouw in Holland, Birmingham, Germany, and Austria; with an all-expenses paid tour to Hong Kong in 1995 to provide valuable experience and serve as an entrée to the main course of the anniversary year. The modest profit of 1994 was another excellent reason for the orchestra's expectation of a brighter future.

On New Year's Day, Eduardo Mata's appointment as principal guest conductor officially took effect. The acceptance of the position by the distinguished Mexican maestro, aged 52, was seen as tangible endorsement of the NZSO's growing international reputation, and a "great watershed in this country's development", according to chairman Dr Hylton LeGrice.

Three days later Eduardo Mata died along with his partner, while piloting his own plane in Mexico. Players on holiday learned of the tragedy in stunned disbelief.

"He was one of the world's ten great conductors," says Dr LeGrice. "He could have chosen any of a hundred orchestras around the world... His death was a huge artistic setback for the orchestra."

As chief conductor, Eduardo Mata was to have conducted the NZSO on its 1996 overseas tour. For a mission as important as this, it was imperative to choose the right replacement, a conductor of equal status, available to come at very short notice. It was only 19 months before the tour was to begin.

Roger Lloyd spent the next three weeks making long distance phone calls. Inevitably there were disappointments but then came success. Alexander Lazarev, principal guest conductor of the Scottish National Orchestra, the sensation of the 1992 New Zealand International Festival, agreed to rearrange his own 1996 schedule to take over the NZSO's tour. It was an incredible coup.

Then, barely more than one month later, the unthinkable happened again. The tour was off. The orchestra's planned international showcase and centrepiece of its 50th year, cancelled. Financial restraints were blamed; $1.3 million was not easily found in these cash-strapped times. NZSO musicians, reading it in their evening newspapers, found it hard to believe that it had happened, and that they had not been told first. Some were quick to say that not all avenues had been explored, sponsors would have come forward had they known, 'in 18 months funds could have been found. Remember Seville?'

But this was not another Seville. The Proms and the entire tour bookings were cancelled. It could only be hoped that this would not prejudice chances for a subsequent tour when, or if, finances improved.

"It reflects badly on New Zealand," warned Lindis Taylor in a hard-hitting article.[45] "An invitation to the Proms is like playing a test at Lords – a crowning point in New Zealand's slow cultural maturation. To turn it down marks our country as one led by barbarians... placing value on nothing but a balance sheet... After the on-again, off-again drama of the trip to Expo Seville... will anyone in the music world risk making plans that involve the NZSO again?"

The answer to that question[46] came some weeks later, from Dan Quinton of Harold Holt's, agents for the cancelled tour. He would have to know there is sound financial backing before starting work on the next visit he said, but having worked hard to "make all the contacts and generate interest... in all the major cities", he would like to try and put the tour back on again. Concert houses that had booked the NZSO had been told it was only "postponed."

New Zealander Joy Mebus, whose international artist agency had represented Eduardo Mata, was scathing when interviewed in the same article. She said she had been told by the British Association of Concert Agents in London that people were saying: "My God, we wouldn't touch that orchestra for a tour for at least another 20 years". In her opinion, Eduardo Mata, who she said had been very proud to have been taking the NZSO to Europe, would

This cartoon, published in The Dominion *in 1981, refers to the cancellation of the overseas tour planned for that year. The comment was as relevant in 1996.*

" SEEMS TO ME THE ONLY WAY THEY CAN GO ON TOUR IS TO ACCOMPANY THE ALL BLACKS AS CHEER LEADERS."

ERIC HEATH/THE DOMINION

have probably "cancelled his contract" if the tour by the orchestra had been cancelled.

"It is critical that a rearranged tour go ahead," Dan Quinton said. International touring is a high-cost and risky activity and "only works with massive subsidy and funding. The next time we start talking to people it's got to happen, otherwise that would be extremely damaging. You can't postpone more than once without causing problems. People are only understanding once."

In view of the long-standing rivalry between Australia and New Zealand, in any field of endeavour, it was no help to be reminded of the largesse handed out across the Tasman by Prime Minister Paul Keating to the Sydney Symphony. The announcement in October 1994, that the SSO was to be withdrawn from the ABC's stable of orchestras, was a surprise. It would be allowed to develop world status with increased government subsidies to broaden its reputation and techniques, including the raising of musicians' salaries. First up in this brave new world was a tour to Europe in August-September 1995, with performances at the BBC Proms.[47]

In the midst of the recriminations and soul-searching about the tour, a letter appeared in *The Evening Post* from composer Edwin Carr, who called the cancellation of the tour "a deliverance... Without a permanent conductor... the orchestra cannot be of world standard in interpretation, and while efficient could not do itself justice when measured against London's four great orchestras". **A Letter to the Editor**

This was a suprising view from Edwin Carr whose works have been performed, commissioned and premiered by the NZSO over 40 years, and whose CD was recorded and released by the orchestra in 1995. During a recent television documentary, *In Bed with the Orchestra*,[48] Mr Carr repeats himself in his praise for the NZSO's performance of his *4th Symphony*: "I couldn't imagine anything better, it had bite, they know the work. I couldn't imagine anything better. It's because they are all so young, they understand 20th century music".

Now his short letter acted as a magnet attracting replies from those rushing to the NZSO's defence and others taking the opportunity for a few potshots. Sir Neville Marriner, writing from England, called Carr "disloyal".[49]

Sir Neville was one of the NZSO's "hit and run conductors", an unrepentant Edwin Carr retaliated:[50] "To accuse me of disloyalty is hypocritical, sentimental and superficial... The opposite is the case. I certainly would have been disloyal to flatter them into thinking they are ready to play in London..."

Side by side with Carr's reply was a response from conductor Yan Pascal Tortelier and Trevor Green, BBC Head Of Music[51] who viewed the cancellation "with great sadness". They said the amount required was a "real pittance when the cultural returns are so high.

You have a great treasure in the NZSO. In recent years it has been recognised as an orchestra with energy, high artistic standards and a real commitment to place itself at the forefront of world music... By 'exporting' these talents overseas you, as a nation, not only demonstrate confidence and pride in the ensemble, you also register, and reflect, the cultural achievements of your country".

Another Cancellation   The cancelled Proms tour and the Carr controversy were still the subject of much debate when the Hong Kong Mid-Summer Classics Festival tour, due to start in two months, was cancelled.

This was a cancellation that brought little regret. The offer of the 10-day tour had come from Klaus Heymann, managing director of Naxos, the budget label, non-royalty paying recording company.

As details emerged, the Mid-Summer Classics Festival, not to be confused with the main Hong Kong Arts Festival at which the NZSO performed in 1980, began to sound much less attractive. The repertoire was mainly light music: love songs and music from shows, with cost-saving measures that included leaving 12 NZSO players, plus the harp, double basses, timpani and percussion instruments at home, to be replaced by players and instruments hired in Hong Kong.

In these circumstances standards were liable to drop, and players felt the NZSO's image would have been tarnished, while sharing hotel rooms on tour, and having to play on hired, possibly inferior instruments, was unacceptable. A planned tour to Japan to coincide with the Hong Kong performances had earlier fallen through.

In reply[52] to an earlier *Listener* article in which Klaus Heymann was presented as a patron of the arts, sub-principal viola Brian Shillito (writing unofficially), aired his view and that of colleagues (based on two years' experience in recording with Naxos), about the tactics employed by Mr Heymann, who was, Shillito claimed, "getting the NZSO at bargain-basement rates... subsidised by the New Zealand taxpayer".

Heymann[53] refuted the accusation that he recorded on the cheap. He paid the NZSO a "market rate" he said, but it cost more to record here because conductors had to be flown in, halls hired and, unlike the English and Irish orchestras which have two three-hour calls with only one break, the NZSO, like U.S. union orchestras, insists on two two-and-a-half hour calls with two breaks.

The Festival was for young people with low ticket prices so expenses are kept low, Heymann said. He had agreed to subsidise the tour with $70,000 when the NZSO's bid to extend the tour to Japan was unsuccessful. To take extra players and instruments would have increased that deficit by $20,000 and, afraid musicians were about to take industrial action, he decided to cancel the tour "then and there".

By this time even the most un-newsworthy items had been elevated in status. This happened when a temporary timpanist missed the opening item in an Auckland concert. His absence went unnoticed until conductor Odaline de la Martinez came on stage, and after about six bars, noticed there was no timpanist. She stopped the concert and walked off stage.

The Case of the
Missing Timpanist

Interpretation of this action varied from insinuations of gender bias towards a woman conductor to *Listener* writer Brian Rudman's expressed view that it was an "outward sign of the general disenchantment and sheer bloody-mindedness infecting the orchestra".[54]

"It is a slur on the professionalism of members of the NZSO... We take strong exception to it," said Robert Adair, then chair of the NZSO's Players Committee.[55] The suggestion that NZSO musicians "knew the timpanist was missing and deliberately refrained from telling the conductor to embarrass her is pure fantasy. Why did no one mention that he was absent? Very simple: no one noticed. The timpani are behind the rest of the orchestra, which was reduced for the opening piece. Everyone except the conductor is seated facing front, and we were busy warming up. The timpanist himself had been there shortly before, doing just that..."

The visiting player, on his first tour with the NZSO, had merely mistaken the start time of 7.30pm for 8pm. Bruce McKinnon, principal percussionist, usually seated at the back, would have noticed but was not required, and from backstage at the Aotea Centre, the stage is not visible. Robert Adair summed up: "Unfortunately... [he] went for a short walk. The incident has been filed under 'it's moments like these...'"

Exit Stage Left

In March long-serving music executive Murray Alford was made redundant and set off on early retirement with a spring in his step and a relieved smile on his face.

Five months later he was back, helping out part-time in his old job; Roger Lloyd, artistic manager, had resigned. It was an open secret by this time that differences had arisen in the company and it was time for a rethink. It can happen anywhere.

This was another setback for orchestral stability but fears that this vital position might disappear, or be shared out between existing staff to save costs, were without substance. Advertisements were placed internationally and brought an encouraging response; a shortlist was expected before Christmas.

The departure of Roger Lloyd attracted more media comment. 'Top Level Power Struggle' was one headline[56] in which it was claimed that a "definition of roles and functions and lack of a clear artistic vision was a major problem". It was assumed by most people that Roger Lloyd would be returning to Britain, so the news of his appointment as general manager of the semi-professional Wellington Sinfonia, came as some surprise.

Roger Lloyd had given notice but it was Tony Lenton, the NZSO's long-serving accountant and secretary to the Board who was the next to leave, planning to spend more time with his young family. Much of the pressure and constant demands made on the orchestra since it left

the shelter of Broadcasting, had fallen on his shoulders and this had proved a heavy burden.

In an interview shortly before he left he told me it had not been that enjoyable since Day One. "The orchestra has been punched over for so long that it's actually quite difficult to think why on earth you stay. There's probably just some intrinsic love affair with what you are trying to achieve and [you] hope that in spite of everything, it will all be better. The sad thing is that this should be one of the fun jobs. What greater fun can you have than putting on concerts and working with some of the great artists of the world? Here I am, a fully qualified accountant, and I spend a substantial amount of my time not managing the company, which has actually achieved some quite significant things, but reporting to government departments."

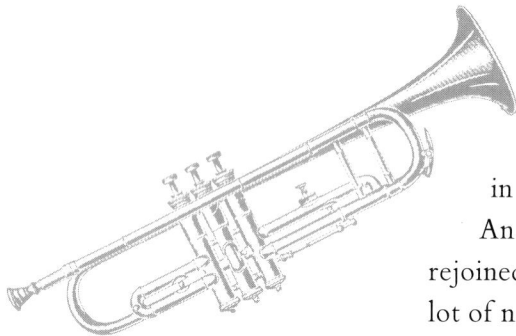

The fourth person to leave in a short period was John Taber, principal trumpet. Unlike Tony Lenton, whose departure was very low-key, John Taber's was very public – as were his views on the orchestra's problems: the heavy workload, the type of music it played, "like a musical prostitute", the inexpensive recordings, and the quality of its concerts and conductors. He reiterated these on National Radio in a hard-hitting interview conducted by Kim Hill, in company with Mark Keyworth.[57]

An American who had first joined the orchestra in the 1960s, John recalled that when he rejoined it in 1992 for the Expo tour, he found "a group of musicians, some old friends and a lot of new ones that were playing extremely well and I was really impressed... [but in his view] We have been going downhill since I arrived". This is why he had decided to leave. "Constant penny-pinching had reflected on the musical quality of concerts," he claimed.

Mark Keyworth was subjected to some abrasive questioning from Kim Hill, who accused him of "propping a corpse up – [the orchestra] was alive in name only". Mark had agreed earlier that the orchestra had had to "move away quite significantly from our core business and take on a whole range of income-earning activities to keep the orchestra afloat..."

Those activities had been at a cost to the musicians "in over-scheduling and putting them at risk to health". He did not disagree with John in most of what he said: "The players have had to bear the brunt... of the need to cut costs and to improve income status."

Opinions that had seemed poles apart at the outset, were not really so distant after all but did show the unenviable position of the Board and management, caught between Government demands and orchestral concerns. John Taber left New Zealand two weeks later, returning to his former orchestra in Bordeaux.

In the Spotlight

1995 was a year when players and those closely associated with the NZSO opened the newspapers or turned on the radio with caution, for fear of some new revelation or doom-and-gloom orchestra story. With livelihoods at stake and the knowledge of so many other New Zealand arts organisations lost, no one could feel complacent about the future.

Much of the action was played out in the news media, exposing the very real problems faced by the orchestra: the uncertainty of its funding, and OOS problems suffered by players.

Everyone, it seemed, had formed their own opinion on the situation and their own personal solutions. Jenny Pattrick, former chair of the QE II Arts Council, made the comparison with the birth of regional opera companies after National Opera "went bust for the last time" – and the four "lean and hungry regional orchestras baring their teeth" at the NZSO's $8 million funding. Perhaps the day of the large touring orchestra was over, she suggested, and smaller, better-funded regional orchestras may be a "more flexible, more vigorous and ultimately more appropriate way to go".[58]

"The orchestra could close," warned composer Martin Lodge, on radio and in print, "if the board and management do not sit down and work out a clear artistic vision... and make a cogent case, the Government will say OK, all orchestral funding is open to competition".[59] Other comments in press reports pinned to the NZSO noticeboard, about 'low orchestral morale' brought a response from players, Mark Keyworth remembers: "One had written 'Who is this Martin Lodge to say what my morale is?'"[60]

Haydn Rawstron, an international arts agent, came up with a complicated plan to divide up the musicians of the NZSO between Wellington and Christchurch, and then put them back together at certain times of the year. This, he said, would "improve the standard of music-making in the whole country."[61]

The loss at this time of the NZSO's biggest sponsorship, Mastercard International, for the NZSO Subscription series, was widely reported. The three-year sponsorship would end as planned at the outset, in 1995. It would not continue for the important 1996 Anniversary Season, with 43 concerts in six different concert centres, but it would, said Mark Keyworth, "be coming on board in a new contract".

Replacement sponsor Montana Wines was already confirmed, but delaying their announcement, even as the media discussed this latest "threat" to the orchestra's survival.

Several articles had been genuinely supportive, as in a feature by John Button, 'What's Wrong with the Orchestra?' and a leader article in the same issue: 'Our Culture Under Threat',[62] cataloguing the "unrealistic demands on players", with onerous travel and OOS, "run-outs", one-day tours and cheap recordings. He gave a clear message: "The NZSO must not be allowed to drift."

It is a vicious circle: run-out tours, concert cuts, contracts with budget recording companies, cancelled concerts, and increased workloads are measures that have been introduced for one reason – because there is not enough money for the orchestra to continue to do what it was set up to be, the National Orchestra of New Zealand.

By late 1995, there were hopeful signs that the orchestra was entering more peaceful waters. *Reports*

Either that or it was the lull before the storm. But in November, within days of each other, came two reports that seemed to suggest the latter. The first announced a joint decision between the Board and Finance Minister Bill Birch, that former Treasury Secretary Graham Scott would "review the orchestra's business strategies, resources and future needs".[63]

Judith Tizard, Labour's Cultural Affairs spokesperson, said she was appalled. "The problems of the NZSO are obvious and known to the National Government... The organisation has already cut itself to the bone. The last thing the NZSO needs is an 'investigation' by an ex-Treasury staffer and yet another restructuring."[64]

Ms Tizard had spoken out previously for the orchestra when at Labour's prodding, Cultural Affairs Minister Doug Graham had said he thought the orchestra needed an extra $1 million. That was in June; in August she had accused him of "fiddling and quibbling with the future of our most important cultural organisations". It was November and nothing had been done.

The second article[65] reported a loss of $173,000 recorded in the 1994/95 year. This was a big disappointment after the remarkable $29,000 profit only 12 months earlier, and monitoring had indicated that they were on target to increase that to $50,000. This result was despite all the extra measures that had been taken to save money; a 35 percent cut in concerts, cancellations in Dunedin, Hamilton, Palmerston North and Hawkes Bay – and the overseas tour.

The loss could be attributed to a $345,000 increase in labour costs through having to replace permanent players on ACC suffering from work-related injuries. About 804 work days had been lost in the last financial year. A dozen people had been off at times for these reasons, and one had been forced to retire. The ACC Employer Experience Rating had risen over three years from $80,000 to $200,000. Deferred tax of $59,000 had contributed to the loss, while the actual before-tax loss was $104,000, Mark Keyworth reported. "Efforts to build up the infrastructure and the rising cost of services had strained [the orchestra's] finances."

Cultural Affairs Minister Doug Graham commented: "The figure of [an extra] $1 million comes from the orchestra – that's what they tell me they need. I think that's probably right. Even the Minister of Finance accepts they will probably need more money. But to have a case for extra funding before we go into the Budget bidding round in February we have to prove the money is needed.

"The orchestra had made a good effort to increase funding from sponsorship," he said, "but proof was needed that having increased its revenue it also needed more funding."[66]

The NZSO that had achieved a 26 percent increase in its self-generated income, to $5.326 million, would nevertheless enter its 50th anniversary year with a deficit, and the prospect of another internal investigation.

Voluptuous
n almost
very way

New Zealand Symphony Orchestra conducted
-Paul Decker with Alicia de Larrocha (piano).
e Espagnole and Alborada del Gracioso,
apsodia Sinfonica and Alborada del Gracioso,
m Iberia (Albeniz) and El Pelele (Granados):
he Gardens of Spain (Falla), Piano solos: El
Espagnole (Albeniz), arr. Fruhbeck de
nel Fowler Co ? i SEP 1995
Lindia Taylc
conclusion that Dr Decker's last
distinctly lightweight didn't meet
Smiles! o

Musicians unite
over testing

Concert FM will broadcast tonight a concert
musicians from three orchestras u
ss their opposition to French n

oncert, being played to coincide
e rally in Tahiti, was recorded lat
: the Wellington Opera House an
sicians from the New Zealand Sy
estra, 'the Auckland Philharmoni
ington Sinfonia.
tation's manager, Elizabeth Kerr
ion to record the concert was a dif
l time, which raised doubts abou
artistic merit.
err says the result is a "spirite
occasion.
nusual to see players from three
s on the same stage, but they ga
concert to a very receptive
programme, cond.
e, begins

Two scenes from the BP Summer Pops Tour, 1996: (Above) Napier experiences the outdoors classical music phenomenon. (Left) Concert in the Dunedin Town Hall.

PHOTOGRAPHS: STEPHEN HARKER

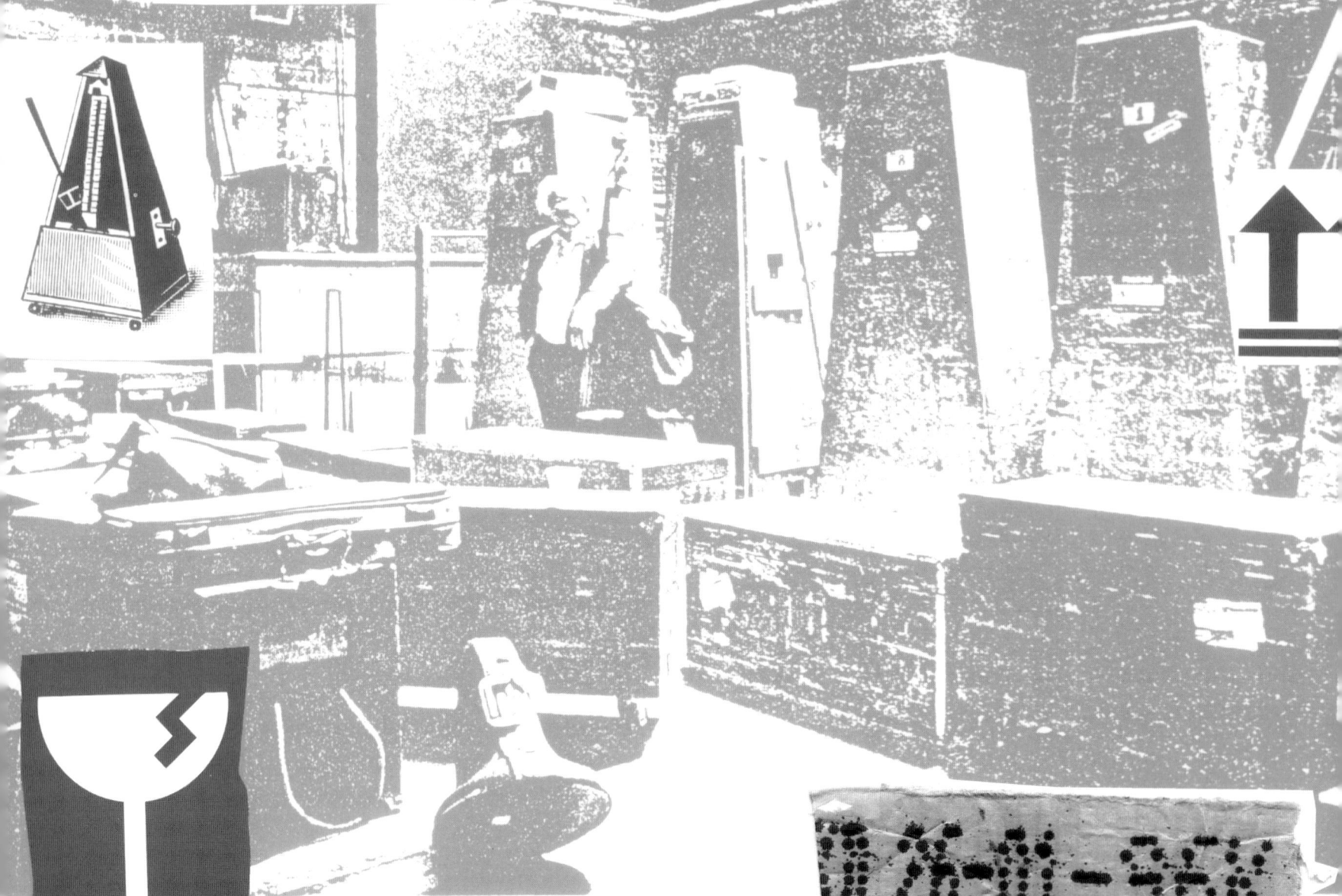

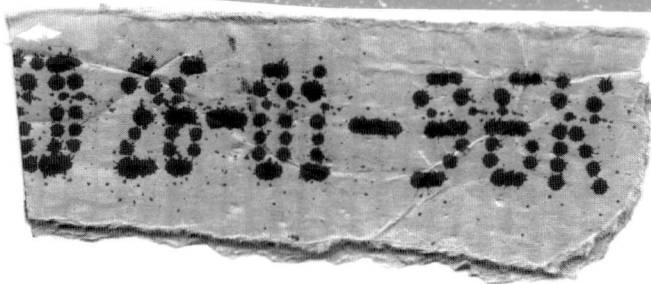

Pack-out Day:
At Home in Symphony House

"I've always envied string players who can give a little smile when they are playing something they really enjoy. Brass players can't smile or frown; they have to keep the same embouchure set. There's no way to show how you feel – except by giving a thumbs-up.
– Kenneth Young, principal tuba.

8.00AM: Stage manager Grant Gilbert is on patrol in the Symphony House carpark. It's pack-out day for tomorrow's Auckland concert. Van Lines owner/driver Colin Isaac will be here this afternoon, with his truck and double articulated trailer rig ready to back up to the loading bay, and pack-out 45 cubic metres of orchestral instruments and equipment. An access corridor is marked out between carparks, but Grant knows that if he is not there it will be parked on, no matter how many lines and NO PARKING signs, by players running late for rehearsal.

Planning for the concert was finalised months ago, so today there are only last-minute details and any special requirements to check up on: if any staging or risers are needed, the piano needs tuning, or the conductor wants a PA system to address the audience. Grant will liaise with section principals to confirm which players are going on tour, information he needs to mark the attendance register at each call; and for the exact number of chairs, music stands and risers to be taken. Principal Bruce McKinnon will confirm which percussion instruments are required. By the time Colin arrives the load schedule will be prepared.

8.30: In the front of the building management staff have been arriving, parking their cars in the small basement below, and making a coffee to start the day.

8.50: Upstairs, the adjoining staff tearoom and board room has been opened up, chairs and tables cleared aside, for 'Trishercise'. NZSO receptionist Trish Popperwell is a former member of the RNZ Ballet, a dancer and choreographer for TVNZ (20 years) and is known for professional musical productions around the country.

The winner of two national awards (Feltex and Golden Disc), she was choreographer of

GRAEME BROWNE

Morning warm-up session before rehearsal. Trish Popperwell demonstrates to NZSO players Rebecca Jackson, Liz Patchett, Janet Armstrong, Peter Barber, Nicky Newton, Vicki Jones, Jane Freed, Andrew Kasza, Simon Miller, Stephen Popperwell, Dean Major and Robert Ibell.

the New Zealand dance drama at the 1988 Brisbane Expo. That's too much talent to be left at a reception desk.

Now Trish holds warm-up sessions before morning rehearsals, with two 12-minute sessions at 8.50 and 9.10am. Numbers vary, but average around 20, depending on what is happening in the studio that day, and tend to drop when there is new music to be learned.

An aerobics manager for 16 years, Trish says she has designed a programme for the special needs of orchestral musicians who "spend much of their time sitting and playing instruments in awkward, unnatural positions, and are prone to OOS problems: warming up and stretching exercises for the muscles used for playing, and strengthening exercises for the opposing muscle groups to keep the body in balance."

9.00: Chief executive Mark Keyworth has seen his first irate player of the day. It still surprises him, he says, that every member of the orchestra "feels they have the right, and they exercise it, to call into my office any time they want to with any little problem they may have, or to give me the benefit of their particular view." There was another article about the NZSO in last night's paper, with an off-the-cuff remark by Mark with which this player disagrees, and goes to great lengths to explain why. When he has got that off his chest Mark tells his side of the story and then slips in a joke; they are both laughing when the player leaves. "It's a great leveller, laughter," he says. Now he must hurry everyone along for the Quarterly Report due today.

9.15: David Pawsey, orchestra manager, arrives with the conductor whom he collected from the hotel on the way. This is the maestro's first visit to New Zealand. He arrived on Wednesday and had his first rehearsals yesterday. In the old days artists liked to have a couple of days to get over their jet-lag, but not this new breed of jet-setters.

The soloist will be here later. A veteran of previous tours, he feels at home in New Zealand and plans to walk from his city apartment, a favourite place where he can cook his own meals, taking the opportunity to get some fresh air and exercise.

Players mill around in the common room and studio, unpacking their instruments, shedding outer garments or, already at their stands, running over today's music. 'Trishercise' has finished, and those from the last session arrive in the studio looking happy and relaxed, exuding camaraderie.

9.25: Grant is moving around the studio with his clipboard, talking to the principals and marking the orchestral register. There are several gaps today, in addition to the 10 players off with occupational health problems; the 'flu is doing the rounds.

9.30: Everyone is at their stands in the studio, the conductor standing beside the rostrum talking to concertmaster Wilma Smith. Principal oboe John Snow from New York sounds the A, and the tune-up begins. The conductor takes his place, wishes the orchestra good morning and raises his baton to start the symphony.

"...You'll hear the composer's blood boiling, heart racing, or tears streaming. Behind the music you'll sense gales of laughter, rumbles of rage or delightful moments of pure peace..." The 1995 Subscription brochure was a little too passionate for some.

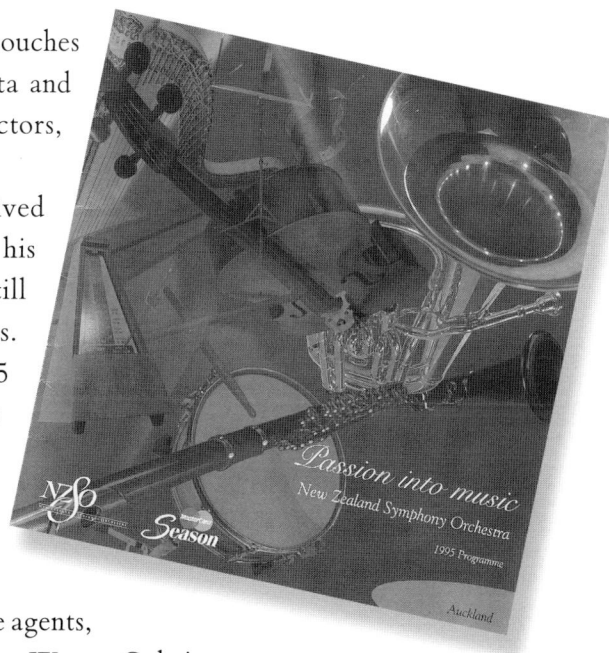

10.00: The artistic department is closeted together to put the finishing touches to 1996 for the new Subscription brochure. The death of Eduardo Mata and cancellation of the BBC Proms tour meant a lot of re-scheduling of conductors, soloists and programmes .

Everything was in place again, had been for months, when a fax arrived from one of the soloists, a Big Name; wanting to change his tour dates, his agent has double-booked. This was greeted with some scepticism, but it still means going back to the drawing board again to consider alternative artists.

Now the sales and subscription people are pressing for details. The 1995 'Passion into Music' brochure was enjoyed by newer concert-goers but its vivid language shocked some subscribers, many of who wrote or rang the NZSO to complain. This year's brochure is aimed at the middle ground but there is not much time: it is going out earlier this year and the tele-marketers are standing by.

10.20: The music library is covered in boxes – old music going back to the agents, checked and packed; new music coming in to be unpacked for the next tour. Wynne Cole is checking parts as she goes. This looks better than the music for next week's recording, which arrived late from America in a grubby condition. It took a lot of time to rub out the old markings for Wilma Smith to do her bowings, and for Wynne to copy them onto the other violin parts. It was all new music and the players were anxious to start practising it.

The Library has 4000 works, catalogued on computer and has to hire about 40 percent of its music. The orchestra plays more than ever now and sometimes Wynne has four sets of six folders on the go at one time: for subscriptions, Tea and Symphony concerts, recordings and one-off specials. The 1996 Skitch Henderson Summer Pops has 30 or so different pieces of music, with 60 parts for each piece, so the extra space here helps. Willis Street was very cramped.

The stage manager looks after the music on tour, so Wynne gives Grant the balance scores required by the recording engineers for tomorrow night's broadcast – this can be handy if the conductor misplaces his score. There have been few mishaps since Wynne joined the orchestra 23 years ago, soon after completing a B.Mus with a double major in composition and music history. Only once has a programme had to be changed: the agent sent a cello concerto by surface instead of airmail, and it arrived three weeks after the concert.

10.40: Elenoa Eyles has everything in place for the orchestra's 15-minute tea break. It can be a rush but she is always cheerful and unflustered, always has a smile – an oasis of calm in a turbulent environment. A primary school teacher back home in Fiji, Elenoa, who is married to respected former Radio New Zealand recording engineer Geoff Eyles, specialised in home science teaching on completing her studies at Seaford College in Sussex. After 11 years, she still thinks her NZSO duties, as tea-attendant and filing clerk, are the best in Symphony House. "I am the luckiest person here: no stress, no deadlines. It's a lovely job."

Backstage can be a noisy gathering place or the quietest spot in town. Barry Johnstone backstage at Invercargill, BP Summer Pops, 1995.

STEPHEN HARKER

Marketing manager Gillian Vosper is on the phone to the NZSO's Auckland office, checking that everything is in place for tomorrow's concert: VIP tickets, programmes and other merchandise. It's a Subscription concert, so it's pre-sold but for the door sales, one of well over a hundred concerts she markets each year for the NZSO and the New Zealand Chamber Orchestra, working up to 18 months in advance.

The long-term marketing strategy for the 1996 Subscription season will be Gillian's priority once Artistic completes the details. In the meantime there is a Christchurch concert to sell, ensuring that radio, newspaper and publicity campaigns are all comprehensive and properly planned. One-off concerts are harder to sell than a whole series. In four weeks there were seven concerts in Wellington, four of them with no subscriber base, whereas the Tower Beethoven Festival is a compact package. The crucial day-to-day servicing of existing sponsors is on-going and Gillian's view that the NZSO is a "delight to sell" is reflected in the dramatic increase in its sponsorship base. Pauline Sheddan, who replaced Gillian when Ruby was born, has been retained as sponsorship manager.

The two have a meeting at 11:00am, pulling together Lotto's Twilight Opera at the Basin; everything from the marketing plan and sponsorship liaison to the physical logistics of putting it on, the selling of the hospitality marquees, right down to where the trucks are going to park. Stage manager Grant Gilbert deals with everything from the stage back while Gillian handles everything from the stage front. Seeing it all come together is the best part, like Opera in the Basin last year: a huge amount of work but a fantastic concert, a full house, the orchestra played wonderfully and the audience loved it.

11.00: Personnel. One of the players with OOS has brought a new ACC certificate for personnel manager Sally Mitchell. He has been off work for three months and had hoped to return but the doctor said no, and extended it for another month. It is a real worry. Other colleagues start off like this, a few weeks' absence, then a few months', and some end up retiring early. Music is their life, not just a profession; few are trained for anything else and the only music jobs outside the orchestra are teaching, hardly the same thing. Who would have expected orchestral playing to become a health hazard?

Sally's immediate problem is a replacement. The casual player currently doing the job expects to be free after this tour and has other work lined up. She will have to consult the section principal: is this player still the preferred choice or should someone else be given a chance in the job?

11.30: David Pawsey is at the photocopier running off the *Friday Flash*. An NZSO institution for over 20 years, players took its distinctive name from the racing newspaper published on the same day.

The *Flash* provides essential information on orchestral calls, programmes, travel arrangements, general notices, changes to the annual call diary, and the odd cartoon if David can

find a good one – preferably musical. This coming week a scheduled day off has become a working day, which was unavoidable. David expects complaints.

Friday Afternoon   12.00: Morning rehearsal ends with the new conductor taking them right up to the dot on the new synchronised clock system. No one can argue that the studio clock is wrong now, but in the old days one minute over and some players would have left the studio.

There is an hour to shop, go to the bank, take a walk, have lunch up the road at Caffe L'Affare or round the corner in Courtenay Place. Some have brought lunch, or will buy something and bring it back to eat in the common room. The chessboard will come out and the playing cards and magazines. The more energetic can play table tennis on the table from the Terrace studio, stored at Willis Street for 14 years with nowhere there to put it up. Now it serves a new generation of musicians.

It's a working lunch for the Players Committee: there is a meeting with Mark Keyworth in the boardroom. Stephen Popperwell, chairman for the "umpteenth time" and the other five members have brought their mugs of coffee, juice and lunch in paper bags. A sub-branch of the Public Service Association, the committee is elected annually as the official representatives of their colleagues to bring orchestral issues to management, especially contract negotiations. They take this responsibility very seriously, although some of their duties have been taken over by the new committees.

Today there is a new report on the studio acoustic to discuss and Mark has a few issues on touring that he wants to try out on the committee before he takes them, as he is expected to do now as a matter of course, to the full orchestra.

12.50: Grant is distributing the *Friday Flash* and new programme advices to each stand. When that is done he has the register to mark for the afternoon call. There are no casual players this afternoon; those who played in the symphony are not required for the overture or concerto.

1.00: Before he starts the overture the conductor tells the orchestra about the background to the music, a rarely played work by a fellow countryman. Some players are interested, others just want him to get on with the music; talkative conductors are not always appreciated. But this story is short and adds insight to the music; now he lifts the baton. Players are still making up their minds about him.

The soloist arrived during the lunch hour and has been practising on the small piano in the soloist's room. He joins the orchestra in the studio after afternoon tea and is given a warm round of applause; his concerts are remembered with pleasure.

2.30: PR manager and editor Joy Aberdein is proofing *Symphony Quarterly*. The door is shut, the phone switched back to reception to stop it ringing 30 times an hour, but people still knock or wave messages through the glass partition. Proofs have to be back in Auckland

tonight, 24 pages to read, one blurred, even with the magnifying glass; faxing proofs isn't ideal but it is fast. This is the third set; next week she will go to Auckland to see the final print. It's a three month turn-round to a very tight schedule, and planning for the next issue, on Douglas Lilburn and New Zealand music, is already well advanced.

The PR side does not stop for that. It's a different job now from when she joined the NZSO almost 11 years ago, with two music degrees and a background in radio and television, and piano performing. Then there were 40 programmes a year to produce, information *Symphony Quarterly* covers now.

Concert FM wants to interview the visiting conductor but his English is not good; there is an urgent press release to write for the Board; programme notes to complete for the Tower Beethoven Festival but nothing's arrived from the Vienna Philharmonic. Time is short.

3:00: Colin Isaac and the three Van Lines crew crowd into David and Grant's office for a cup of tea before pack-out. Colin has had no problem backing the rig into the carpark. Not like the old Symphony House, with 20 parking spaces for 110 NZSO people, and cars squeezed in one after another, right up to the footpath. If they were still there when he arrived, there was nowhere to stop and he had to keep driving around the one-way system for several blocks to get back again. Manoeuvering-in stopped the traffic in Willis Street, and it was even worse on The Terrace. There is less traffic this end of town.

3.15: The first candidate arrives early for this afternoon's auditions, wanting somewhere to practise. It's violins again, the biggest section of the orchestra with 28 players, and the highest turnover. This position is vacant as a result of a retirement. It's rank and file, so it was not advertised overseas. In addition to six live auditions there are five on tape, more than usual, all from young New Zealanders who have been studying or working overseas and want to come back home. Standards keep rising so they will have to be very good.

3.30: The conductor takes the rehearsal right up to the last minute, as he did this morning. He is still feeling his way with this new orchestra, but becoming more relaxed now he knows their worth. There is growing respect on both sides, and anticipation of some good concerts. David explains the arrangements for their flight tomorrow and sends him back to the hotel in a taxi, leaving himself free to help with the pack-out.

3.40: Almost all players have left the studio except for a small group chatting as they pack up their instruments. David hurries them along.

"What's going?" Colin shouts from across the studio.

"All the percussion; that's out," Grant yells back from the other side where he is packing up a box of trombones.

"Don't forget to put out the audition screens – eight chairs and stands," David reminds them, because it's unusual to have auditions on pack-out day.

Sometimes when it is noisy they can't hear each other and could end up taking something

Preparing for a pack-out: double bass John de Colville, who joined the NZSO in 1968 after working with leading Australian orchestras.

that's not needed, or worse, leaving something behind that is wanted. The piano stool was left once, many years ago, long before Grant's time of course, but it is still remembered. Pianists can be very fussy about piano stools.

Grant, Colin and the crew are old hands at the job, knowing how to treat expensive instruments with care. The studio becomes a hive of activity when they swing into action. Out go eight double bass cases, ten cello cases, the harp, timpani, bass drum, percussion instruments, perspex sound-deflecter screens (for players who sit in front of the brass and woodwinds), instrument boxes of various shapes and sizes, all packed into padded road cases that roll out of the studio straight into the trailer.

Travel manager Ed White is having his usual pre-tour meeting with the NZSO's two travel officers. John Dodds, principal second violinist, and violist Peter van Drimmelen (who is acting for cellist Chris Salmon, absent with hearing problems) will represent management on tour. They will liaise with airline and coach staff and their own colleagues – and frequently have to use their own initiative. Ed hands them copies of all the bookings, plane and coach, so they have the information if something goes wrong.

In over 20 years as travel officers John and Chris have had to deal with several emergency situations and have seen many NZSO travel managers come and go. So it was a surprise when a colleague took on the job. American Ed White, an orchestral player for 27 years, had to learn new skills as an administrator when, after two operations for glaucoma, he hung up his horn in 1994 and joined management. He is the third player to do so in the orchestra's 50 years: violinist Ted Pople was the first when he became administration officer in the 1970s, and in 1992 flautist Felicity Bunt worked in the artistic department briefly. Violinist Stephen Managh gained his Masters degree in Arts Administration in London and was concerts director for the Bournemouth Symphony Orchestra and then general manager of the English String Orchestra, before returning to the NZSO in mid-1993.

"It's an enormous change," Ed says, "both mentally and physically." A job with no room for error, with the potential for disaster if the arrangements for the 100-strong party are not accurate: flights, coaches, taxis and, except on run-outs (a one-day tour), accommodation. Pack-out days usually mean tickets to distribute and the inevitable reshuffle of names when one player drops out and has to be replaced with another.

3.45: The string audition committee is assembled in the boardroom: concertmaster Wilma Smith, associate concertmaster Donald Armstrong, all string principals, the acting artistic manager and Sally Mitchell. There are the five violin tapes and some unsolicited string tapes to hear before the live auditions, all identified only by number. Sally never usually schedules auditions on pack-out day, but today there is no alternative. It takes time to hear all the tapes and compare impressions, but eventually a shortlist is decided. Now for the live ones.

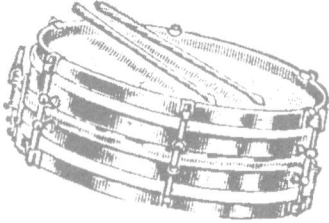

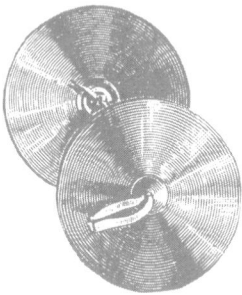

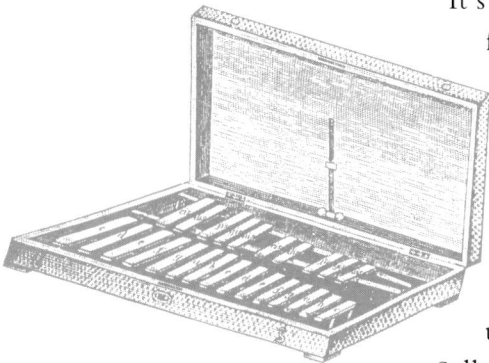

4.30: The last of the gear has been packed on the truck with maximum speed and efficiency. Colin shuts the large swing doors and drives out onto Tennyson Street, down Tory to Wakefield, already congested, and onto the motorway. This is good timing: he is on the road before the big traffic build-up – the weather report for the central North Island is not good.

The Audition Committee arrives in the studio as Grant finishes setting out their row of chairs and music stands behind large screens. They settle down with their music and audition sheets, the impartial artistic manager seated where he can see committee and candidate, to help if needed. Anonymity is maintained throughout, as it must be in a country with a music community as small as this one.

Sally asks the committee to decide which orchestral excerpts are to be played now, and which ones are to be held over for round two. When the committee is ready she leads 'number 1' through the bare studio to where a solitary music stand is set up in front of the screens.

When the first round finishes the six candidates wait nervously. This is the worst part, while the committee debates their relative merits. Two are recalled, the other four can go home. After the recalls the committee listens to the shortlisted tapes again and a unanimous decision is made. Now the names can be revealed. There is surprise at the improvement in some players and that others have not done so well.

5.30: David Pawsey is on the phone, ringing names on the casual list to replace players on long-term sick and accident leave. He's not having much luck. No one is at home waiting for him to call: they are all probably playing in other orchestras. Tracking them down at short notice is time-consuming, but answerphones are a boon. Casuals always help if they can.

Bassoonist Ruth Brinkman is the shining example of that. She spent several days commuting between APO and NZSO rehearsals and concerts when the NZSO had an emergency in the bassoon section. On the morning of the NZSO's Auckland concert she rang to say she would not be in for rehearsal, but would be there for the concert, which she was. She had given birth to her son at 1:00am that morning, left National Women's to do the concert as promised, and then returned to hospital afterwards.[67]

6.00: David is still not having any luck. None of the casuals are home yet. He decides to pack it in, pick up his suit for tomorrow and phone them again from home. Then he notices the time – he's missed the cleaners again...

Colin is making good time in the truck, driving from Wellington to Paraparaumu, the longest part of the whole trip in the rush hour. Next stop Waiouru, to stretch his legs and hope that the Desert Road, where snow is expected, will stay open until he gets through.

Friday Evening

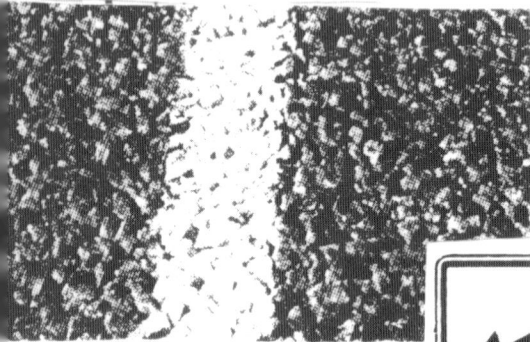

DETOUR

Run-out:
The NZSO on Tour

"What keeps an orchestra happy is playing good repertoire under good conductors; musical satisfaction in the job is very, very important." – Alexa Still, principal flute.

Saturday Morning

6.00AM: Colin Isaac wakes up in his truck parked on the Desert Road. After Waiouru the weather deteriorated very quickly as he made that long, slow haul up the centre of the island. Somewhere on the Desert Road the traffic ahead came to a standstill, the road impassable from a recent heavy dump of snow, the blizzard raging around them. He was there for the rest of the night.

It's only happened once in 20 years. All those tours, both North and South Islands, 40,000 kilometres a year and just the one concert missed. Colin was there waiting in Napier with the rig, ready to pack-in. It was the band that was stranded, unable to fly out of Wellington.

The soloist Gillian Weir, international organist from Wanganui, saved the day with a recital in the Cathedral. David Pawsey drove her up from Wellington, working out the programme as they went. There was nothing Colin could do but turn the truck around and drive home again.

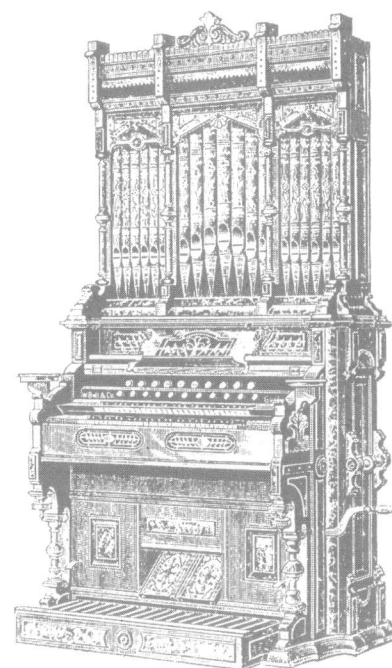

Since then there has been the odd close shave, like the trip to Hamilton when the truck was diverted around National Park, or when the brakes failed going to Palmerston North and Van Lines sent a back-up truck from Wellington.

Outside it is well below zero but it is warm inside the truck and its precious cargo is safe, protected by a special heating unit to keep a constant, even temperature and humidity. That is important for all instruments, especially woodwinds, the most susceptible to temperature change. At 18°C it's warmer than some of the halls they go to around the country.

BASIL CHARLES

On tour in the 1950s meant many hours travelling by train. This one advertises the orchestra's next concert in Greymouth, on a tour of the South Island.

The wind dropped overnight but more snow has fallen so the truck and all the other vehicles around it must wait for the snow-plough. With luck Colin will still meet the deadline in Auckland.

7.00: Wellington. David Pawsey's alarm goes off. It's cold, with heavy rain falling and an ominous cloud bank hanging low over the hills. Soon the phone calls will start, players asking: "Do you think the airport will be open?" Hoping that on a miserable day like this he will say No, so that they can stay at home by the fire and listen to someone else playing music on the stereo.

The airport is still open, so far, and stage manager Grant Gilbert is on the first flight out, the red-eye special at 7am... It is Saturday so there is not a business suit or briefcase in sight. He likes to get to the venue soon after Colin arrives, but this time he will be there first. Colin is still five hours away, and no one knows if or when the Desert Road will re-open.

8.30: Around Wellington players are waking up, having breakfast, telling their children they cannot take them to play soccer or netball.

In violist Peter Barber's household, Jacqueline aged nine, James, six and Felix, four, are going to Saturday Music School; the elder two have piano lessons in the afternoon. Peter likes to go with them but today he will miss that. Saturday is usually a working day for him.

"The job is very good from a family point of view," he says. "It's something you can share with the children because of the hours, and music's a much more healthy activity than many other professions or occupations, although the kids may get sick of hearing me sawing away for hours at a time."

The longer tours are harder on family life, working most weekends and having days off during the week when everyone else is at work or school. For many years it was 85 days touring a year and management wanted to make it 100. That was before funding cuts started in 1991, and long tours became unsustainable. So 'run-outs' were invented. One-day tours with no overnight accommodation, fewer meals to pay for, and if the orchestra is there within three-and-a-half hours of concert call, no dayrooms.

That way the NZSO fulfills its obligations as a national orchestra, saves $10,000 a night and the budget stretches that much further. Ten run-outs pay for another concert. Players understand the reasons, but no one likes them.

All tours were long in the 1940s. One like this to Auckland could mean several weeks away from home. Rehearsing new programmes every day because each concert was broadcast live, wherever the orchestra played, symphony and schools concerts. Travelling up there and back on the Limited, the overnight train, sitting up with a pillow behind your head and

Packing into the hall in Timaru, from the back of an open truck. Former bass player and stage manager Bill Barsby (right) supervises. In wet weather a tarpaulin would be used to cover the load, but sometimes the rain got through.

a rug over your knees, rushing to buy a solid meat pie and a thick cup of tea when the train stopped at the station.

A run-out is hardly a tour, but it still has to be planned for: babysitters arranged, someone to feed the cat, walk the dog, or collect the newspaper so that it's not obvious the house is empty.

Wilma Smith has no need of a babysitter this trip. Her two small daughters, Jessye and Rosie, both born since she became concertmaster three years ago, are coming too, and her partner Peter. They will be staying on in Auckland with her parents who are part of the national support system that makes it all possible – a fulltime nanny on hand with her babies for orchestral breaks; Peter in Wellington, her parents in Auckland, his in Christchurch, friends around the country to babysit on longer tours. At Symphony House as a baby, Jessye attended lunchtime meetings, in Wilma's arms or beside her in the pram – and like her famous namesake Jessye Norman, she won hearts.

10.15: Grant phones David with good news from Auckland. The Desert Road is open, Colin is on his way. Fantastic. David's news from Wellington is not so good: the weather is deteriorating, the airport marginal. He hears this as he goes to collect the artists, leaving ahead of the orchestral flight so he can get them there without pressure and with plenty of time to have a meal, relax and get ready for the concert. The way it used to be for the players.

He is on the motorway when his cellphone rings again. Another player has 'flu: she was alright yesterday. Winter colds and viruses are hard to avoid in an orchestral environment where everyone works in such close contact; this year's strain is affecting entire sections.

Strings sections are not such a problem but wind and brass players may have no one to replace them. The harp is worst of all, with only three or four professional harpists in the country. When Carolyn Mills had pneumonia, there was no one available here or in Australia so one of her students, a schoolgirl, played the concert. She did a marvellous job, but it was scary stuff.

At the James Cook Centra David phones the airport again. "It's still marginal," he tells the conductor as they leave to collect the soloist.

11.00: The airport is full of travellers whose plans have been disrupted by the bad weather around the country. A handful of NZSO players are among them, travelling ahead of the orchestral group for lessons with their Auckland students. Some who left after rehearsal yesterday stayed privately overnight.

It is less crowded in the Golden Wing Lounge where the artists and David wait, their flight delayed, but not cancelled. The cellphone rings again. Another 'flu victim, the third, quite bad it seems, and this time a wind player. He thinks the section can cover him, and when David phones his principal at home, he confirms it: "As long as no one else gets sick!"

This is a relief. If they cannot cover him the conductor may demand a replacement, someone of comparable calibre and experience, who can step in at the last minute, with only a half-hour rehearsal. This may not be a problem in music capitals overseas, but in New Zealand the pool of such players is very small.

1.00: At the other end of the island Colin is making good time in his rig. The trip has been problem-free since the Desert Road re-opened, and he is on target to meet Grant and the crew at the Aotea Centre. Usually it takes 10 hours from Symphony House, arriving at the Aotea Centre or Town Hall at 4am, 5am at the latest, and waiting until 7am when they open the hall. Any later and city workers will have taken all the carparks, even on Saturdays, despite Grant's signs.

1.15: David and the artists arrive at their Auckland hotel half an hour late because of the flight delay. He gives them his cellphone number and reminds them of the rehearsal and concert arrangements. All three are staying overnight. David used to return on the orchestral flight, but it was always a nightmare trying to hustle artists away immediately after a performance. They like to unwind, talk to people who have come backstage to meet them, eat a leisurely supper and relax. It makes the tour much more satisfying and can influence their feelings about a return visit.

For this conductor everything is new and a bit strange. He will lunch here in the hotel, take a walk and then rest until David collects him. The soloist says he is not feeling so good, his throat is sore and he has a headache. Players have told him about the 'flu and he is afraid he has caught it. Artists travelling around the world are susceptible to infections and many over the years have had to cancel performances. David feels uneasy. This is how it happens without warning, and usually at the last minute. His mind races through possible scenarios. Engage a replacement soloist? Too late. Play a work from the other programme? Yes, if librarian Wynne Cole can send the music up from Wellington in time, if he can contact her, and if the airport is still open.

No, the pianist says, he does not want a doctor. He has his own medication, he takes it everywhere, an impressive array of tablets, medicines, mixtures, gargles and throat sprays spread out on the bathroom unit. He will not risk a walk or even practice at the hall. He will stay inside where it's warm, sleep and eat in his room. Tonight will be OK, he is convinced of it. He has not come all this way to miss concerts.

The conductor is not worried. They have worked together before; they are professionals. He shrugs; this pianist always worries about his health, there is no need to send for more music. David hopes he is right. At this stage he is not sure if the orchestra itself will get here in time, or if there will be a concert. Perhaps this soloist could give a recital like Gillian Weir did in Napier that time.

Grant Gilbert has used the long wait backstage at the Aotea Centre to talk to its lighting engineer. Theatre has been Grant's life for the past 20 years: touring around the country with stage shows and rock bands, then at the Michael Fowler Centre, where he first worked with the NZSO. He became its stage manager four years ago and always enjoys applying his theatrical skills and experience to the orchestra's advantage.

He and the stage crew are waiting when the distinctive-looking rig pulls in. "What took you so long?" Grant shouts as Colin jumps down grinning from the truck and throws open the trailer doors.

In the old days Broadcasting made all the NZSO's backstage arrangements, engaged the crew and the piano tuner, and managed front-of-house. Now David and Grant must find their own contacts when something goes wrong in any centre. The men here today have been hired by Van Lines, and like those in Wellington have worked with the orchestra for years. The pack-in gets underway as the trailer disgorges its treasures, rolling out through the loading doors and onto the stage, in the opposite order to when it was packed-out.

Set up, the stage looks exactly the same as it did in the studio, Michael Fowler Centre, Dunedin Town Hall or any one of a dozen or so concert halls up and down the country – give

In the video arcade on tour: from left, Deborah Rawson, Ed White, Colin Hemmingsen, David Angus, Greg Hill.

GRAEME BROWNE

or take a little more space at newer venues, and a little less, usually, in those that are older. Some conductors prefer a different configuration, with first and second violins on opposite sides of the rostrum, cellos in the middle – whereas the Summer Pops concerts have a rhythm section of drum kit, keyboards and bass at centre stage, with screens around them so that strings and winds can hear themselves.

It is a straightforward set-up today and all finished in under two hours; half an hour less at the Aotea Centre because of its loading bay, than at the Auckland Town Hall. The players arriving for practice, with everything in place, have little idea of what it has taken to get it there. Grant and Colin suspect that many of them think that each venue has its own chairs and music stands, identical to those at Symphony House.

"Some may not have cottoned-on to the fact we have worked all day for them to arrive and find it all laid out the way they need it," says Grant. "Moving the orchestra around has specific requirements to moving the gear, how the band is set up on stage, and it's taken me three to four years to learn that."

Colin goes off now for his regulation time off, a 10-hour break before the trip home tonight. Because of the delay he must leave later than usual.

1.30: Wellington airport: players arriving for their 2:00pm flight are met by travel officers John Dodds and Peter van Drimmelen. They have been on duty now for half an hour and have just learned that their flight, along with several others, has been delayed.

An airline employee beckons them to the counter for a phone call. Ed White had warned that a couple of players might not make it today: this is one of them, the doctor has told him not to fly. They cancel his ticket and tell his principal as soon as he arrives. The section will be down in numbers but it's too late to do anything about that now.

News of the delay is relayed as more players arrive. Some grumble that they should have been told to come later; most are resigned to waiting. It happens so often. They wander upstairs to the Golden Wing Lounge on the right, or the airport café on the left. Others go in search of a seat, bury their heads in the newspaper or pull out a crumpled paperback. There is little talk.

A further delay is announced. The boredom continues. So many people are waiting now it's impossible to find a seat and no one risks leaving theirs. At 2:50pm, almost an hour after it was due to leave, their flight is announced. A Wellington northerly has sprung up, dispersing the thick cloud hanging over the city. The sky clears and they are on their way.

The flight to Auckland seems slow today, with nothing outside the windows but swirling grey cloud. There is a lot of turbulence; not as bad as on that last trip back to Wellington, but they were heading home then, with the evening's concert behind them. Flying affects people differently; some feel queasy, others suffer from a blocked nose or painful sinuses; some may experience ear pressure or temporary deafness. Some of these symptoms may persist long

GRAEME BROWNE

after the flight is over – and that can be frightening with a concert to play in a few hours.

It's warmer in Auckland, although fine rain is falling as they leave the terminal and board the two coaches, one travel officer to each. It would be good to rest and freshen up, but no welcoming hotel room waits at the end of this coach trip.

Run-outs are tiring and stressful for players, spending five hours travelling with a two-hour concert sandwiched in the middle. Some of this may even come across to the audience, in the performance. The coaches deposit players at the Aotea Centre with two hours to kill and few options: to eat, walk, practise or wait around. On a wet winter Saturday the first two are not inviting and few restaurants serve dinner this early. Not that everyone feels like eating after a bumpy flight; some musicians never eat before performing; others, who ate on the plane, will wait until they get back home tonight. Many will happily use all their spare time practising either on stage, backstage, or in the auditorium. Most opt to wait around backstage.

Were they at home, or had a hotel room, they could rest and channel their energies as part of their concert preparation. David Chickering, principal cellist, spent eight years with the prestigious Chicago Symphony and was principal cellist with the National Symphony Orchestra of Costa Rica (four years) and the Auckland Philharmonia (two years) before appointment to the NZSO in 1993: "It's hard for me personally because I am a nap convert and naps before concerts are something I do religiously for about an hour around 4 o'clock... to make sure I am at my peak for the performance. It's OK on tour but it's almost impossible on run-outs, unless we have a dayroom."

Violinist Jane Freed wants to feel "warm, clean and fresh" before a concert. She likes to spend an hour in the bath, "to relax and warm up my muscles before getting dressed, ready for a beautiful night out, excited about the music we are going to play."

Dressing on a run-out can be a problem. Whether to travel in concert dress, which would look out of place, or carry it up from Wellington, and risk its becoming crushed. Many women wear trousers or culottes for that reason. In some venues it is difficult to find somewhere to change and freshen; professional musicians are expected to look well-groomed on stage. Here in the Aotea Centre colleagues share dressing rooms. Other halls have only rest rooms: toilets and hand basins with nowhere to rest, and no real privacy.

(Opposite) Interval, backstage at Palmerston North Opera House; from left, Stephen Harker, Andrew Lawrence, David Pawsey, Sue Warner, Bruce McKinnon, Nicholas Sandle.

Saturday Evening

6.30: Everyone is onstage with their instruments, for the acoustic rehearsal. This is a recent innovation, a half-hour run-through one hour before the concert in halls where no full rehearsal is able to be scheduled. Visiting conductors appreciate it, especially those who, like the current one, have never played in the hall before. The acoustic is not perfect, but that is not unusual in a new hall, no matter what efforts have been made.

The soloist is fully recovered. Whatever he took has worked. He slept all afternoon and when he awoke he felt wonderful. The conductor looks at David and raises an eyebrow: "Did I not tell you so?" his look says. David is relieved – one thing less to worry about.

7.00: Players leave the stage again, the ushers open the doors, and the Aotea Centre starts to fill up. The hall built for Kiri Te Kanawa was hailed as a great performing centre when first opened but soon gained a reputation as a white elephant – a typical New Zealand reaction. Still hugely expensive to run, it seems to have settled down as performers and audiences come to terms with its acoustic. From NZSO members it receives grudging acceptance now. It is the old town halls in the main centres that musicians love best. The old-fashioned, rectangular shaped shoebox which gives the best sound but not always the best view.

There is half an hour to fill before the concert starts. Everyone is dressed, or almost, with only jackets and ties to add. The travelling tea urn brought up on the truck from Wellington has been kept busy this afternoon. It used to be that two players looked after it on a roster basis; now violinist Lisa Egen looks after it on contract.

This is the time when players remember questions they have been meaning to ask David for weeks. They are ready and there is nothing else to do. "No, this is not the time," David says, looking distracted, "can't it wait until next week?"

Concert FM is recording the concert tonight. The equipment was set up this morning and tested during the acoustic rehearsal. It is a live broadcast so timing is important, something that David, an ex-broadcaster himself, appreciates. Before that it was theatre, over 70 full-scale theatrical productions stage managed; Radio New Zealand publicity and promotions for 13 years; his own promotions company; then NZSO in 1982. He has worked to ensure that NZSO concerts start on time – both orchestra and audience had to be trained, although to see the latter you might not think so tonight. They are wandering in like Brown's cows, though the bells have been ringing for several minutes.

7.15: Grant cues the lighting engineer and the stagelights dim; all players have left the stage. David checks that the conductor is happy, collects the score he has been studying and carries it on stage, placing it on the rostrum.

7.25: Backstage the adrenalin is running high. David is walking around, clapping his hands loudly as he passes the dressing rooms, his trademark signal for everyone to get ready. Despite the difficulties, a transformation has taken place. The casually dressed musicians who boarded the plane in Wellington have emerged sleek and elegant in evening wear: white tie and black tail suits, long black dresses, trousers or culottes.

The orchestral dress code, vigorously debated over many years, has become more flexible. Individuality, at least in women's wear, is more acceptable, although a standard medium-length ensemble is still not resolved. Men have their white tuxedos at last, not for tonight's Subscription concert, for which convention dictates traditional black, but for the glamour nights, the outdoor extravaganzas and Summer Pops concerts.

Lined up on either side of the stage, players seem lighthearted as they chat and laugh together, with the occasional one staring ahead blankly, playing in his head that difficult bit in the second movement. David gives the conductor a five minute warning, and he waits out of sight, baton in hand, for the first sounds of applause. In another dressing room the pianist flexes his fingers – playing imaginary scales in the air – and regrets missing his afternoon practice. At the back of the line of players, Wilma awaits her cue.

Grant is on the phone to the hall manager, the audience is seated, and he signals to David on the opposite side of the stage. The audience is hushed. David sends the players on, they go to their chairs, sit down and wait. Wilma Smith enters and the applause starts up; this is her home town and they are proud of her. She bows to them, turns to face the orchestra and the tuning begins, that evocative sound that anticipates the pleasures to come. There is a pause, the conductor walks on and the audience greets him warmly. This is his first NZSO tour but his reputation has preceded him. He raises his baton and the eyes of 90 musicians follow it. The concert begins.

At interval a queue forms at the tea urn. Smokers go outside for a puff, others cluster around the TV to watch excerpts from the big All Blacks game. It is an incongruous sight. Two great national teams, both in black, both playing for New Zealand.

Colin has joined Grant and David backstage. He has had his rest and anyway it's hard to keep away. Almost 80 percent of his work now is with the orchestra and he loves it, not just as the driver, but as an integral part of the team. Moving the grand piano is one example of that teamwork, and they have got it down to a fine art: two minutes flat to shift chairs and music stands for the violins, the conductor's rostrum, roll the piano on, lift the lid, place the piano stool – and then replace everything and get everyone seated again. He can set up the stage on his own now, put out the music at a pinch, knows when something is wrong, but still feels "nervous going on stage" he says and always avoids looking at the audience.

Once he put the piano lid up on the wrong peg. Pianists won't play with it like that, "It looks wrong and it's bad luck". Someone else had to sort it out.

9.30: The music reaches its passionate conclusion and the audience erupts with enthusiasm. Spontaneous whistles and foot stomping indicate a good smattering of younger people amongst the grey heads; a brave few even rise to their feet. New Zealanders are not usually demonstrative about their music.

It has all gone very well. Everybody is pleased. Later at supper the conductor will praise the orchestra, talk of "next time" and of the

music he would like to do with them. The pianist, too, is on a high. There is no sign of the 'flu. "It must have been jet-lag," he says and the concerto was outstanding. He has generous praise for the orchestra.

The players' response to the conductor will be reflected in the assessment they complete after he leaves, a process that provides a valuable indicator of how players perceive the effectiveness or otherwise of these conductors, and how they measure up one to another. Sometimes the orchestra's assessment can differ markedly from that of the music critics. If favourable it could be the start of a long-term relationship. But players are wary. The NZSO has a long history of conductors who, after a spectacular first tour, fail to live up to expectations on their second: 'The Second Visit Syndrome'.

Grant, Colin and the crew begin the pack-out before the last of the audience has moved out the doors. Players pack their instruments into their cases and hurry to the dressing rooms to get ready to return home. Family and friends may have been in the audience tonight, but there is no chance to see or talk to them, to share tonight's magic. Like Cinderella they must leave now to get back to Wellington before midnight, the airport's noise curfew – if the planes are still flying, that is.

The two coaches stand outside, engines throbbing as the early players climb on and claim favourite seats. Once one entire coach would have been designated for smokers only. Now there are not enough of them to fill one coach, although numbers have recently risen, a worrying sign.

The last stragglers are taunted by those who have been kept waiting. Most would prefer to stay overnight, but if that is not possible, then they are impatient to go. The travel officers check numbers and then give the OK to their respective drivers. The doors shut and the coaches speed off through the dark streets towards the airport.

The performers are gone before half the audience reaches the foyer. Backstage the pack-out will take another hour to complete, so Grant too will stay over and fly back tomorrow. If anything goes wrong on the orchestral flight he and David are here to sort it out, as they did once on a Christchurch run-out when the flight back to Wellington could not land there and had to return to Christchurch. Being on the spot, they had the hotel accommodation all arranged, for 90 people, by the time the plane landed again after midnight.

A few people have come backstage to talk to the conductor and soloist while NZSO Board chairman Hylton LeGrice and his wife Angela arrive to take them both out to supper.

Several others have come to see orchestral friends and look very disappointed to hear they have gone. This happens a lot now, says David, most noticeably in Christchurch: "Anything up to 25-30 people would come backstage to talk to players, the conductor or soloists. It's a very musical city and they loved it, and a lot of our players are from there. We are losing our relationship with the people of the communities we play to."

The atmosphere aboard the two coaches is relaxed with much laughter, the opposite of their arrival earlier in the day. There is satisfaction for a successful concert, but some tension lingers beneath the laughter, because there is still the flight home and one can never be sure about that.

This time their fears are groundless. A small backlog of passengers waits to be rescheduled but the delay to the orchestral flight is minimal. They fly off into a beautiful night sky and there is no turbulence when they make their descent into Wellington 50 minutes later.

Players drift away in their separate directions, to cars left in the airport carpark or to share taxis, which they hope are still waiting.

Sunday morning they can sleep in, if the kids let them, catch up on household or garden chores, practise and try to relax, ready for a week of studio recordings. Lower Hutt Town Hall is the venue, like "playing in a bathroom, noisy and cold", according to violinist Jane Freed. A lot of new music by a composer some players have never heard of before, not even on a recording, because none have been made. Theirs will be the first.

At the Aotea Centre the instruments and equipment are all packed away in the truck, ready for an early start in the morning. Grant and the crew have gone off for a couple of beers and David hopes to join them when he gets through. Colin prepares for his solitary drive back to Wellington. Usually he is gone as soon as pack-out is completed, but his 10 hours will not be up until 1.00. Then he can get back on the road. The weather report was not too bad but you cannot rely on that in winter. He has to be back in time to pack-in and to set up for Monday's recording.

Colin is driving back along the Desert Road. Snow and ice is banked up on either side, **Sunday Morning** deposited by the snow-plough. All the stranded vehicles have gone. The sky is clear and the moon shines on Ruapehu's snow-covered peak. Another run-out almost over.

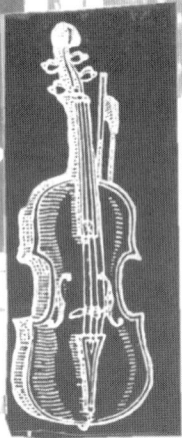

The Concertmasters

"The best of musicians... a paragon among orchestral players."

– Owen Jensen, former music critic.[68]

THE role of concertmaster is the vital position in any orchestra. It provides the vital link between orchestra and conductor, orchestra and management. The person James Robertson referred to as his "left hand man".

The NZSO's present "left hand man" and the orchestra's fifth concertmaster is a woman and mother. Fijian-born but brought up in New Zealand, Wilma Smith achieved success against the competitive odds in the United States, and as first leader of the New Zealand String Quartet. Wilma left the NZSO from the back desk of the second violins and came back 15 years later to take the first chair.

"It's an enormous responsibility," Wilma says. "The focus of the job must always be musical, that's my main function, a kind of musical overseeing. It's all too easy to loose sight of that when all this other stuff comes along. I was amazed at how much extra musical activity there is."

The other responsibilities have grown and evolved over the years, reflecting the increased demands on the orchestra, and to some extent the personality of each incumbent. Wilma's present workload of committees and responsibilities was never foreseen in the early days.

Vincent Aspey MBE

Doctor of Music, Honoris Causa, Victoria University of Wellington, 1974

Leader October 1946-August 1967

When Andersen Tyrer set out with his shopping list for players for the new National Orchestra in 1946, there was one obvious choice for leader, Vincent Aspey. The son of an illiterate miner from Huntly, Vince was a professional violinist from the age of 12, playing for the silent movies at the Huntly pictures, three nights a week, five shillings a night. He was often in trouble with his uncle Herbert Farrimand, his first teacher, for watching Tom Mix or Hopalong Cassidy on the screen and losing his place in the music. He left school in standard five to play in Auckland theatre orchestras, like the Civic, accompanying major films such as *Ben Hur* which had complete scores. He later credited the movies for his exceptional skill at sight-reading.

When the family moved to Australia, 19-year-old Vince studied briefly at the then New South Wales State Conservatorium, then led the Australian Broadcasting Orchestra, the ABC's first studio orchestra, from 1928-32. He could have possibly filled a more important role in Australian orchestral history but chose instead, after an absence of almost four years, to come home.

He became leader of the 1YA Studio Orchestra and went on to lead the National Broadcasting String Orchestra established in December 1939. A year later he was sub-leader of the 1940 Centennial Orchestra. Although that orchestra was disbanded, the NBS String Orchestra was retained and Vince led this, and the NBS String Quartet, throughout the war years.

By 1946 Vincent Aspey had come a long way from the Huntly pictures: he was by then the first leader of the National Orchestra. He held this chair for 21 years. In 1967 he chose to move further back in the section until his retirement in 1973, after 40 years in Broadcasting orchestras.

"He was a fabulous fiddle player," the late James Robertson told me, "and though you might not expect it of a person like that, with little formal music training, he read magnificently well, no matter how many ledger lines; he used to shoot up the fiddle and arrive ahead of people with much more training. I admire leaders who do concertos [along] with the strain and responsibility of leading."

John Hopkins: "He was one of the most remarkable men. He could not put the bow on the instrument and not make a beautiful sound for all the romantic literature. He was a great player."

Twenty years after his retirement, Vincent Aspey is still quoted by former colleagues like John Dodds: "His dry wit and sensible comments have stuck by me over the years. When I was an impatient and over-enthusiastic young person, Vince patted me on the back, 'John, it's a long road', in other words, pace yourself. I wasn't sure what he meant then. Thirty years later I do!"

In 1984, at the instigation of NZSO violinist Dean Major, Kiwi Pacific Records released a recording of two live performances by Vincent Aspey and the National Orchestra in the 1960s, the Bruch and Mendelssohn Violin Concertos. These are Vince's only commercial recordings and he was greatly moved that they were recorded.

(Above) Vincent Aspey after receiving his MBE at Government House, Wellington. (Opposite) Leader from 1946 to 1967, Vincent Aspey retired from the orchestra in 1973.

Vincent Aspey attended the orchestra's 40th birthday celebrations on 24 October 1986 and launched my first book on the NZSO. He died suddenly five months later.

Eric Lawson
Sub-leader May 1948-March 1971

When Alex Lindsay stepped down as sub-leader in 1947, Andersen Tyrer planned to replace him with Francis Rosner from Vienna. Vince was not having any of that. He rang the conductor at his hotel and told him so: "Look Tyrer," he said, "I'd rather be a tram conductor unless I have Lawson!"

He got his way. Eric Lawson became sub-leader and he and Vincent Aspey were a dream team front desk for the next 19 years. An incredible partnership of two musicians and two great friends.

Eric Lawson was one of Andersen Tyrer's British recruits. He had followed both his father, a violinist, and grandfather, an organist at Liverpool Cathedral, into music, training with Sir Hamilton Harty and going on to play in the Liverpool Philharmonic and Hallé Orchestras. After four years' war service he joined the London Symphony and then the BBC Northern Symphony, under its then conductor Sir Charles Groves, a post later held by John Hopkins who remembers that whenever he went back there "the first thing they asked was 'How's Eric?'"

"His professionalism and unstinting musical loyalty to his leader helped establish the front desk as second to none in Australasia," said Ashley Heenan. "It was known in the profession that, even though he may never be required to perform it, every leader's solo was well and truly prepared by Eric... 'Just in case!'"[69]

Said Vincent Aspey of his great 'cobber', with whom he played snooker between rehearsals and concerts: "Eric and I were the same make-up, otherwise I wouldn't have lasted as well as I did. A leader has to have an assistant to take some of the weight off."

James Robertson said of Eric: "A splendid desk together with Aspey, it was very rare indeed... exactly what you want of No. 2."

Alex Lindsay MBE
Sub-leader October 1946-December 1947

Leader August 1967-July 1969

Concertmaster July 1969-December 1974

As a 17-year-old, Alex Lindsay set out from Invercargill with a scholarship to the Royal Academy. He worked his passage on a ship to England, "doing skivvy jobs in the day and playing in the ship's orchestra at night".[70]

His first job after finishing his studies was as leader of the chamber orchestra at Stratford-

Vincent Aspey and Eric Lawson, a rare front desk partnership for 19 years.

upon-Avon. He then joined the London Philharmonic for the last six months under the legendary Sir Thomas Beecham. Drafted into the Royal Navy during the war, he had an unhappy time before being transferred to the New Zealand Navy, where he served in the Pacific until the war finished.

From there he joined the National Orchestra as foundation sub-leader. He "loathed" it and its "apalling" conductor, he said later,[71] and "hated every aspect of New Zealand. I thought I had done the wrong thing". He left to start the important Alex Lindsay String Orchestra in 1948, forerunner of the Wellington Regional (now Sinfonia) Orchestra.

In 1956 James Robertson persuaded him to return to the National Orchestra as principal second violin and in 1958 he co-founded the New Zealand String Quartet. In 1963 an Arts Council Travel Grant took him back to Europe, where he studied conducting, violin and chamber music at the Mozarteum in Salzburg. Joining the LSO for its 15th Anniversary World Tour, he became principal second violin, LPO, spending part of that time with Glyndebourne Opera, and then held the same position with the LSO.

When Vincent Aspey retired, Broadcasting turned to Alex Lindsay. They wanted to appoint a New Zealander. It was the first time they had not looked towards Britain and the significance was not lost on him. He returned and took up the job in August 1967.

For the next seven years he led the orchestra, conducted it occasionally, despite the protests of some subscribers, and performed as a soloist, all with very great distinction. His initial appointment was, like Vincent Aspey, as leader. But in 1969, after 23 years, the title changed, reflecting new responsibilities when the resident conductor system ceased. It was recognised that as more would now, inevitably, fall on the Leader's shoulders, the American term 'concertmaster' was more appropriate.

Alex Lindsay was enthusiastic about the change. He felt the orchestra was ready to stand on its own two feet and did not need a permanent conductor. It would be up to him to "preserve the esprit de corps and the musical integrity of the players".[72]

In the same interview he described his duties. The leader, he said, "decides on matters of bowing".[52] The conductor indicates the phrasing he wants and the leader 'translates' it into the appropriate bowing. "Conductors usually accept the leader's bowing but clashes of taste and personality can occur. As leader, he is responsible for the general artistic standards of the orchestra. He is a spokesman for the players with management... concerned with orchestral discipline, and acts as a 'means of contact between conductor and orchestra'; artistic and personal problems of individual players can be brought to his notice." He does "a good deal of conducting between guest conductors", and is required to play solo violin parts. "It's a hell of a job!" he said.

Then, in 1974, Alex Lindsay took on what was possibly his greatest challenge when the orchestra was invited to Australia at short notice. Chief Conductor Brian Priestman was out

Alex Lindsay MBE, 1974, at Christchurch Airport. He died the same year soon after the Australian tour.

of the country so it was left to him, in addition to his duties as concertmaster, to study scores and prepare the orchestra for the conductor to take on tour. Some works selected by Priestman had not been performed by the orchestra for two years and needed much work. The strain must have been enormous and indeed, though a critical success, there was pressure on all players, and a feeling of insecurity about the conductor's hold on things.

In December, six weeks after the orchestra returned to Wellington, Alex Lindsay died suddenly while on holiday, aged 55. Players had lost "not only a concertmaster and colleague, but also a friend – a comrade of great warmth, humanity and gentleness", said horn player Bob Burch.[53]

Alex Lindsay's tremendous contribution to music in New Zealand lives on in the Alex Lindsay Memorial Awards, operated by orchestral players to fund advanced studies for young instrumentalists.

Margaret (Sicely) Tibbles

Acting sub-leader December 1974-June 1976

Although she was never officially leader or assistant leader, Margaret Sicely as principal first violin, deserves recognition for the part she played, acting as sub-leader and occasional leader to Alex Lindsay for almost three years whenever he conducted, and then again for 18 months as sub-leader to John Chisholm after Alex Lindsay's death.

A foundation member of the orchestra, she was born in Marton but spent much of her musical life in Christchurch, where she studied with Maurice Clare and played in trios and in the 3YA Studio Orchestra.

In 1976 Margaret Sicely elected to stand down from the first violins and moved to the seconds, retiring in 1980.

John Chisholm

Sub-leader January 1973-December 1974

Acting leader (later concertmaster) December 1974-June 1976

Assistant concertmaster June 1976-December 1984

At 27, half the age of Alex Lindsay, sub-leader John Chisholm became acting leader, later concertmaster in December 1974, until the appointment of Peter Schaffer in June 1976.

Born in Hamilton, John Chisholm grew up in Dunedin and Christchurch where he did two years of an arts degree at Canterbury University. He studied at the New South Wales Conservatorium under Carl Pini and held positions as deputy leader of both the Melbourne Elizabethan Trust Orchestra, and the Christchurch Civic Orchestra.

John joined the orchestra in October 1970, then spent six months leave overseas in 1972, freelancing and as a member of the Philomusica of London. He married NZSO cellist Vivien

John Chisholm: premature finale to a brilliant career.

TOM SHANAHAN

Thomas, a former trainee, in 1973 and the following year his twin brother Allan, now associate principal cello, joined the orchestra. The brothers shared a love of chamber music, forming in 1975 the esteemed Gagliano Trio with pianist Bruce Greenfield, which toured in New Zealand for the then Music Federation, to Australia in 1983, and made an historic cultural visit to China the same year. John took very seriously the wider implications of the trio's visit as musical ambassadors.

John Chisholm led the NZSO in the important recording of the Mahler 4 under Uri Segal, with Malvina Major in September 1975 .

Ten years after Alex Lindsay's death, and his move into the leader's chair, John Chisholm died, tragically young aged 37, from cancer. The loss affected the orchestra deeply.

There were many who wanted to see him become concertmaster but it was not a position he sought. It was the music, not the chair, that was important to him, he said, and he preferred to spend time playing the violin and chamber music, "which is a great love of mine". The assistant concertmaster should be able to lead the orchestra, and lead it well, "without necessarily aiming to be the leader", he said.

As a leader of the then National (later New Zealand Post) Youth Orchestra on two occasions, it is appropriate that his memorial, the John Chisholm Award, established in 1988, is awarded each year to the leader of that orchestra.

Peter Schaffer was highly regarded by players and conductors, but departed in 1984 after irreconcilable artistic differences arose.

Peter Schaffer

Concertmaster June 1976-July 1984

The first non-New Zealander to lead the orchestra, Peter Schaffer was born in Munich and emigrated to the United States when he was nine years old. His mother was a dancer, his father in vaudeville. A visit by the famous violinist Fritz Kreisler to their home inspired Peter's father that his son should be a violinist.

He joined NZSO in June 1976, from the position of associate concertmaster San Francisco Symphony, and concertmaster of the San Francisco Opera Orchestra. It was almost eight years to the day when he left, at short notice on 7 July 1984, irreconcilable artistic differences having arisen between him, his wife Zoe Fisher Schaffer and principal horn David Cripps. John Chisholm could not take over the chair this time and he died five months later.

A charming and sincere man, Peter Schaffer was always respected as a musician, and highly regarded by visiting conductors and soloists. Franz-Paul Decker wanted him to join his orchestra in Barcelona when he left.

There is no doubt that he found some of his administrative responsibilities such as player assessments very difficult. In an interview before leaving, he gave an exaggerated account of his job description, which was, he said, much longer than that of a comparable position abroad.[54] "He has to lead the orchestra, he has to show by example, he has the bowings to do

TOM SHANAHAN

Concertmaster Peter Schaffer and co-principal cellist
Wilfred Simenauer rehearsing the Brahms double
concerto, 1977.

TOM SHANAHAN

for the string parts, he has to be good at public relations, he has to meet and consult with the conductor, he has to see that everybody's alright on tour, to take care of people's problems and be there to consult with..."

"It's a very difficult job as leader of this orchestra because of the varied responsibilities and the absence of a musical director," he told me as editor of *Concert Pitch*.[76] There was a closer involvement with players here, and a lot more falls back on the concertmaster.

John Chisholm, his desk partner for eight years, said it was a good relationship.[77] "He was an excellent violinist and I learnt a great deal sitting beside him... He was a very gentle man who perhaps didn't like the conflicts which inevitably arise in an orchestra, but I think that is possibly a nice side of his nature... he was always a gentleman."

In return, Peter Schaffer said: "I'm particularly fond of my partner, John Chisholm – I couldn't have had a better one... He is a marvellous violinist and he supports, which is what that chair really is, a supporting chair, not a lesser chair... You are living together on the job, you know each other's quirks and shortcomings, and you try to help each other. It's not just concertmaster and assistant concertmaster, it's two people working together in complete harmony."[78]

Acting Leaders

Replacing Peter Schaffer was a long process with several trials, among them those with Morry Kernaman, assistant concertmaster of the Toronto Symphony, and Carl Pini, former leader of the Philharmonia Orchestra in London and Hugh Maguire, Bournemouth Symphony.

Marian Tache, a Romanian who had escaped from his home country while on a tour with the Bucharest Philharmonic in Germany, joined the NZSO from the position of assistant concertmaster in the South African Broadcasting Corporation. A deteriorating political situation there led him and his family here. An excellent player, although unsuccessful in his bid for concertmaster, he had accepted appointment as principal first violin only to escape again, this time from New Zealand, over the Christmas holidays. His empty chair at the first rehearsal in January was the NZSO's first indication that he and his family had left the country and returned to Europe.

A much more reliable recruit was Yury Gezentsvey. He, too, had escaped his homeland, in his case Russia, and had to give up his citizenship and leave everything, including his beloved violin. Yury went first to the United States and was concertmaster of the Chicago Civic Orchestra, before taking up a similar position with the Caracas Philharmonic in Venezuela.

After his initial trial in February, Yury returned in 1985, and said: "Since I was born in Russia 32 years ago I have been searching for the place where I should have been born. This is where I should have been born." The Gezentsvey family, Yury, his wife Desiree and three small daughters, have since been joined by Yury's parents from Kiev.[79]

Yury was not appointed concertmaster but as principal first violin, frequently moves to the front in the absence of either front desk player and acted as assistant concertmaster after the departure of Isidor Saslav. He is active in chamber music and as a solo performer.

NZSO players on the front desk between trialists were Valerie Rigg, who now lives in Canada, as acting assistant concertmaster; alternating with Richard Panting, who was acting concertmaster, and now lives in Melbourne, and Zita Outtrim, sub-principal first violin who occasionally moved up as assistant concertmaster. Zita retired in 1990 and was awarded a QSM in 1991.

Isidor Saslav

Concertmaster August 1986-December 1992

It took two years to appoint a new concertmaster. Isidor Saslav was the orchestra's choice and in August 1986 he became the fourth appointed to the chair, the second American.

Isidor was born in Jerusalem. He joined the Detroit Symphony at the age of 17 (its youngest member), and was concertmaster of three major American orchestras for 12 years, the Buffalo Philharmonic, Minnesota Orchestra and Baltimore Symphony.

Recognised internationally as a Haydn scholar through his work as co-editor of the Josef Haydn Institute in Cologne and published editions of the Haydn String Quartets, he had been a faculty member of the prestigious Peabody Institute of the Johns Hopkins University of Baltimore. He also had a passion for the works of George Bernard Shaw, and had amassed a huge collection of books and other memorabilia which he brought with him to New Zealand.

The NZSO was "virtually unique", Dr Saslav said on his arrival. It had "no permanent musical director, and I felt that this was an advantage, and a rare one, to be able to work in that sort of environment with guest conductors as continual leadership... I will provide an environment in which I can really do the job in what I consider a proper way..."[80]

Isidor's family remained based in the United States, where his wife Ann Heiligman had her own career as a pianist. He returned there for three months each year and the pair performed together as a violin-piano duo during the North American winter months. In autumn Isidor flew back to New Zealand, either accompanied by Ann, or she would join him later. The couple performed concerts throughout the country, including many for schools, in between NZSO engagements. It seemed a demanding lifestyle for an NZSO concertmaster.

Donald Armstrong as associate concertmaster, was his desk partner for six years. "Isidor was an absolute enthusiast; however, he did not really fit into the tradition of the orchestra and New Zealand ways. Personally we had some nice times, but musically we had very different approaches which made it difficult sometimes."

Dr Saslav's tenure as concertmaster ended soon after he led the orchestra on its important tour to Seville; his contract expired and was not renewed. At the end of 1992 he returned to the United States.

Isidor Saslav with his wife Ann Heiligman, 1990: an energetic and demanding lifestyle.

Donald Armstrong

Associate concertmaster January 1987

Acting concertmaster December 1992–September 1993

Born and raised in Wellington, Donald spent three years in the Schola Musica (1974-77), and was a member of the National Youth Orchestra, including the world tour in 1975 along with another young violinist, Wilma Smith. In January 1977 he joined the NZSO and two months later, in March, so did Wilma. The two of them, the section's newest recruits in those days before rotation, sat together at the back of the seconds, and seemed to spend every spare moment vigorously practising; outside the orchestra they played in a string quartet together.

In August 1978 they left for the United States within a week of each other – Wilma to study in Boston, and Donald to New York for two years at Mannes College, then three years in Boston, completing his M.Mus (with distinction) at the New England Conservatory and spending summers at the Aspen Music Festival. He played in a string quartet for a year then left for Europe to become principal second violin in the Tivoli Gardens Orchestra in Copenhagen.

When it began to get "cold and dark" after six months in Denmark, Donald moved south. He was appointed second concertmaster of the Orchestre Philharmonique de Nice, leading the 100-strong opera and symphony orchestra for most of the time, a challenge to his fifth form French.

In 1986 he returned to New Zealand after an absence of eight years, initially for a trial as concertmaster to replace Peter Schaffer, and became the NZSO's first associate concertmaster when Isidor Saslav was made concertmaster, replacing him in this position for two months of each year.

When Isidor Saslav returned to the United States at the end of 1992, Donald slipped easily into the role of acting concertmaster until Wilma Smith's appointment took effect in September 1993. The two back desk partners were now a front desk team.

"If you are a second chair, the biggest issue is who is in the first chair," Donald says. "If they're good and you respect them it can be a very good job. If there is a clash, and you don't respect them, it can be the worst job in the world. That's a crucial point, and a lot of luck comes into it. For myself I find that for two months it's really fun [in the first chair] and I really enjoy that time but I'm also quite happy sitting in the second chair for the time. There isn't quite the pressure and the expectation on you and I feel I'm quite good in a supportive role and seeing from both sides."

As leader and musical director of the New Zealand Chamber Orchestra, in addition to being the NZSO's associate concertmaster, Donald says he has "time to have a personal life outside the orchestra, so there's a great satisfaction there, and for me the balance couldn't be better."

Donald Armstrong: a front desk team with his old back desk partner Wilma Smith.

TOM SHANAHAN

Wilma Smith

Concertmaster September 1993-

Wilma started playing the violin because "my primary school teacher in standard one or two, wanted all the kids to play an instrument. If you had a good ear he would suggest one of the harder instruments. That's how I got started. I still remember going home and I had to ask my parents for $10, to buy a violin, a lot of money. They had been thinking of a recorder, but they agreed and I brought it home. I remember being quite fascinated."

"When I was a kid there wasn't much of a tradition of having to work hard at an instrument and compete as they do in some countries. I didn't know anyone who did. I just did it for fun." She is impressed by the technical standard and obvious dedication of today's Youth Orchestra players.

In Boston she was a special student at the New England Conservatory, doing the performance side without completing a degree, and in 1980 was appointed first violin with the prestigious Lydian String Quartet based at Brandeis University in Massachussetts. In 1987 she accepted an invitation to establish and lead the new New Zealand String Quartet.

When the job of NZSO concertmaster came up, Wilma was the only applicant to audition live. "It was excruciatingly traumatic!" she says. "These were all my old friends, I'd kept in touch with them over the years, and here I was showing up for this new job. The first rehearsal was quite nerve-wracking. I got a lot of support from my colleagues and basically I've always had the feeling in anything I do, you just go and do your best and what comes out is what you've got to offer. If people like it well, good. If not, too bad! It's not that nerve-wracking any more but I do feel it's an enormous responsibility."

(Opposite) Concertmaster Wilma Smith got started as a child with a $10 violin.

She agrees that more responsibility falls back on the concertmaster in this orchestra because there is no musical director. Being a woman in the job does not seem to have an effect, although sometimes a conductor will give her the impression, "'A woman, Oh dear!' But even that is fairly seldom, the world has changed," she says. "It's more accepted now, even though there aren't that many women concertmasters."

Desk partner Donald Armstrong has the last word: "I feel what's important with an orchestra is its identity. Having a New Zealand concertmaster of a New Zealand orchestra is a real stamp on that orchestra. While it's not a criterion, it's a settling influence on all around. With Wilma's characteristics it was like a wave of calm has gone through the orchestra, starting from the front and going back. It's been a really nice thing to see."

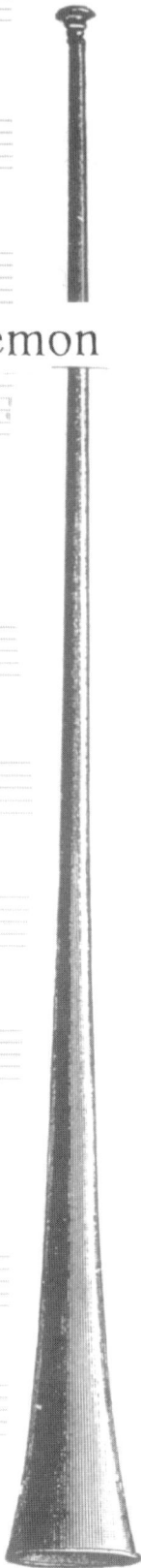

Fl. 1

1, 2

Trb.

Tba.

mp

246

rc. 1

rc. 2

rc. 3

In. 1

24

Vla

Lilith's Dream of Ecstasy

night demon

OEDIPVS REX

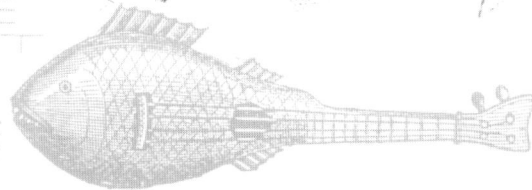

and *A Pacific Piece* by Gareth Farr,

Making Music

"You sit down and play pages and pages and pages of notes, and the red light is on and you are recording the whole way. You get to the end of the day and think, what did I actually do today? What was that? Was there music there somewhere or just pages of black dots?"

– Lisa Egen, Viola.

CONCERTS, venues, times and audiences have moved on since the 1940s when the National Orchestra played symphony concerts in a hall – and basically that was that. Music-making now covers a broad spectrum of activities for the NZSO which in any given year may be expected to play symphony concerts, schools concerts, family concerts; accompany opera and ballet in the pit, record commercially in the studio, perform indoors for pops concerts, prom concerts, sponsored concerts; and outdoors in sound shells, in parks, on pontoons, at cricket grounds and in vineyards; or play contemporary music, pop music, ethnic music – at morning concerts, matinée concerts, early evening or Sunday concerts and in an ironic twist, given the background of many of its foundation players, accompany silent movies.

In the Pit: Opera

A Broadcasting production of Bizet's opera *Carmen* was the National Orchestra's first experience of working in the pit. In 1948, its second season, it accompanied a four-month, four-centre, 33-performance tour with principals Arthur Sevent and Janet Howe from England and New Zealanders Dora and Bryan Drake. Minor principals, the chorus and ballet changed in each centre.

A much larger and more important tour followed a year later. The International (Italian) Grand Opera Company, stranded in Australia and unable to continue to New Zealand because of the cost, was rescued on the personal intervention of Prime Minister Peter Fraser. He assigned the National Orchestra to accompany the 180-strong company, without charge – and Broadcasting to pay the bill. This extraordinary gesture brought a feast of opera to a

New Zealand audience of 120,000, at 104 performances, 61 of them broadcast on radio, in 10 centres, under conductors Franco Ghione, Manno Wolf-Ferrari and Umberto Vedovelli.

Home-grown opera came in 1954 with the establishment of the New Zealand Opera Company. Resident conductors James Robertson and John Hopkins were successive musical directors and individual National Orchestra players the mainstay in accompanying both opera and ballet. As demand increased, the need for another orchestra became clear, and the ill-fated Concert Orchestra was formed, disbanding two years later.

In 1969 the National Orchestra accompanied two operas under James Robertson: *Carmen*, with a young Kiri Te Kanawa creating a sensation, and *The Mikado*. Two years later, *Aida* and *The Marriage of Figaro* were performed, conducted by Vanco Cavdarski and Alex Lindsay respectively.

Australian opera came to New Zealand in 1976, in an exciting collaboration with the NZSO, instigated at government level. Two operas were performed: Verdi's *Rigoletto* under the baton of Richard Bonynge and *Jenůfa* by Janáček, conducted by Georg Tintner. In the same year, although not in the pit, James Robertson conducted New Zealand's first concert performance of *Turandot*, for the Golden Jubilee of Radio.

Other significant concert versions include *The Flying Dutchman* in 1977, with Robert Allman and other principals from the Australian Opera Company, again conducted by Georg Tintner; Verdi's *Macbeth* in 1978, conducted by Vanco Cavdarski with Donald McIntrye; Stravinsky's *Oedipus Rex,* conducted by Elyakum Shapirra, also in 1978; and *Hansel and Gretel* by Humperdinck, conducted by Kenneth Montgomery in 1983.

Since national opera in New Zealand gave way to regional opera, the NZSO has performed with Auckland Opera, now Opera New Zealand, for Wagner's *The Flying Dutchman* with Sir Donald McIntyre in 1992; Puccini's *Turandot* in 1994 and Benjamin Britten's *Peter Grimes* with Richard Greager and Wendy Dixon for Wellington City Opera in 1995.

Wellington's Michael Fowler Centre has no pit and was never envisaged as an opera venue but remarkable results have been achieved there for New Zealand International Arts Festival operas, *Die Meistersinger Von Nürnberg* in 1990, *Salome* in 1992, *Madame Butterfly* in 1994, and in 1996 *Katya Kabanová*.

Donald Armstrong: "I played in the opera orchestra in Nice. It was unbelievable: top, fantastic singers, marathon scale productions with 200 people on stage, unlimited funds. I came back thinking I'd never see anything like that again. Two years later we did a *Meistersinger* that left Nice for dead!"

In the Pit: Ballet

Given the almost parallel establishment of New Zealand's professional orchestra and ballet within a few years of each other, it is surprising that it was not until 1985 that these two leading performing arts organisations appeared together in performance.

Accompanied by the National Orchestra, The International (Italian) Grand Opera Company brought a feast of opera to New Zealand audiences in 1948.

The orchestra had performed previously with overseas ballet companies, the first being the Maly Ballet from Leningrad in 1961/62, an arrangement made through theatrical agents Kerridge, which in 1955 had become the first company to hire the National Orchestra when it accompanied the acclaimed American pianist Julius Katchen.

For their first collaboration the NZSO and Royal New Zealand Ballet chose Tchaikovsky's *Swan Lake*, conducted by New Zealander John Matheson. It was significant for being the first full-length version of the ballet performed by The Royal New Zealand Ballet, and one of only a handful of such performances in the country. The success of this four-centre tour ensured successive collaborations later: *Romeo and Juliet* under Ashley Lawrence in 1988, with 76 musicians in the pit, the largest number of players to accompany any New Zealand production; Prokofiev's *Cinderella* in 1991 with Varujan Kojian; Stravinsky's *Petroucka* in 1993, conducted by Brian Law; and *Romeo and Juliet* in 1994 and *Cinderella* in 1995, both conducted by Peter Bandy. In latter performances the cost of touring the NZSO proved prohibitive, and performances have been restricted to the Wellington season only.

The orchestra also accompanied two disappointing performances of a sadly aged Rudolf Nureyev with members of the the Paris Opera Ballet, conducted by Varujan Kojian in the 1988 New Zealand International Festival of the Arts.

Accompanying opera and ballet can add variety to orchestral life but there are perils of playing in the pit, according to three of its longest-serving players, principals John Dodds and Vyvyan Yendoll (second violins and viola respectively) and cellist Christopher Salmon. Christopher recalls the pit in Palmerston North, where he knocked the wooden tip off his expensive Hill cello bow during a performance. Knowing he would need to find the tip to get it repaired, "I put my cello down, got down on my hands and knees and began crawling around the floor. Conductor Georg Tintner was tearing his hair out saying 'What are you doing?!' But I found the tip, about as big as the tip of a needle – and it is in the bow to this day."

In the same pit, conductor James Robertson badly gashed his head on a protruding nail. He suffered another accident in Christchurch, as John Dodds remembers: "He was a great ballerina as a conductor, [but] he stepped too far back on the rostrum and disappeared into the organ pit." A subterranean voice was heard to call out "I'm alright, I'm alright!"

In Vyvyan Yendoll's experience, even sitting in the pit can be dangerous, especially with a spirited sword-fight on the stage above. "During *Romeo and Juliet* in 1994, one of the swords came down over Brian Shillito [sub-principal viola] and it went boinngg! into the floor between us. It was déja vu because something similiar happened during *The Bartered Bride* when the hoops from the fair used to come clattering down on the instruments." During *Peter Grimes*, a barely visible net was strung across the pit,

Perils of the Pit

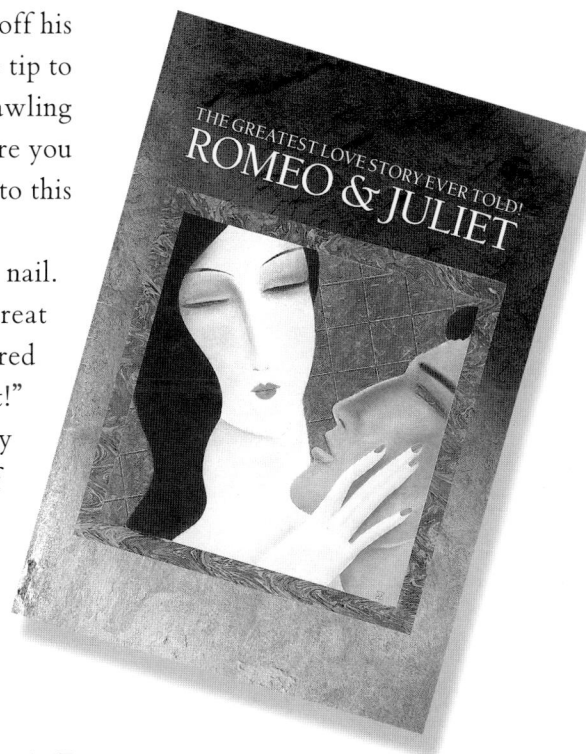

and just as well because this time a dagger came off stage and hung suspended over the violas. Says Vyvyan, it could be time for the viola section to move somewhere else: "They're trying to get us!"

Outdoor Concerts

A series of three 'open-air serenade concerts' to conclude the Carnival for Auckland's 111th Birthday at Epsom Showgrounds in 1951, were the orchestra's first experience of outdoor concerts. Under its second resident conductor Michael Bowles, the orchestra faced the now-familiar problems of music flying away, mosquitoes that were thirsty for musicians' blood and the sound disappearing skywards.

A long gap followed until the late 1970s, when concerts in more exotic locations began to appear on the orchestral schedule: at Turangawaewae Marae in 1979, and there again with the National Maori Choir on a floating pontoon in 1992.

Inspired by the hugely successful 'Kiri's Homecoming' concerts in 1990, with Dame Kiri Te Kanawa and the NZSO under John Hopkins, the idea really took off. A rainy Wellington concert attracted 70,000, while the Auckland Domain broke all existing records for an NZSO concert, with an audience of 140,000.

Since then outdoor concerts have been staged at many venues, including the Mission Estate in Hawkes Bay and at Montana Wines' Brancott Estate, Marlborough, where in 1993, the orchestra was under a large marquee when the heavens opened. They were happy to keep playing – while the audience under large umbrellas was happy to keep listening; both were doomed to be disappointed.

Says David Pawsey: "The design of the marquee proved inadequate. The water was supposed to drain out onto the ground – but we were playing on hardboard so it just drained out and started to flood the stage to a level of an inch or so. With all those electric cables lying around it was potentially too dangerous, and the instruments were getting wet." The concert was abandoned mid-*1812 Overture* before guest artist guitarist Laurind Almaeda even played a note.

Wellington people, who tend to be somewhat self-conscious of their city when it comes to outdoor activities, finally joined the club with Montana's 'Opera in the Basin' in 1994. On a perfect evening, the NZSO conducted by Patrick Flynn with Dame Malvina Major and tenor Anson Austin delighted an appreciative crowd of 13,000 at the Basin Reserve, the city's premier cricket ground. This figure seems rather insignficant when compared with the 250,000 who saw and heard the NZSO play in the Coca-Cola Christmas in the Park concert in Auckland's Domain.

Youth Music

School concerts were there from the beginning, interspersed between symphony concerts in a deliberate move to train the next generation of concert-goers. These were mini-symphony

KIRI'S HOMECOMING

HAGLEY PARK JANUARY 9 1990
AUCKLAND DOMAIN JANUARY 14 1990
TRENTHAM MEMORIAL PARK JANUARY 28 1990

SOUVENIR PROGRAMME

Made possible by Bank of New Zealand   In support of Child Cancer FOUNDATION

The first of the big outdoor performances, featuring Dame Kiri Te Kanawa with the NZSO under John Hopkins, struck a chord with New Zealand audiences in 1990.

TEATRO DE

La Maestranza

26 de junio

NEW ZEALAND SYMPHONY ORCHESTRA

Director
Franz-Paul Decker

Solista
Kiri Te Kanawa, soprano

I

El Amor Brujo
de Manuel de Falla

Aotearoa (Obertura)
de Douglas Lilburn

Exsultate Jubilate
de Wolfgang Amadeus Mozart

II

Obras de Richard Strauss

El Caballero de la Rosa, (Suite)

Cuatro Ultimas Canciones

Programación del Pabellón de Nueva Zelanda

El concierto dará
comienzo a las
21:00 horas

EXPO'92 *Sevilla*

Poster for the NZSO's triumphant concert at Teatro de la Maestranza, 26 June 1992.

(Above) Dame Kiri Te Kanawa and Franz-Paul Decker with the NZSO, Teatro de la Maestranza, Seville. (Right) The orchestra staged a highly popular free concert for the people of Seville in the Plaza de San Francisco.

GRAEME BROWNE

(Above) NZSO musicians relaxing in the colourful heart of Seville, June 1992.

The
New Zealand
Symphony Orchestra
presents

OVERTURES TO Seville

(Right, Lower and Opposite Page) Making music, Michael Fowler Centre, Wellington, 1995.

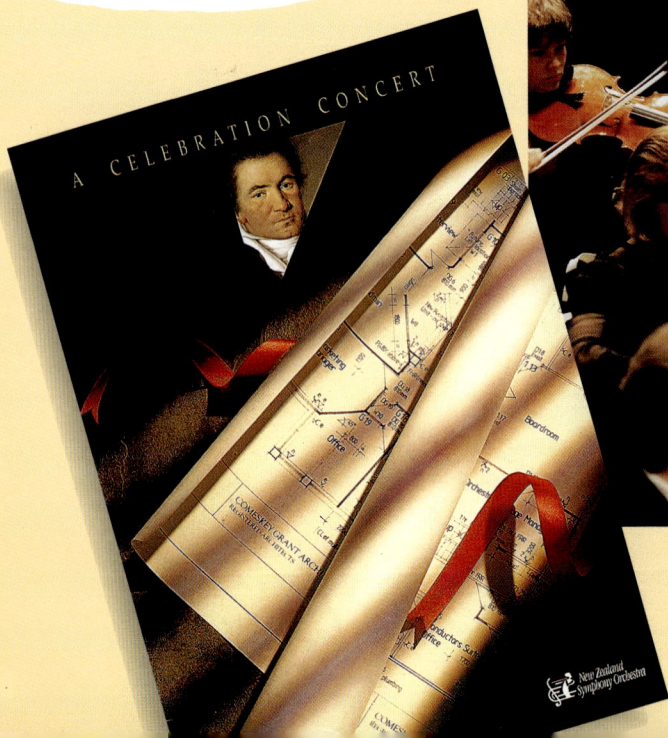

A CELEBRATION CONCERT

New Zealand Symphony Orchestra

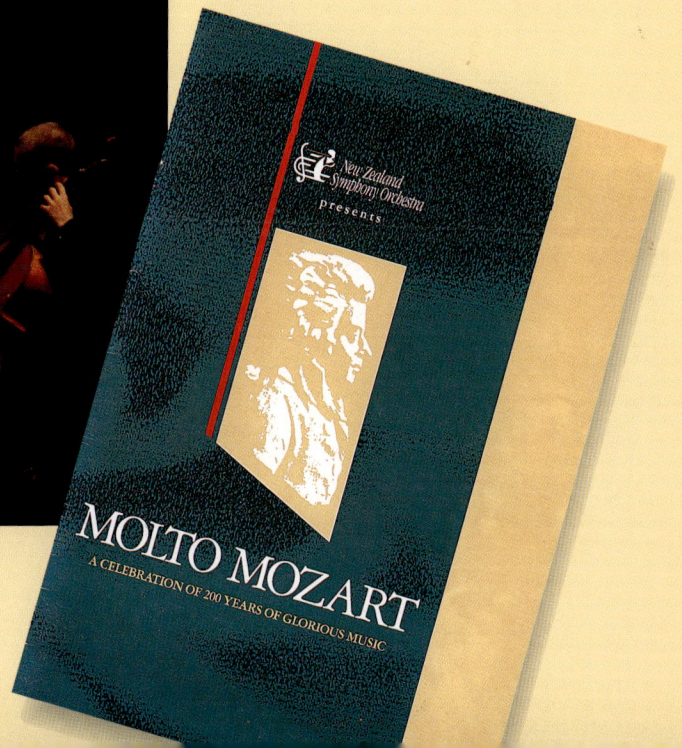

New Zealand
Symphony Orchestra
presents

MOLTO MOZART

A CELEBRATION OF 200 YEARS OF GLORIOUS MUSIC

(Opposite page, from Top Left) Wellington's mayor Fran Wilde (alto) was a guest artist at NZSO Corporate Concert, to launch the NZSO Foundation, Michael Fowler Centre, August 1995; Dame Malvina Major with Prime Minister Jim Bolger, Montana Opera at the Basin, 1994; the New Zealand Trio is Wilma Smith, David Chickering and Vyvyan Yendoll; Bruce McKinnon as 'the typewriter', Corporate Concert, August 1995. (This page, clockwise from Top Left) Last Night of the Proms, Wellington Town Hall, June 1994; Rima Te Wiata was a popular guest artist with the NZSO in BP Summer Pops, 1995; Visiting smaller centres in New Zealand is an important function of the orchestra; Concertmaster Wilma Smith's daughter Jessye started learning about music early in life.

concerts, 'heavy' by today's standards, a collaboration between Broadcasting and the Department of Education. It was many years before there was any noticeable change in format or any question of charging children to attend: serious music was viewed as an integral part of education.

Various formats have been tried in the years since. One of the better ones split the orchestra into smaller groups to perform in individual schools, allowing closer interaction with the pupils.

Programme experiments have ranged from the solid classics of the 40s, to those hosted by various television presenters, and the popular film and TV themes. Canadian Mario Duschene achieved some worthwhile results over a couple of visits, with children receiving recorder pieces to practise for performance with the orchestra. Each section was identifiable by matching coloured sweatshirts, an idea oboist Stephen Popperwell brought back after his exchange with the Sydney Symphony.

In 1985 the funding shortage put schools concerts on hold, until an education policy could be established. This was a disappointment to Kenneth Young who, with Stephen Popperwell, and writer/producer/director John Banas, spent six months developing an alternative children's programme with actor Mark Hadlow. Despite an encouraging reaction from children, only three or four performances were given.

NZSO
NEW ZEALAND SYMPHONY ORCHESTRA

MONTANA
**Opera
at the
Basin**

The first orchestra concert
at
The Basin Reserve

Dame Malvina Major - Soprano
Edmund Barham - Tenor
Patrick Flynn - Conductor

Saturday 3 December 7pm
(Rain Day 4 December)

In support of the International Year of the Family

NEW ZEALAND HERALD

PHOTOGRAPH OPPOSITE: STEPHEN LA PLANT

(Above) Handbill advertising NZSO's first outdoor concert at Wellington's Basin Reserve, 1994. (Left) Greg Hill and Ed Allen perform a duet for horn and garden hose with kitchen funnel, to the delight of children from Waimauku School, Auckland. This was one of several schools visited by groups of NZSO players for the BP Schools Concert Tour in 1992. (Opposite page) The NZSO, Michael Fowler Centre, Wellington, 1995.

Recent questionnaires have shown that despite the somewhat negative images of unimaginative schools concerts, it remains the primary source for children to experience music, and the starting point for many professional musicians.

Family concerts for children and parents are usually held in the early evening, unlike the schools concerts held during the day, and these began in the 1970s with varying degrees of success. Among them have been Brian Priestman's 'Magic and Spells' concerts; Rolf Harris and Coogee Bear; and 'Around the World in 80 Minutes', a programme of popular symphonic excerpts with New Zealand entertainer Jackie Clarke, conducted by Kenneth Young.

Orchestra Trainees/
Schola Musica 1961-1989

Music-making in the NZSO owes a debt to the unique orchestral training scheme set up by John Hopkins to train young musicians for a career as orchestral players. As the first national scheme of its kind, it addressed the lack of a New Zealand conservatorium and provided a pool of potential players for the orchestra. A variety of instruments was accepted initially, even percussion and brass, before becoming restricted to strings.

Trainees were treated as bursars, received an annual retainer, free individual tuition from principal players and occasional master classes from visiting conductors. Housed in the orchestral buildings from 1964, they experienced a professional musical environment first-

Schola Musica, 1988 (from left, standing): Catherine Hambly, Slava Fainitski, Michael Vinten (musical director), Craig Utting, Thorsten Engel, Sam Konise; (seated) Peter Black, Elspeth Gray.

NIGEL MORRIS

hand, performing in the NZSO as part of their training and also as casual players when required. From its initial aim as a training orchestra, it developed into a performing ensemble in its own right, known as the Schola Musica from the 1970s. Public and schools concerts were performed in Wellington and on tour out of town, it made regular radio broadcasts and commercially recorded a considerable volume of New Zealand music. The Schola performed overseas twice: in 1974 in Perth, Western Australia, and in 1975, on the National Youth Orchestra World Tour, as members of that orchestra, and also as a separate entity.

Ashley Heenan, its musical director, retired in 1984 after 23 years. Michael Vinten, who took over the formidable task, says: "By that stage the standard of the NZSO had risen and it had become less likely that trainees could go straight into the orchestra, although some did. Others who went overseas to further their studies came back and took up jobs with the NZSO or other New Zealand orchestras."

By this time many alternative tertiary music opportunities had been established and Michael consciously tried to broaden the Schola's scope of activities by performing with both Victoria University and Wellington Polytechnic. Engagements outside of Wellington were fewer but demands from the NZSO for more casual players increased. Three trainees from that time became NZSO violinists: Sharon (Tongs) Callaghan in 1987, Lisa Egen and Elspeth Gray 1988; another, Sam Konise of the Turnovsky Trio, is on contract.

"It was important for the Schola to find its own niche, but we were not given time to fully settle on a 'new look' before the Board abandoned the scheme at the end of 1989," says Michael Vinten. He and Flora Edwards, head of Wellington Polytechnic's Conservatorium of Music, had been working on a compromise scheme and "trying to get sponsorship to keep Schola alive, but time ran out and the project died before I could put my mark on the scheme and get it moving in a direction relevant for the time we were in".

New Zealand Post National Youth Orchestra 1959-

The National Youth Orchestra, preceding the training scheme by two years, serves a similar purpose: providing access and insight into the world of professional music. It has endured, though at times shakily, for almost 40 years.

John Hopkins set it up as a professionally-run orchestra and it has always been treated as such. He conducted it himself for its first few years. Ashley Heenan followed, and since 1977 guest conductors have been engaged, often in conjunction with NZSO engagements: a who's who of conductors includes Uri Segal, Thomas Sanderling, Doron Salomon and Franz-Paul Decker. Some have been more successful than others and more recent conductors have been chosen for their experience in working with young people: Michael Vinten in 1988, and former NZSO timpanist, now Paris-based international conductor Gary Brain, in 1992.

In 1995 Isaiah Jackson, a protégé of both Leopold Stokowski and Leonard Bernstein, and founding conductor of the Asian Youth Orchestra, conducted a NZPYO working together

PHOTOGRAPH: GRAEME BROWNE

with the country's finest young singers and musicians, the National Youth Choir and Combined Regional Youth Choirs. "This was in keeping with a review of the long-running scheme under its sponsor New Zealand Post, says its Manager Allan Badley, "in order to find ways and means of increasing the value of the experience to young musicans."[81]

The Youth Orchestra's first international experience was its World Tour in 1975 to Britain, Japan, Hong Kong and the People's Republic of China, the first Western orchestra to perform there since the Cultural Revolution. Its second tour, to Expo 88 in Brisbane, performing with the International Festival of Youth Orchestras, and with other performances in Australia, was conducted by Michael Vinten, led by NZSO violinist Lisa Egen, with soloist Michael Houstoun who himself conducted the orchestra in 1991.

For several current NZSO musicians the Youth Orchestra was their first experience of orchestral playing, and former leaders include Robin Perks, Simon Miller, Lisa Egen, Mathew Ross, and the late John Chisholm whose name is commemorated in the award for Leader. Lifetime friendships have been forged by young people working together over several years, and it has been the incentive for the start of many professional musical careers.

(Below) The New Zealand Youth Orchestra, 1988: conductor Michael Vinten (absent); leader Lisa Egen. Shown rehearsing for their tour to Brisbane's Expo '88 to perform at the International Festival of Youth Orchestras.

Music Policy   Subscription concerts, the Proms (later Summer Pops) schools, other concerts and touring are part of an on-going music policy that has evolved from the 1950s. Ashley Heenan, who

NIGEL MORRIS

was assistant to both James Robertson and John Hopkins, credits the former with devising a five-year major touring plan for main centre concerts for each year and provincial centres to be visited on the basis of every one to five years. "A basic pattern of repertoire for a city such as Wellington over two years would hear the complete Beethoven, Brahms and three Schubert symphonies etcetera: so that three generations of people would hear the complete basic repertoire without being aware of it."

The number of overseas artists increased during John Hopkins' time and were slotted in, together with local artists, with 12-14 concertos a year, and contemporary and New Zealand music introduced.

The early conductors like Andersen Tyrer and Michael Bowles were contracted as 'musical directors', expected to plan repertoire and artists but the name changed to 'conductor' after internal disagreements and public complaints about Warwick Braithwaite's programmes. Juan Matteucci was supported by a Music Committee and a Concert Committee, and John Gray was on both of them. When Peter Nisbet became head of music, John became his artists and repertoire assistant and both committees were soon scrapped.

"We inherited an artistic policy that was an unwritten thing, that no standard work would be given more than once in three years in any one place," John says. It was followed "slavishly" and he remembers an argument when Andre Kostelanetz and Leonard Pennario wanted to play the Grieg piano concerto in a centre in which it had been played recently. The policy changed in the 1970s when the Sinfonia of Auckland and the Christchurch orchestras entered the market.

When Roger Lloyd became artistic manager he thought the NZSO's repertoire "quite heavily Germanic [with an] earnestness about it", and needed some "fun, excitement and glitter". His artistic policy was to try and widen the perspective with a more even spread of repertoire to "give people things they've never heard before, [because with] concert-going, people should have a sense of discovery".

A plan for the NZSO to diversify as a 'musical resource' was developed for consideration during 1995 and provided for smaller chamber ensembles and split orchestras working within the framework of the NZSO. In early 1996 this was on hold, pending funding decisions.

Contemporary Music

Some of the sense of discovery for concert-goers should come from contemporary repertoire. The New Zealand view on that seems to be that the orchestra plays too much – or not enough – contemporary music; there is rarely a middle ground.

Gone are the days, hopefully, when subscribers leave the hall at interval if the last item is a 20th century work. After several such exoduses the strategy was to conceal the new work in the middle of the concert.

John Hopkins' 'Music of Our Time' concerts created an audience for new music, with an

(Below) Lilith, the night demon of Hebrew mythology, was a nocturnal creature of exquisite beauty. This work by Gareth Farr was commissioned by the New Zealand International Festival of the Arts for the NZSO, and had its sensational world premiere at the Festival in Wellington, 13 March 1996.

annual series 1962-65. Small audiences were expected, so a small hall was used, at Wellington Technical College. The audience no longer seemed small and a more intimate atmosphere was achieved.

The three nights averaged audiences of 600 each, which John considered a very good result. They ceased when he left New Zealand and it took 30 years for a similiar series to return, as it did in the Town Hall Series in 1994. Reviewers were appreciative but the general public stayed away and the series could not be sustained for a second year.

New Zealand Music

Roger Lloyd says that when he arrived in New Zealand "it seemed every other person I met was a New Zealand composer. They all wanted to know what I was going to do as soon as I stepped off the plane."

New Zealand music had been played by the National Orchestra from its first season, with works by Douglas Lilburn and Harry Luscombe but again it was John Hopkins who proved the biggest supporter of New Zealand artists, including its composers.

Under Peter Nisbet's policy New Zealand composers were commissioned to write works for the orchestra, either for studio broadcast or concert performance. After the break-up of Broadcasting, the links with international broadcasting organisations were lost and the funding of commissions became more difficult. The NZSO does not receive assistance from Creative New Zealand as the Regional Orchestras do.

A new policy was needed to provide for the new situation and to ensure the best use was made of NZSO commissions, while continuing to encourage local musicians.

To this end, the New Zealand Music Panel was set up in July 1995.[82] This consisted of the NZSO's artistic manager Roger Lloyd and concertmaster Wilma Smith, with conductor Sir William Southgate, pianist Michael Houstoun and Ken Young, conductor-in-residence. Their first meeting in October 1995 produced a good response of scores to be considered for performance by the NZSO.

New Zealand music produced by the NZSO the same year has included the important concert for Douglas Lilburn's 80th birthday, and recordings which include works by Edwin Carr. In the anniversary year the NZSO will premiere Christopher Blake's eagerly awaited first symphony *The Islands*; *A Pacific Piece* by Gareth Farr (part one in October 1996, part two in March 1997) for the orchestra's first rehearsal and first concert anniversaries, and Farr's *Lilith's Dream of Ecstacy* in the International Festival in March 1996.

Other works commissioned by the NZSO include Anthony Ritchie's overture on the life of Charles Upham VC; Sir William Southgate's work for the black boat and America's Cup; and John Charles whose birthday offering *Ground Rules* for Douglas Lilburn, was performed in October 1995.[83]

The orchestra's first recording *Festive Overtures* was conducted by John Hopkins in 1959 and featured Douglas Lilburn's *Festival Overture* and five other overtures by Dvořák, Berlioz, Glinka, Nicolai and Brahms.

This remained the only recording until the mid-70s and the release of *Donald McIntyre Sings Wagner,* conducted by John Matheson on Kiwi Pacific; Ron Goodwin's *Going Places* which was awarded a platinum disc, and the Mahler *Symphony No. 4* recording with Yuri Segal and Malvina Major.

The most successful of these early recordings was *The Great Classics* conducted by John Hopkins, released by Deutsche Grammophon in 1976, which stunned everyone by becoming the first classical music album ever to top the New Zealand charts – in doing so, replacing pop group Abba from the top slot. New Zealand sales were the equivalent of 10 gold discs.

Seventeen recordings were made in the NZSO's first 40 years, the majority of which were of lighter music. This has not been so in the last decade in which increased commercial recordings of serious repertoire have played an important role in the orchestra's self-generated income, as a result of a more vigorous recording policy.

The orchestra's first digital recording was *Birth of a Nation,* the soundtrack to the D.W. Griffiths silent film, and its first CD was its recording of the music of Samuel Barber, conducted by Andrew Schenck. International acclaim followed when almost immediately this reached the top of the American charts, launching the NZSO into a flourishing recording career which has brought valuable reviews in respected publications; the *1994 Penguin Guide to Compact Discs, Gramophone* (including Critic's Choice 1994) – and the *1995 Gramophone Good CD Guide,* in which Andrew Achenbach states: "My discovery of the year has to be the triptych of symphonies by Douglas Lilburn... the admirable NZSO prove superbly committed advocates."

The NZSO's relationship with budget label Naxos, which pays no royalties, underwent scrutiny over the cancelled Hong Kong tour and has ceased on mutual agreement. "One of those marriages that didn't work out," says Mark Keyworth.

The much more important relationship with Koch International, through its respected vice-president and record producer Michael Fine, continues to flourish, with the NZSO receiving kudos for its recordings of the music of lesser known composers.

New Zealand music was given a boost with the recordings in 1995 of Edwin Carr on Corellia, Lilburn's *Three Symphonies* on Continuum and a two-CD set of nine shorter works by nine New Zealand composers on Continuum.

Recordings

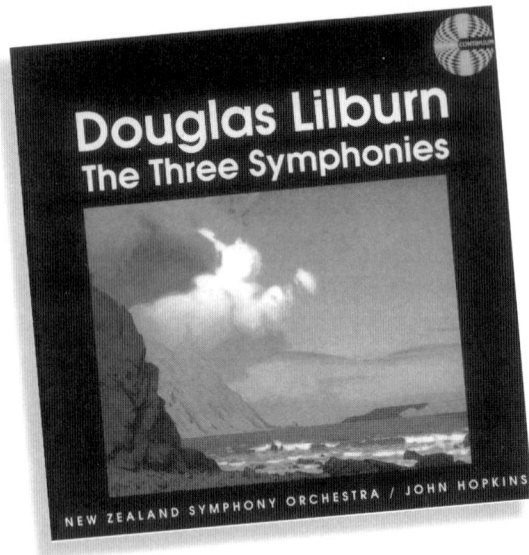

Douglas Lilburn's association with the National Orchestra began in 1947 when the orchestra performed A Song of the Antipodes, *its first work by a New Zealand composer. In October 1985 the NZSO performed the same work, since re-named* A Song of Islands, *in a special concert conducted by Sir William Southgate, to celebrate Douglas Lilburn's 80th birthday.*

JANE USSHER

The old Broadcasting ethos to 'Inform, to educate and to entertain' led to adventurous things and amazingly innovative concerts, says Murray Alford, most of which were the result of Peter Nisbet's "own personal flashes of insights. I got quite used to starting work in the morning and he would come in and say 'Stop what you're doing – I've had an idea in the shower!' I used to groan but nine out of ten times these ideas were really good and gave rise to something interesting".

The innovations had started in the early 1970s with Peter Nisbet's appointment as head of music. In 1973 a 'Musical Marathon' provided a non-stop entertainment as part of a Wellington Festival: beginning with a recital by pianist Andre Tchaikovsky, it led to the NZBCS orchestra and the Orpheus Choir performing Carl Orff's *Carmina Burana*, then to a programme of electronic music, and finally a 'big band', almost half of who were members of the orchestra.

Sonic Circuses began in 1974, a celebration of New Zealand music and musicians that began at Victoria University. Although not an NZSO initiative, by 1975 the NZSO was an enthusiastic participant and in 1978, Sonic Circus 5 was held in the newly-opened Symphony House in Willis Street. Musical activities filled every room on three floors, including both the NZSO and Schola Musica studios, with a continuous programme of performances by the NZSO, Schola Musica, Wellington Youth Orchestra and Junior Choir, various chamber ensembles, dance, electronic and experimental music, over a period of 12 hours. A festive atmosphere prevailed and served to introduce the public to the new building. Subsequent Circuses included one in 1981 in conjunction with New Zealand Composers Foundation and Radio New Zealand.

Cushion concerts were a natural extension to the Marathon Concert, with a series of three concerts in 1974. They broke down perceived musical barriers with unlikely combinations of symphony, avant-garde chamber music, electronic or big-band jazz music. Each concert contained a Beethoven symphony, a contemporary work, such as Messiaen's *Quartet for the End of Time* with Music Players 70, with then NZSO timpanist and percussionist Gary Brain and Trevor Dean, and pianist Barry Margan – with the final item provided by the New Zealand Jazz Orchestra conducted by NZSO percussionist Bud Jones. Cushion concerts were popular for several years until a series in the 1980s indicated the novelty had worn off.

By that time some audiences were becoming reluctant to go out at night and early evening concerts were a solution, with the successful 645 series launched in Auckland. Wellington requests for more Sunday matinées were answered with a 230 Sunday series but were not continued after a disappointing response – unlike Telecom's 'Tea and Symphony' concerts, a winner from the start; short weekday concerts conducted by Kenneth Young which start at 11:00am, and serve free morning tea.

Murray Alford: "Nowadays it is more difficult to do adventurous things because the

.... BUT CAN THEY SING??

This 1976 cartoon comments on the NZSO's album replacing top-selling group Abba at the top of the charts. The Great Classics sold the equivalent of 10 Gold Discs.

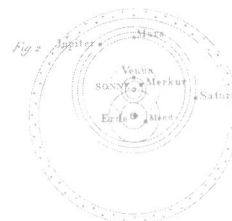

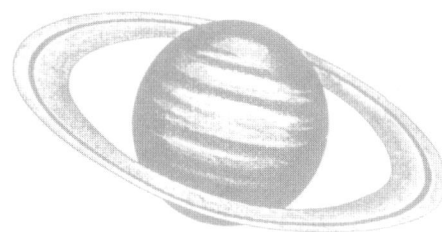

pressure is on the bottom line. The Sonic Circus concept was magnificent. The first were probably more successful, a wild and wonderful wacky situation whereas the later ones were more of a showcase for the established avant-garde."

A more recent innovation was the seven-concert 'The Planets' tour, sponsored by law firm Buddle Findlay, which brought a visual element to Holst's music conducted by James Loughran, with colour space images projected onto large screens behind the orchestra.

Single-composer theme concerts have been very successful. The most adventurous of these was probably 'Molto Mozart' in 1991, which in one weekend celebrated two centuries since the great composer's death with 10 separate concerts given by six orchestras, including the NZSO under Stephen Bishop-Kovacevich. Almost all 41 symphonies were performed in five Wellington venues. The Great Bach Day was a one-day three-venue occasion, while the Tower Beethoven Festival in November 1995 performed all nine symphonies and the *Emperor Concerto* with Michael Houstoun under Janos Fürst in five performances each in Wellington and Christchurch. The finale, Beethoven's first and last symphonies, was relayed by a huge outdoor screen to free cushion concerts in the Civic Square and Victoria Square.

Proms

The introduction of Prom concerts by second resident conductor Michael Bowles was an immediate success in 1952. Based on the Henry Wood/BBC model, New Zealand Proms had their own style, with all seating removed except for in the gallery and around the perimeters of the hall.

Last night of the Proms.
An evening to bring out the British in you.

The music was substantial but lighter than that in Subscription concerts, and to add to the festive look of the concerts, the women left their black dresses at home and appeared in coloured tulle 'frocks'. "We must have looked like lampshades," one foundation player commented. The audience were not so much promenaders, as sitters and loungers on a variety of rugs and camping equipment. These concerts represented a significant breakthrough in changing attitudes and preconceptions about classical music.

Prom areas eventually disappeared. The public still enjoyed sitting on the floor but halls could never be full, and fire and safety regulations restricted the numbers which could be accommodated. When the chairs came back, something was lost. At their peak, there were four or five concerts each season in main centres but eventually trends changed and they evolved into the Summer Pops series.

The name resurfaced as an annual series of Spring Proms held in November 1987 which featured five concerts conducted by Franz-Paul Decker, and continued sponsored by BP in 1990-91.

In 1994-95 the Proms made a comeback with two highly successful 'Last Night of the Proms' charity concerts organised by Rotary for Wellington hospices. A traditional BBC Prom programme was enhanced by the inclusion in 1995 of highlights from Gilbert and Sullivan operettas, topically updated. The madness was contagious, with audiences entering enthusiastically into the spirit of the occasion, with painted faces, Union Jacks, and all the whistles, hooters and balloons of the genuine article.

The inaugural New Zealand Chamber Orchestra, 1987. Back row: Dean Major, Stephen Managh (founding chairman), Simon Miller, Jennie Goldstein, Vyvyan Yendoll, Brian Shillito, Allan Chisholm. Front row: Richard Panting, Vicki Jones, Yury Gezentsvey, Donald Armstrong (leader and musical director), Vivien Chisholm.

TOM SHANAHAN

The New Zealand Chamber Orchestra was founded in 1987 by NZSO violinist Stephen Managh and quickly established itself as an ensemble of the highest quality. Made up of 16 strings with oboes and horns all from the NZSO, the orchestra performs without a conductor, under Donald Armstrong, NZSO associate concertmaster, its founding leader and musical director. It now has its own Subscription series and has notched up major performances at the New Zealand International Festivals and overseas at the Mittagong Easter Festival for Musica Viva in Australia and at Expo 92 in Seville. Seven CDs have been recorded. The orchestra is becoming known for its recordings of rare repertoire of the mid-late 18th century.

Since 1994 the New Zealand Chamber Orchestra has been based at Symphony House and its scheduling more closely co-ordinated with that of the NZSO. Its general manager, music-ologist Dr Alan Badley, the NZSO's artistic development manager, says that disciplined chamber playing has had a stimulating effect on NZCO players, to the benefit of their playing in the NZSO, most noticeably in Mozart.

There have always been chamber music groups, the music of friends, within the orchestra, ranging from the New Zealand Brass Quintet to duos, trios, quartets and other combinations. Following the tradition of John and Allan Chisholm's Gagliano Trio tour to China in 1983, the NZSO Trio, Wilma Smith, Vyvyan Yendoll and David Chickering, performed in Tokyo and Osaka in 1994. On a second tour to Japan in 1995, they performed in Kobe, scene of the devastating earthquake in January of that year, taking a personal message to the city from the Prime Minister Mr Bolger.

The days of regular television productions with the NZSO ceased with the dismantling of Broadcasting. In earlier days television featured the orchestra in live concerts televised for later transmission, in studio productions including opera and light music such as the popular 'Make Mine Music' series with Michael Moores in the 1970s. A series with Franz-Paul Decker conducting the NZSO and pianist Michael Houstoun in the studio was screened in the 1980s.

Working with television was a mixed blessing in those days, says Ed Allen, principal horn: "We used to get so frustrated because we would go over and over until you got it wrong – and the cameras would have it right – and you'd get it broadcast."

A return to a more enlightened policy on televising the arts, such as the orchestra, would provide access for audiences across the country to see and hear the orchestra at a time when its resources preclude the sort of touring it was set up to provide.

The NZSO has frequently accompanied scores for New Zealand films, including *Utu*, *Heart of the Stag* and *The Quiet Earth*, but in 1994 at the International Festival it played film music to a live audience. In a return to its historical roots the NZSO accompanied the D.W. Griffiths silent film *Intolerance*, with score by Carl Davis conducted by Sir William Southgate. This was an amazing performance which had the audience riveted and led in 1995 to a similar

Chamber Music

CHAMBER MUSIC NEW ZEALAND

The New Zealand String Quartet, 1987: Gillian Ansell, Sandro Costantino, Wilma Smith and Josephine Young.

Film and Television

success with the Charlie Chaplin classic film *The Gold Rush*, with the Chaplin score adapted by Carl Davis and conducted by Sir William Southgate.

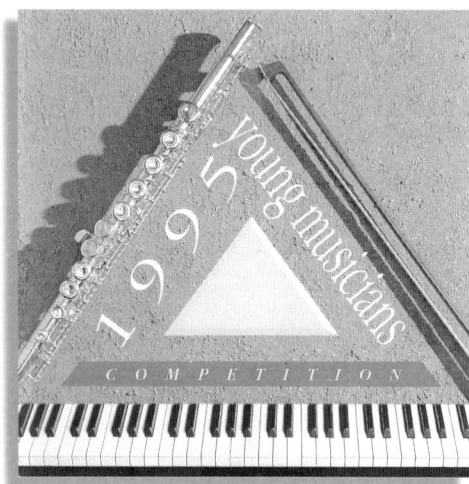

Competitions and Awards

Mobil Song Quest

New Zealand's best-known and longest-running musical competition dates from 1956. The NZSO has been involved only since 1974, accompanying the finals in concert. The opportunity to study and perform overseas provided the first step in international careers for former winners including Dame Kiri Te Kanawa, Dame Malvina Major and Christopher Doig.

Young Musicians Competition

In 1982, the biennial competition began as a collaboration between television and the orchestra, then still stablemates under Broadcasting. It continues now under the auspices of the NZSO with various sponsors.

In that time, some of this country's finest young instrumentalists have competed, under independent judges with the final performance by four semi-finalists in concert with the NZSO televised to reach a nationwide audience.

NZSO players have been well-represented in the contest, either as current players or those who have subsequently joined the orchestra. In the first competition in 1982, NZSO violist Belinda Prentice, a former trainee, was a finalist. Cellist Christopher Kane, a semi-finalist in 1982, was third-equal in 1984. Former trainee and NZSO contract violinist Sam Konise from Samoa, a finalist in 1988, was the winner in 1990, with NZSO violinist Justine Cormack runner-up, Elspeth Gray and Mathew Ross, semi-finalists. Peter Sharman and Dianne Cochrane were semi-finalists in 1987 and 1990 respectively.

Alexa Still, principal flute, on tour with flute and motorcycle outside Christ Church Cathedral, Nelson.

Alex Lindsay Awards

Celebrating its 21st birthday in 1995, the Awards were set up to commemorate a beloved concertmaster with a fund set up at his Memorial Concert in 1975, and are still administered by a Trust Board of elected members of the NZSO.

Envisaged as an "investment in the future of orchestral playing in New Zealand",[84] it was hoped that recipients would consider this country as their "musical homeland" and ultimately return. Since then almost all of the past winners have become professional musicians, and of these 26 percent have returned to play as members of the NZSO. In early 1996 these were: Wilma Smith (concertmaster), Donald Armstrong (associate concertmaster), Alexa Still, (principal flute), Robert Orr (prinicpal cor anglais), Rachel Vernon (principal bass clarinet), Peter Sharman (sub-principal horn), Justine Cormack (1st violins) and Robert Ibell (cello). Brian Shillito: "There can have been no better way to remember Alex Lindsay than to invest in the young players who are the orchestra's future."

It is a decade since the International Festival started in Wellington in 1986, and it has made a huge contribution to the arts and to artistic standards in that time.

Since the beginning, the NZSO has been a mainstay of the music programme and there has been a succession of major performing artists since then. In 1986 the stars were Dame Joan Sutherland and her husband, conductor Richard Bonynge, who performed in concert with the NZSO; 1988 brought conductor Maxim Shostakovich, son of the great Russian composer and his countryman, Mstislav Rostropovich, generally regarded as the world's greatest cellist, who performed two cello concerti and a solo recital. The orchestra also accompanied Nureyev, once the world's greatest male dancer.

Subsequent years have brought conductors Sir Neville Marriner and Alexander Lazarev, and four operas: *Die Meistersinger* with New Zealander Donald McIntyre, *Salome*, *Madame Butterfly* and *Katya Kabanová* in 1996. This feast of music is appreciated by members of the NZSO, says cellist Vivien Chisholm. "Every Festival has brought us something very good or memorable. Just to know that every two years we will have the chance to perform a significant opera is a thrill and it's refreshing to be part of it."

The Summer Tours which took over from the Proms has been a unique institution in New Zealand's summer entertainment for over 20 years. Very few shows tour during the summer months, with even fewer visiting provincial centres. The NZSO Pops begin at the end of January usually, with a series of several concerts, broken into groups of four or five with time off in between. Once there were up to 22 concerts in a five week period, encompassing large halls in main centres to sports stadiums in smaller ones, and more frequently now, outdoor venues where families can watch the action under the stars. Many NZSO players like to take their own families with them for part of the tour, taking advantage of school holidays and good weather.

These tend to be more relaxed concerts, not because the music is taken any less seriously in the matter of standards, but with several concerts and only two different programmes, the pressure is greatly reduced. It is summer, everyone can enjoy themselves, playing to new audiences, with the chance for a game of golf or a trip to the beach during the day.

"The Pops tours give me lots to do and I can rave around on the drums and have a good time. We always have fun," says percussionist Bud Jones, who is usually located centre stage in the rhythm group, the 'heartbeat of the orchestra'. "Pops conductors Ron Goodwin and John Dankworth may not be the world's best conductors, but they love doing it and they just let the orchestra play. I always enjoy Ron Goodwin concerts because you can tell by the crowd when they are on their feet singing *The White Cliffs of Dover* at the end of the concert that they have enjoyed themselves. That's what it's all about. We are here to entertain people and if they walk out whistling and singing to themselves, we've done the job."

New Zealand International Festival of the Arts

Summer Pops

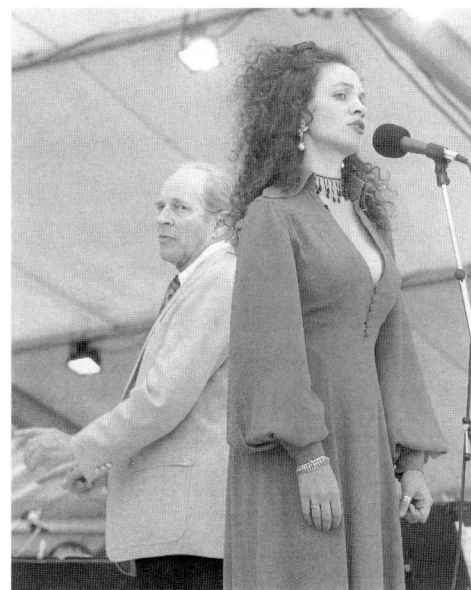

John and Jacqueline Dankworth performing at 1994 BP Summer Pops, Brancott Estate, Marlborough.

MARLBOROUGH EXPRESS

appassionato

Michael Houston

d *The Protecting Veil* (c
cent of Byzantine churches,

The Guest Artists

"One of the most significant developments in the last quarter-century is that soloists of the international calibre and reputation of Michael Houstoun and Dame Malvina Major have chosen to live and work in New Zealand."

— Peter Nisbet, former general manager, 1992.

NEW Zealand has always been fortunate with its solo artists. The NZSO has built on a tradition that goes back to colonial days when a succession of travelling artists made their way here, apparently undeterred by often arduous travel conditions. There were opera companies, chamber groups, instrumentalists, singers and pianists who brought their own pianos. Some of the biggest names of the times performed here in the early part of the century: singers Dame Nellie Melba in 1903; Amelita Galli-Curci in 1925 and 1932; ballerina Anna Pavlova and Russian bass Chaliapin, both in 1926; pianists Ignace Paderewski, before and after being premier of Poland, 1904 and 1927, Percy Grainger, 1903 and Boris Moiseiwitsch, 1923; violinists Jascha Heifetz 1921; Fritz Kreisler 1925 and Yehudi Menuhin 1935 (returning 1951 and 1962).

With the establishment of radio broadcasting another medium for artists became available and it was not long before a special Concert Section was set up to play a more active role in arranging concerts in addition to radio recitals. The arrival of the National Orchestra on the scene in 1947 became a catalyst, attracting more artists to perform in concert, recital and radio broadcasts.

From a few solo artists in those early years the orchestra's list grew steadily as standards improved, and Broadcasting itself became more entrepreneurial. By the 1960s it was touring the country with a variety of light entertainers as well as classical artists, many of who were major international performers.

Those heady days could not last once television arrived, and shrinking audiences sounded the dead knell for recitals from all but the best-known artists. The days when performers

THE GUEST ARTISTS *191*

like British pianist Solomon, first here in 1947, attracted overnight queues for tickets and full houses, are now long gone. Most superstars today demand fees that are beyond what is possible in New Zealand's small population-base, and even for those on the next rung down promoters will need convincing before taking the risk. This may change, given the phenomenal revival of interest in opera and classical music, especially when performed outdoors.

The orchestra benefited enormously from its exposure to so many high calibre artists. Space precludes an in-depth review of them all, although they are listed in Appendix C. This chapter concentrates on those who have been the special friends, as well as the superstars of the last decade.

A very special performer: pianist Lili Kraus, the first to appear in a celebrity orchestral concert with the National Orchestra, later became a New Zealand citizen.

Pianists   Lili Kraus in 1947 and New Zealander Richard Farrell in 1948 were two soloists who appeared with the National Orchestra in its first two seasons, in a decade that included first visits from Louis Kentner in 1953, Julius Katchen in 1955, Solomon and Bela Siki in 1954, Paul Badura-Skoda in 1956 and Eileen Joyce in 1958.

Lili Kraus

A very special link existed between the orchestra and Lili Kraus who was the first international artist to perform in New Zealand after the war. She was also the first to appear in a celebrity orchestral concert with the new National Orchestra of New Zealand, on 29 March 1947, three weeks after its inaugural concert.

Born in Budapest where she made her debut, Lili Kraus studied under Kodaly and Bartók, and at 20, was a professor at the Vienna Conservatory. She had just begun another overseas tour in 1942, when she was captured by the Japanese in Java and interned there, together with her husband and two children for three years, until the end of the war.

New Zealand granted her citizenship afterwards and for this she was always grateful. She never forgot that this country had given her a home. In a touring career that spanned almost 50 years, Lili Kraus continued to perform here regularly over the next 33 years until 1979. She died in 1986 aged 81, three months after the NZSO received her last letter:[85]

There is no circle of people, consisting of professional and human friends, who are nearer my heart, whom I cherish and appreciate more, than you New Zealanders. You are loyal, concerned and loving towards me since the first minute of our acquaintanceship to this day, when the physical discrepancy between my will and desires grew so big that it is not possible for me to come and visit you. However, my heart never left. You are in my thoughts and prayers as my next of kin. I wish you all the richest blessings of the Lord, accompanied by my timeless love.

The trickle of piano soloists that had started in the 1950s, increased to a flood during the

1960s. A succession of outstanding artists visited for the first time and many returned several times in coming years, including Shura Cherkassky who made his first visit in 1961, his last visit in 1992 and died in 1995. Claudio Arrau in 1962 (and again in 1968 and 1974) was followed by Alfred Brendel in 1963 and Jorge Bolet in 1964, who returned almost 30 years later. In 1965 Russian Paul Serebriakov toured as did American pianist Rudolf Serkin, and Chinese pianist Fou T'Song, who was a frequent visitor for several years.

Moura Lympany and John Ogdon each toured first in 1966, and made a subsequent tour some years later; Andre Tchaikovsky was here in 1967 and made four further tours; with Vladimir Ashkenazy and Stephen Bishop-Kovacevich both making their first of several visits in 1969.

From the 1970s onwards there were fewer new major artists appearing: Anthony di Bonaventura in 1970; Spanish pianist Alicia de Larrocha came here in 1973, 1977 and made a welcome return with Dr Franz-Paul Decker in 1995; Radu Lupu and duo artists Alfons and Aloys Kontarsky in 1974; Pascal Roge and Peter Frankl began their long-term relationships with the NZSO in 1975; Hans Richter-Haaser toured once in 1976, the same year as Christina Ortiz who has made several return visits, most recently in 1995; Andras Schiff 1983; French pianist Cecile Ousset toured in 1986; the controversial Ivo Pogorelich in 1984; Imogen Cooper, 1987; Dmitri Alexeev in 1988, and Louis Lortie, 1994. Barry Douglas (1988) and Peter Donohoe (1989) are outstanding artists with whom the orchestra has worked most frequently in recent years.

(Above) Vladimir Ashkenazy at the keyboard, 1982. (Left) A welcome return visit in 1995 from Spanish pianist Alicia de Larrocha, here in rehearsal with Dr Franz-Paul Decker and Donald Armstrong, associate concertmaster.

Richard Farrell

The young New Zealand pianist was already acknowledged as a virtuoso performer who seemed assured of reaching the ultimate heights of his profession, when he was killed in a car accident near London aged 31. As a child prodigy he performed in New Zealand and Australia before commencing studies with Madame Olga Samaroff-Stokowski at the prestigious Juilliard School of Music in New York. Richard Farrell made his debut at Carnegie Hall in 1948, and toured extensively in the United States and Britain.

He performed the Lizst *Piano Concerto No. 1* as soloist in the first Royal Concert in 1954, but a later concerto and recital tour in New Zealand in 1956 was not as successful as earlier ones, and NZBS decided to defer a return visit. Only two years later he was dead, a tragic loss on the brink of the international recognition he was confidently expected to achieve.

The contribution made by New Zealand pianists working with the orchestra cannot be overlooked. Relationships that began in the early days in some cases continued for decades afterwards and include the following artists, and the date they first performed with the NZSO:

Oswald Cheesman and Colin Horsley, 1947; Peter Cooper and Shirley Carter, 1948; Maurice Till, 1951; Jocelyn Walker, 1952; Frederick Page and Janetta McStay, 1954; David Galbraith, 1955; Lola Johnston and Colleen Rae-Gerrard, 1961; Tessa Birnie, 1963; David James and Rae de Lisle, 1969; Richard Beauchamp, 1970; Georgina Zellan-Smith and Richard Mapp, 1972; David Guerin and Deidre Irons, 1978; Sharon-Joy Vogan, 1982; Tamas Vesmas, 1983; Patrick O'Byrne, 1987; Eugene Albulescu, 1987; and Jeffrey Grice, 1988.

Michael Houstoun

(Opposite) The moment captured: Eduardo Mata conducting Michael Houstoun in Beethoven's Piano Concerto No. 4, *in 1993. For Michael Houstoun this was the most memorable of all his performances with the NZSO.*

Best known of pianists now working with the NZSO is Timaru's Michael Houstoun, who in 1971 at the age of 20 made his debut with the orchestra. Since then he has played with them almost every year, returning to do so even when living overseas.

"I think this is a unique relationship involving soloist and orchestra and it has been of inestimable value for me," he says. "It has enabled me to build a large concerto repertoire and helped develop a strong audience base. I have also monitored my development as an artist through the reactions of the orchestral players and visiting conductors to my performances. Many have remarked how 'easy' it is to conduct them and I see this as a direct result of the long association between myself and the players. We play together and are involved in true concerted music-making."

Michael has no hesitation in choosing the most memorable of his many performances with the orchestra: "Without doubt this was with Eduardo Mata in Wellington, Beethoven *Concerto No. 4*, in 1993. His commitment to every note of the score was inspiring and we enjoyed a matched vision of the work. Many conductors are rather dismissive of the concerto repertoire and it is always a joy, and a boon, to find one who loves it."

GRAEME BROWNE

On several occasions over the years Michael Houstoun has stepped in to save the day for the NZSO when scheduled soloists have cancelled. He is always happy to do this, he says, "if it is a concerto I know well and the orchestra is also familiar with it. Although it is not an ideal situation, such a happening produces its own certain 'electricity'. The standard repertoire can usually be handled, without peril to quality, on one rehearsal."

In 1995 Michael Houstoun conducted the NZSO in concerts in Auckland and Hamilton, having previously conducted the New Zealand Chamber Orchestra, the New Zealand Youth Orchestra and the Auckland Philharmonia. He admits to feeling some apprehension about this, having had no training in this field, and because of concern not to jeopardise his long-standing relationship with the orchestra.

"The players were very generous towards me," he says, "but I realised after the first concert in Auckland that it was not what I should be doing with the NZSO. An orchestra of such prowess, at that level, should always be working with fulltime professional conductors in its Subscription series performances. I needed to conduct them in order to fully realise all this and so I am pleased to have had the opportunity."

(Right) Resident conductor John Hopkins with Yehudi Menuhin in 1962. (Opposite, Top) Flyer for the esteemed Canterbury Trio, each of them distinguished soloists. The close relationship that has existed between the NZSO and Canadian pianist Diedre Irons since her arrival in New Zealand in 1976 will be renewed with performances in 1996. (Opposite, Lower) Superstar violinist Nigel Kennedy busked in Cuba Mall to publicise his second visit in 1990, but was deadly serious about his music.

TOM SHANAHAN

The list of violinists is no less impressive than that of the pianists. Isaac Stern was first here in 1947 and returned in 1971; Alfredo Campoli made the first of several visits in 1950 while Leo Cherniavski, one of the Cherniavski Trio of brothers who first toured in New Zealand in 1908, made his last visit the same year.

Sir Yehudi Menuhin who appeared first as a recitalist in 1935, returned as a soloist with the orchestra in 1951 and again in 1962; Maurice Clare, leader of the Centennial Orchestra in 1940, appeared as a soloist in 1953, the same year as New Zealander Alan Loveday, who also appeared in 1971. Ida Haendel first appeared with the orchestra in 1958 and returned with Franz-Paul Decker in 1992.

The great violinist David Oistrakh also came in 1958 and was followed by other Russian artists, including Igor Ozim in 1959 and Valeri Klimov in 1962, a year that also brought Ruggiero Ricci and Leonid Kogan. Tibor Varga came in 1963, and Gyorgy Pauk first visited in 1965. Henri Temianka was the former leader of the Temianka Strings, a violin soloist and conductor of Broadcasting's short-lived Little Symphony, in 1966.

Israeli Zvi Zeitlin came in 1967, and Henryk Szeryng in 1968 and 1976; with Maurice Hasson 1975. Russian Boris Belkin has toured several times since 1980. In 1991 former leader of the Polish Chamber Orchestra Jan Tawroszewicz visited, later becoming a New Zealand resident, a senior lecturer in violin at Canterbury University and a member of the Canterbury Trio. Ernst Kovacic toured here in 1995.

Nigel Kennedy

Best known of the more recent superstar violinists, Nigel Kennedy from Britain was definitely not in the usual mould of artists who have appeared with the NZSO. On his first visit in 1987 he was not so well known in New Zealand, nor as eccentric as he had become when he made his second visit in 1990, sporting a punk haircut, designer stubble and blue glasses.

Piero Gamba was to conduct the first tour but cancelled at very short notice because of a severe wasp sting. Nigel Kennedy was delighted when asked to take over, recalls public relations manager Joy Aberdein: "He decided to conduct from the violin, and changed the programme to include Vivaldi's *Four Seasons* – which caused some subscribers to ring and complain because they really wanted to hear the [scheduled] Elgar concerto. It was only a short time after this that we heard he was the first classical artist to hit No. 1 on the overall charts, with the Vivaldi – quite ironic really.

"As a publicity stunt we borrowed a shop violin and a shop cello, still with their price tags on them, a couple of music stands and my Bach *Two-part Inventions*, and sat Nigel and his girlfriend down in Cuba Mall to busk. They didn't earn much at all! I actually found Nigel Kennedy deadly serious [about his work]. He had the persona for the public but he always did everything he said he would."

The NZSO has worked with some of the world's major cellists including William Pleeth, 1961; Pierre Fournier, 1967; Julian Lloyd-Webber, 1983; Heinrich Schiff in 1989; and Janos Starker in 1991. New Zealander Ross Pople, former principal cello of the BBC Symphony, toured with the orchestra in 1980.

Raphael Wallfisch has made two tours with the NZSO, most recently in 1994, a year in which Steven Isserlis premiered John Taverner's *The Protecting Veil*. Another to perform with the NZSO in 1994 was Alexander Ivashkin, former solo cellist of the Bolshoi Theatre Orchestra and Artistic Director of the Bolshoi Soloists Ensemble, who now lectures in cello at Canterbury University and is a member of the Canterbury Trio.

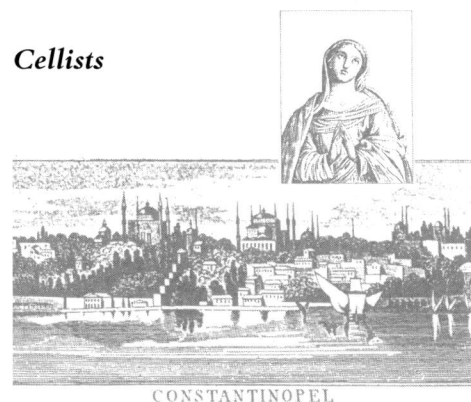

Cellists

CONSTANTINOPEL

Jacqueline du Pré

The young British cellist made two visits to this country, one in a non-playing role, accompanying her husband Daniel Barenboim on tour with the English Chamber Orchestra in 1969, the other a flying solo visit from across the Tasman in 1970 to perform one Wellington concert, playing both the Haydn *Concerto in C* and the Dvořák Concerto. Negotiations had been taking place for a tour by Jacqueline du Pré since 1966, and this short visit increased interest in a longer visit, but at the height of her career she was struck down with multiple sclerosis, with which she was later paralysed.

Her performance made an indelible impression on two members of the NZSO. Chris Salmon's baby daughter was named after the inspiring cellist, so it was a wonderful experience, he says, to be part of her New Zealand performance – and he brought baby Jacqueline to meet her namesake. Years later, in London on the Orchestral Bursary, Chris attended possibly her last recital, and going backstage afterwards, was surprised to find she remembered this.

Brigid O'Meeghan was a schoolgirl learning the cello, when she came up from Christchurch for the concert, and saw Jacqueline du Pré leaving the stage door: "I only had this tiny piece of paper with me, and she autographed it with a pencil. I have it to this day on a fading photograph by Tom Shanahan. She really was my hero. I had a lot of her recordings and read everything about her. It was so amazing she came to New Zealand."

On stage Jacqueline du Pré made a physical impact, Brigid recalls. "She had these very strong big bones and long legs and she just embraced the cello; it seemed like a tiny instrument, it was dwarfed, she totally enveloped it. The fact that she was so tall made it look more romantic when she was playing somehow, with this blonde hair that flew around, her pale skin and penetrating blue eyes. She wasn't pretty but there was an extraordinary beauty about her and she had such charisma and magnetism you were drawn to her.

"She did extraordinary glissando slides up the cello, which only she could do, and they were just gorgeous coming from her; she had an inspiring way of expressing herself. Jacqueline

NZSO COLLECTION

(Above) Steven Isserlis, the original interpreter of John Taverner's The Protecting Veil, *performed its southern hemisphere premiere in New Zealand in 1994. The inspiration for* The Protecting Veil *(of the Mother of God) was an alleged appearance of the Virgin Mary at Constantinople in the 10th century. (Opposite) Jacqueline du Pré, seen here with John Hyatt and Farquhar Wilkinson, principal. Her 1970 visit left an indelible impression on members of the NZSO.*

du Pré was an extraordinary talent who played the cello like no one else, before or since."

Brigid became a professional cellist herself, and spent 19 months with the NZSO until going overseas in 1978. It was 11 years before she returned home, eight of which she spent with the Hong Kong Philharmonic Orchestra. "I had a lesson and played for her and it was quite a severe shock to see how seriously her health had deteriorated, but the spirit that came through in her music was still there." Brigid rejoined the NZSO in 1989, and is now assistant sub-principal cello.

Mstislav Rostropovich

"What wondrous cello playing... What an amazing concert! What an appreciative and enthusiastic audience!" reviewer John Button wrote about the recital given by Russian cellist Mstislav Rostropovich, with American pianist Lambert Orkis, in which he performed Beethoven's *Cello Sonata No. 5*, *Suite for Unaccompanied Cello* by Bach, Shostakovich's *Cello Sonata in D Minor*, *Vocalise* by Rachmaninov and his own *Humoresque in C*.

The words apply equally to all three performances by the cellist recognized as the world's best, during the 1988 New Zealand International Festival. In the final programme Rostropovich had combined the two Haydn and Shostakovich cello concertos under the baton of Maxim Shostakovich, son of his old friend the great Russian composer Dmitri Shostakovich.

Even more astonishing was the programme that began the series, with Rostropovich playing the Dvořák *Cello Concerto*, and Maxim Shostakovich conducting his father's *5th Symphony*. These were performances that will long remain among the most memorable of the orchestra's recent concerts and the enthusiasm of the audience then was something rarely experienced. For many orchestral players, who in John Button's words "played as if possessed" they have become supreme highlights of their playing careers.

The rapport between Rostropovich and his compatriots Maxim Shostakovich, whom he had known as a child, and Russian former World Chess Champion Boris Spassky, was wonderful to see, but led to some anxious moments for me as his 'minder'. I was left to guard his Stradivarius cello, said to be worth US$1 million, while he slipped out of rehearsal "for a few minutes" before one of his performances with the orchestra. Time rolled on, the rehearsal ended, all the musicians packed up and went home; still no cellist. The cello was too valuable to leave backstage unattended or to carry around town searching for its owner, who might at any minute return – I could only wait. When a colleague returned he agreed to take over while I began my search, at his suggestion, at the international chess tournament. Sure enough, there was Mstislav Rostropovich seated in the front row, where he had been for three hours, totally absorbed in Boris Spassky's game – time, concert, cello completely forgotten – but my concern acknowledged by one of his all-enveloping Russian bear hugs.

Sensational performances with two great names at the 1988 New Zealand International Festival. (Above) Maxim Shostakovich, Mstislav Rostropovich and David Pawsey. (Left) Rostropovich rehearsing as conductor Shostakovich looks on from the stalls.

EARP-JONES ORIGINALS

Other Instrumentalists

Gary Karr

American bassist Gary Karr was a surprise success as soloist in concert with the NZSO under Nicholas Braithwaite and also in recital performances. Surprise because the bass is rarely heard as a solo or concerto instrument and its concerto repertoire is not large.

"His playing was a revelation to me," says sub-principal double bass Vicki Jones. "I was amazed at the incredible cantabile sound he produces on the bass. Although I had often listened to his recordings, hearing him live was a remarkable experience.

"Gary's warm personality was even more apparent in the recitals organised by the NZSO which he gave with his partner Harmon Lewis, and also when we had the privilege of playing Beethoven 7 with him in Christchurch, where, after playing the Koussevitsky *Bass Concerto*, he slipped into the back of the bass section to play the symphony.

"I recently attended a bass convention in the USA, at which he was the special guest, and his recital received a standing ovation from a hall full of bassists. I also saw his wonderful kids concerts called 'Karr-tunes' – the kids loved him too."

Woodwind soloists include British oboist Leon Goossens in 1954; New Zealand flutist Marya Martin, now based in New York, who has returned to perform with the orchestra on

(Above) Gary Karr with his Amati bass: his playing was "a revelation". (Right) A performance in 1995 by Lucero Tena, castanet player and classical Spanish dancer, delighted most concert-goers but shocked others, prompting some to walk out. Also shown, from left: Michael Monaghan, Yury Gezentsvey, Donald Armstrong.

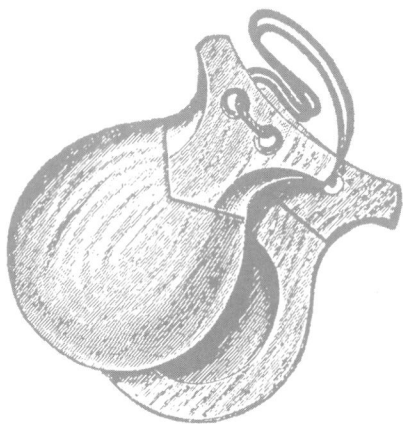

several occasions since 1981; Irish flutist James Galway has appeared in solo concerts and with the orchestra in two tours in 1983 and 1986; horn player Barry Tuckwell made one visit in 1977; and bassoonist George Zuckerman made two, in 1972 and 1976.

Organists include New Zealander Dame Gillian Weir, honoured in the 1996 New Year's Honours List, who has returned home frequently since 1968; George Thalben-Ball in 1971; and France's distinguished Marie-Claire Alain in 1978.

Virtuoso guitarists have toured with the NZSO: John Williams in 1977, and Julian Bream in 1983, 1986 and 1989. New Zealander Mathew Marshall was soloist in the 1992 BP Summer Pops Tour.

Evelyn Glennie

The multi-talented Evelyn Glennie made her first visit to New Zealand as a percussion recitalist in the 1992 International Arts Festival, where she was an overwhelming success.

Born in Scotland where she began playing percussion and timpani at the age of 12, she has gained worldwide acclaim for her virtuosity and claims to be the world's only full-time solo percussionist – something that is all the more amazing because she is profoundly deaf, and has to feel the rhythm through her feet.

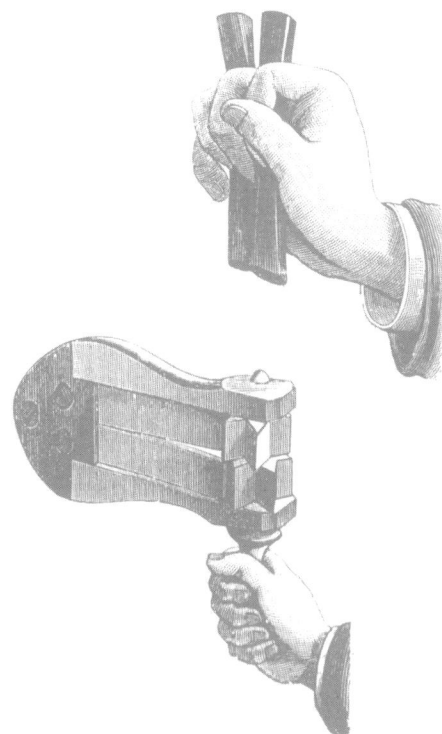

The charismatic Evelyn Glennie, virtuoso percussionist, who performed with the NZSO in 1994.

Alessandra Marc

Alessandra Marc arrived with an enormous personality and a sense of fun. She had been a last-minute replacement in the 1990 Festival, and made several visits afterwards to sing with the orchestra, feeling a real rapport with both the NZSO and the country.

Joy Aberdein: "She would call us up at night to say how much she loved us all, or call in on the way to Melbourne to say Hi. She cut her first recording here and told appalling jokes. Now her career has taken off and we can't afford her."

Sopranos

As with instrumentalists, the NZSO has performed with some of the world's top singers: Dame Isobel Baillie who sang with the Centennial Orchestra in 1940, returned to sing with the National Orchestra in 1948; Victoria de los Angeles, 1956; Rita Streich made four visits from 1960-72; Dame Elisabeth Schwarzkopf, 1967; Dame Joan Sutherland, 1976 and 1986.

Mezzo sopranos and contraltos

Zara Dolukhanova, 1966; Dame Janet Baker, 1968; Sarah Walker, 1982; Jard van Nes from Holland in 1989 and 1993. Bernadette Greevy made the first of her frequent visits in 1977. She returns to sing Mahler, Wagner and Richard Strauss in 1996.

Tenors

Jan Peerce, 1967.

Basses and Baritones

Yi Kwei Sze 1953 and 1960; Gerard Souzay made three visits from 1959-79; John Shirley-Quirk 1981 and 1984.

Dame Kiri Te Kanawa

Dame Kiri Te Kanawa's long relationship with the orchestra began in 1965 with a modest lunch-hour concert conducted by Oswald Cheesman. The concert attracted record numbers, setting a pattern that continues to this day; everyone wanted to hear the winner of the Mobil Song Quest and the Melbourne Sun Aria Contest, and they still do. By the time of her next appearance, two performances in the 1967 Proms tour with the Little Symphony Orchestra, Kiri Te Kanawa was a student at the London Opera Centre.

Kiri returned home in 1970 to sing in Dunedin at the concert for HRH Queen Elizabeth and Prince Philip the Duke of Edinburgh, with Walter Susskind conducting. It was her first Royal Concert. In 1974 she accompanied the Orchestra on its first overseas tour to Australia, where she caused a sensation singing Strauss's *Four Last Songs*. She was to have accompanied

(Opposite) The outgoing Alessandra Marc's star was rising when she performed with the NZSO at the 1990 New Zealand International Festival of the Arts.

New Zealand Singers

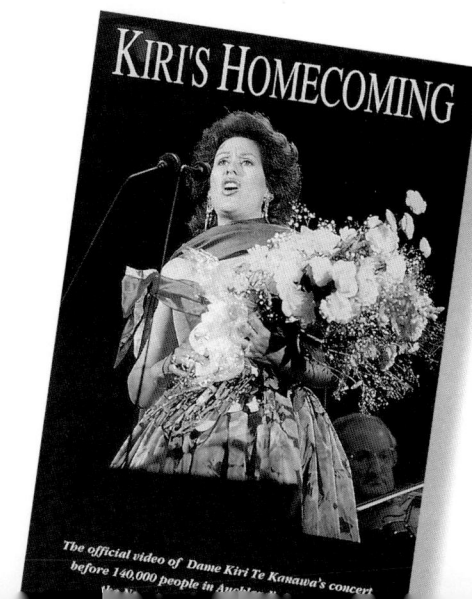

The official video of Dame Kiri Te Kanawa's concert before 140,000 people in Auckland.

the orchestra on its planned European tour in 1981, but this was cancelled by Government.

After a gap of 16 years, in which she had achieved international acclaim and celebrity status, Dame Kiri Te Kanawa returned home in 1990 to sing with the NZSO under John Hopkins, in 'Kiri's Homecoming' concerts.

In the same year she sang with the NZSO for the opening of the Aotea Centre in Auckland, a venue with which she had been closely associated. She has appeared with the orchestra on a regular basis since then, at the Mission Estate in Hawkes Bay, and in Seville for Expo 92, where her stunning performance at the Teatro de la Maestranza will forever be a milestone in the history of the orchestra.

Dame Malvina Major

Malvina Major is a special friend who also made her orchestral debut as a 20-year-old: "A nerve-wracking experience," she remembers, as "James Robertson never stopped reminding me how difficult it was, making it all the more traumatic."

The NZSO took good care of her in those early tours, she says. "I was always met at the airport and chauffeur-driven to hotels and venues. A schedule of rehearsals and performances, times and places were given to me so that I knew exactly what was required of me. It is such a pity it doesn't happen any more, probably through lack of money. The 'to be preserved at any cost' status of the NZSO by those who allocate money does not seem to exist anymore."

Dame Malvina has performed almost every year with the orchestra, apart from several years when she was living in Europe. She says that she still feels like the 'Daughter of the Regiment' after a 30-year association with it. "It is great! In earlier days the ladies of the orchestra took more than a casual interest in my costumes. They delighted in admiring me 'good, not so good or not glamorous enough!'"

There have been times when things have almost gone wrong: "During the recording with Uri Segal of Mahler *4th* I was exceedingly ill. I remember getting out of my sickbed hardly able to stand to record on the second day. Another recording session I had with John Matheson I had lost my speaking voice and my lower singing voice. I was still able to complete the recording of *Martern Aller Arten* with all 15 coloratura in place. It was like experiencing two voices."

Since its earliest days, the orchestra has regularly featured New Zealand artists, many with international careers, and others who have remained based in this country. The following is a list of major New Zealand singers and the date they first sang with NZSO:

Sopranos
Dora Drake, 1948; Mina Foley, 1950, Vincente Major, 1957; Mary O'Brien, 1958; Rosemary

Dame Malvina Major's first performance with the orchestra was as a 20-year-old.

Gordon and Angela Shaw 1959; Emily Mair 1965; Beverley Bergen 1973; Lynne Cantlon 1975; Wendy Dixon and Niccola Ferner-Waite 1979; Patricia Wright and Jenny Wollerman, 1995.

Mezzo Sopranos/Contraltos
Mary Pratt 1948; Corrine Bridge 1954; Heather Begg 1964; Patricia Lawrey 1972; Flora Edwards and Patricia Payne, 1973; Anthea Moller, 1986; Isabel Cunningham, 1987; Judy Bellingham, Carmel Carroll and Margaret Medlyn, 1989.

Tenors
George Metcalfe, 1959; Noel Signal, 1962; Peter Baillie, 1963; Richard Greager, 1968; Anson Austin, 1970; Anthony Benfell, 1972; Patrick Power, 1973; Christopher Doig, 1985 (previously baritone, 1973); Keith Lewis, 1993.

Baritones and Basses
Ninian Walden and Donald Munro, 1955; Noel Mangin, 1959; Grant Dickson, 1962; Rodney Macann, 1970; Barry Mora, 1972; Roger Creagh, 1973; Roger Wilson, 1979; Richard Green, 1987; Michael Leighton Jones, Ted Rhodes and Paul Whelan, 1988; Conal Coad, 1991; Kerry Henderson, 1995.

Sir Donald McIntyre

New Zealander Sir Donald McIntyre has a long-established international reputation as a Wagnerian bass, especially for the role of Wotan in *The Ring Cycle* at Bayreuth. He has returned to New Zealand at regular intervals since he left to study in London at Guildhall, singing with the orchestra in concert and on record *Donald McIntyre Sings Wagner* with John Matheson in the 1975 Proms. In 1977 he sang in a concert version of the Verdi opera *Macbeth*, and in 1982 he appeared in an all-New Zealand performance of the Verdi *Requiem* with Malvina Major, Heather Begg and Anthony Benfell.

Other notable performances with the orchestra include a concert version of *Valkyrie, Act III* in the 1989 November Proms under Franz-Paul Decker; in the role of Hans Sach in *Die Meistersinger* for the 1990 New Zealand International Festival of the Arts, with conductor Heinz Wallberg; and *The Flying Dutchman* with the Auckland Opera at the Aotea Centre in 1992.

Renowned Wagnerian bass Sir Donald McIntyre has performed regularly with the NZSO.

Over the past 40 years several international orchestras have come to New Zealand. Many, like the Czech Philharmonic, the Boston Symphony, the Israeli Philharmonic and the Cleveland Orchestra have been toured here by Broadcasting. Others like the New York

USSR State Symphony Orchestra

Philharmonic and the USSR State Orchestra arrived through different agencies. NZSO musicians have few chances to see international orchestras so when the 106-member USSR orchestra bypassed Wellington they were bitterly disappointed. Almost one third of the orchestra flew down to Christchurch for the concert at which Russian musicians wore red carnations, a gift from their NZSO colleagues.

On the next visit, in 1989, Wellington was included. Most NZSO members attended the concert and the special after-concert supper was hurriedly arranged at the old Symphony House in Willis Street. Those cramped quarters were almost bursting at the seams with two orchestras but the Russian guests clearly enjoyed themselves and if verbal communication was limited, smiles and nods conveyed the message. Later, as the night wore on, instruments were unpacked, and musicians spoke to one another in the universal language of music.

NZSO Soloists

Many NZSO players have performed as soloists over the years, and it is a pleasure to see and hear them in that role. In the last decade NZSO soloists have included Gary Brain, timpani and Trevor Dean, percussion, 1986-87; Anna Christensen, harp, 1987; Bruce McKinnon, percussion, 1987; Yury Gezentsvey, violin, 1987-88; Alan Gold, clarinet, 1988; Stanley Friedman, trumpet, 1988 and 1990; Isidor Saslav, concertmaster, 1987-88; Kenneth Young, tuba, 1989; John Taber, trumpet, 1993.

In 1990 Alexa Still, principal flute and Carolyn Mills, harp, appeared together as soloists

NZSO soloists with maestro, 1993 (from left): Alexa Still, Michael Monaghan, Franz-Paul Decker, Juliana Radaich, Robin Perks, David Gilling, Marc Taddei, Dale Gold, Ed Allen.

NZSO COLLECTION

in the Mozart Flute and Harp concerto. In 1992 in Auckland and 1994 in Wellington, Franz-Paul Decker introduced a new concept with a concert featuring orchestral members as soloists: four principals, Dale Gold, double bass (also 1978); Ed Allen, horn (also in 1984-88); Marc Taddei, trombone; and Alexa Still, flute; and four violin section players: Juliana Radaich, David Gilling, Michael Monaghan and Robin Perks performing Vivaldi's *Concerto for Four Violins*.

The 1995 soloists were Alexa Still, principal flute, and David Chickering and Vyvyan Yendoll (also 1986, 1988 and 1992), respectively principal cello and viola, in Richard Strauss's *Don Quixote*.

On Tour Stories

It is often the things that don't go according to plan that are remembered as the funniest moments. In an orchestral situation, things tend to go wrong on tour, and usually to pianists, their pianos and piano stools, about which some pianists can be very particular. One international artist, more particular than most, was not happy with any of the regular piano stools for his Auckland concert. He found one for himself backstage, old and scruffy, and used it in rehearsal.

After he left, the hall manager came by. Thinking it looked too shabby for such a distinguished visitor, he took it away and replaced it with his own piano stool from home.

That evening the pianist came on stage, bowed to the audience, and sat down at the piano. Suddenly he leapt up and rushed off stage, with the manager in hot pursuit, down the corridor, out the stage door, across Grey's Avenue and into a nearby restaurant. The pianist was huddled under the table, in concert dress, saying "Wrong seat! Wrong seat!"

The manager dusted him off and coaxed him back, the old scruffy stool was found and reinstated, and the concert went on. The audience and radio announcer (valiantly ad-libbing for the live broadcast), were still waiting, with no idea of what caused the delay.

The second story involves another pianist, but could have as easily happened to any artist who travels the world, living out of a suitcase. This one was lucky to have a former scoutmaster for orchestra manager. It happened to Peter Donohoe during the International Festival, just as the concert was starting, David Pawsey recalls:

"There was a 15-minute overture, and then he was due on. He came to me and said 'David, I haven't got any studs or cufflinks – I haven't brought any!' There was no time to try and buy some, and all I could think of as a pipe-smoker, was pipecleaners. To make a stud I folded one over, cut it off with a pair of nail-clippers and poked it through, then folded over the top – so Peter ended up with a series of pipecleaner studs and he said 'They look so neat, why don't we have the whole set?' So I made a couple of pipecleaner cufflinks as well, and Peter Donohoe went on stage and played this magnificent concerto with studs and cufflinks made out of pipecleaners! He was thrilled with them."

British pianist Peter Donohoe, a regular performer with the NZSO.

NZSO COLLECTION

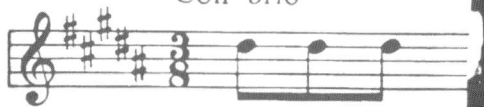

Rigoletto

Con brio

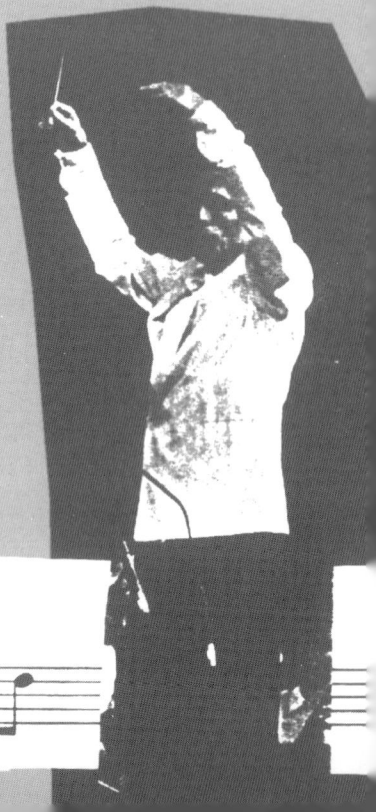

Encore!
Twilight Opera at the Basin

"You must cherish your orchestra – it is yours – and encourage it every way you can."
– James Robertson, former resident conductor.

9 00AM. Saturday 2 December 1995. It's cold and grey, the sky is overcast, the wind blowing and rain threatens. It's an unsettled time of year. Last year they took a risk but it paid off: a beautiful sunny day, a glorious starry night and not a breath of wind. Tonight's concert is not looking good.

Yesterday strong winds buffeted the Basin Reserve. They dropped away during the dress rehearsal, then returned blowing misty rain onto the stage, playing havoc with players' music. The forecast said there was worse to come.

Two days have been set aside. If not today there is still tomorrow, Sunday, but then the alternatives run out. Three days of recording in the studio next week, then on Thursday that is it for the year. Everyone will be on holiday, some with overseas flights to catch, going home for Christmas.

1.00: Decision time. The 'weather committee' confers: NZSO staff, technicians, the groundsmen, to confirm the grass is dry enough to walk on. Overhead the cloud is breaking up, a hint of blue sky; it's definitely improving. Everyone agrees, it's ON.

2.00: Orchestral players check local radio stations for the decision. Once it's confirmed they can prepare for the concert.

3 00: The gates open: the sky is getting bluer and the wind has dropped. With three hours before the concert starts, people are queueing with rugs and chilly bins. They surge inside, towards the stage, staking their claims. Outside the traffic builds up, races around the Basin, everyone trying to find a park. Once it was part of the foreshore, now it's a roundabout, dissecting the artery from city to south coast.

IAN ROBERTSON

Lotto Twilight Opera at the Basin, December 1995: Kerry Henderson, Dame Malvina Major, Anton Austin and Margaret Medlyn under conductor Patrick Flynn.

The Basin Reserve, home to Wellington cricket, has been mowed to resemble a giant green chessboard, with the pitch cordoned off and partly covered by blue tarpaulin. Tonight it's opera to be delivered, next week Shell Cup Cricket. The crowd descends on it, dressed for comfort and warmth in soft soled shoes to protect the grass, spreading out ground sheets, rugs and picnics. The chess squares disappear.

6 00: There's a curtain raiser, just like the football, a half-hour programme from the Titan Hutt Brass Band, conducted by Peter Maunder, the NZSO's second trombonist. It ends at 6.30 and people are still pouring in.

7.00: The gates close, the ground's full; the licence is for 15,000 and they have reached that already. Last year 13,000 came; this year hundreds are being turned away. Someone's been spreading the word.

This time the stage is larger, with a huge new domed canopy from England, like a giant golf ball. Behind the scenes all crews – technical, television and orchestral – finish their preparations. The musicians wait for the signal to walk on stage. The Lotto people hover.

7.15: The Orchestra sits waiting, men in white tuxedos, women wearing bright solid colours for the television cameras, looking out on a sea of people spread out over every part of the grounds and two grandstands.

Conductor Patrick Flynn was here last year, as were Dame Malvina Major and Anson Austin, from the Australian Opera, who are joined tonight by Margaret Medlyn, Kerry

EVENING POST

Henderson and the Wellington City Opera Chorus. The Anvil Chorus from *Il Trovatore* is announced and the first half of the programme commences: a selection of arias from Verdi operas: *Don Carlos, Aida* and *Rigoletto*. A hush falls on the audience as the music begins.

A night to remember: Wellington lights up with the magnificent 1812 *Overture.*

8.00: The first half ends: Lotto presenters are on stage to rehearse the crowd's 'spontaneous' response for the live Lotto draw. Everyone joins in with enthusiasm. The NZSO has several good reasons to be grateful for lottery grants for the Seville tour and the refit of Symphony House. Other arts organisations can be similarly thankful, but being bailed out is no substitute for reliable, secure funding. Arts funding should not have to be a gamble.

Dame Malvina, stunning in an iridescent gown that shimmers under the lights, has extra cause to look radiant, as she tells the audience, she expects to become a grandmother tonight. She and the orchestra are old friends; they have been performing together for 30 years now and have both come a long way, sharing the good times, the bad and sad times.

8.15: The second half is devoted to French opera: *Carmen, The Pearl Fishers, Faust* and *Orpheus in the Underworld*. Much of tonight's music is familiar from television themes and advertisements. Classical music is becoming more accessible and many will know *The Toreador's Song, In the Depths of the Temple* and the Offenbach.

The wind is cooler as the sky darkens. People in their small groups have finished eating, some huddle on their rugs or lie on the grass, eyes shut, while the luscious sound floods over them. The big screen helps, though there is the occasional glitch when the picture disappears.

9.00: The singers make their bows and leave the stage to tumultuous applause. There is another interval while everyone prepares for the finale; the item many have come to hear, Tchaikovsky's mighty *1812 Overture*. Some of the children are starting to tire; they have been busy all night, conducting the orchestra, dancing to the music, watching wide-eyed or just having fun playing around.

A stunning firework display from inside the grounds and two other locations made last year's *1812* both visually and musically exciting. This year's new fireworks legislation means no rockets and only one launch site: no fireworks can be fired inside the grounds, at Wellington College – or at Government House. Until a week ago, a firework-free *1812* was a distinct possibility but permission came through for a disused car yard as a firing site.

Tchaikovsky's exuberant overture has everyone spellbound. The fireworks still amaze, and there are gasps from the audience each time another round goes off, bursting above them in a shower of reds, greens and silver, illuminating every corner. Children add to the scene with their sparklers, and the ground shakes and shudders from the battery of cannon lined up on the skyline. The carillion bells chime in over the top as orchestra and all its forces including the Band of the Royal New Zealand Airforce reach a triumphant conclusion.

As the last sounds fade away a rousing cheer goes up into the night sky. The entire audience is on its feet, cheering and shouting. A man in front is calling "Bravo!" and waving his arms; it's a cry echoed by other voices from different parts of the grounds and the grandstands.

Orchestra players stand to acknowledge their large audience; it is impossible not to be moved by the warmth of the atmosphere and the outpouring of enthusiasm. There is nothing elite about this audience. Twelve months ago some may never have imagined themselves at an evening of opera. Now here they are, and enjoying it too. It is something the musicians hope to keep sharing with all their audiences, this gift of music, not just the ones in Wellington and the main centres.

Tonight is the orchestra's last concert for 1995; the eve of their most important anniversary year. It's a triumphant finale to what has been a traumatic year with more than its share of fireworks and cannon fire: Eduardo Mata's death, the cancelled European and Hong Kong tours, management changes, defections from the orchestra and threats of more to come, revelations, leaks, claims and counter-claims.

There are genuine concerns for health, working conditions and the Government Review but these can be put aside for now as players enjoy the applause. Making music is what they are here for. They are not looking for hand-outs. They want the chance to prove what they can do, playing music for New Zealand.

Encore!

NZSO on the Internet

In September 1994, The New Zealand Symphony Orchestra was the first orchestra in the world to have a site on the Internet via the World Wide Web. As of March 1996, there are at least 70 more orchestras for company, and we are still regarded by many as one of the best and most innovative orchestra sites.

As expected, our schedule, ticket information, and artist biographies are all online, but a lot of overseas visitors come just to browse the collection of links to information for classical performers and listeners. Another popular feature is a collection of classical music humour (which includes quotations from conductors like Leif Segerstam (see pages 92-93 in this book), a SmokeFree version of *Carmen*, and the legendary Bangkok piano recital review). Our rendition of *God Defend New Zealand* and a snippet of Bottesini can be heard, and we will soon have some tempting excerpts from our CDs available online.

The NZSO site has attracted international attention as the official WWW home for *DOS Orchestra*, an online weekly newsletter from the International Conference of Symphony and Opera Musicians (ICSOM) in the USA, and we maintain a database of recommended new compositions for orchestra from an e-mail list for conductors. Information about other New Zealand music groups such as the New Zealand String Quartet and CadeNZa is available as well as pointers to a wealth of general information about New Zealand.

The May 1995 issue of the US magazine *PC Computing* put us on its list of the 101 best Web sites in the world and we've been written up in overseas papers from the UK *Guardian* to the Saginaw, Michigan *Times*. NZSO on the WWW won an award as the Internet's "Cool Site of the Day" a few weeks after we went online and was praised by the Chairman of the

86 New Zealand Symphony Orchestra
The first symphony orchestra on the Web by its own claim, the New Zealand Symphony Orchestra offers the kind of information you'd likely find in performance programs: symphonies around the world, history of the New Zealand Symphony Orchestra, employment opportunities, and viola jokes (in case you didn't think they existed).
URL=http://www.actrix.gen.nz/users/dgold/nzso.html

Association of British Orchestras when it was used as an example of new technology at their conference in 1995. Prodigy, one of the largest commercial Internet providers in the USA, ran ads in all the major computer magazines which listed NZSO as one of a dozen exciting places to visit on the WWW – along with the Louvre, the Whitehouse, and the Slovakian Document Store! Two recent books published in the USA have used the NZSO to illustrate good uses of the WWW and musical resources.

Our site has been sponsored and encouraged by Actrix Networks, New Zealand's first public internet providers, and in 1996 there was a mirror of our site in the USA thanks to Akiko International. This will provide faster access for overseas visitors as well as reducing costs to our NZ network.

Dale Gold
e-mail: dgold@basso.actrix.gen.nz

Anyone with access to the World Wide Web can find the NZSO at:
http://www.nzso.co.nz/

Before our conversation was properly under way Summers was enthusing about the delights of the Internet. 'Do you know,' he announced with a delighted grin, 'that you can call up the New Zealand Symphony Orchestra and get their full season's programme, biographies of all the players and the management, and if you've got the right bits on your computer you can even run a video of someone playing the double-bass or whatever.'

Perhaps the NZ orchestra needs to communicate in that way because it is so far from everywhere? If Summers is to drag the ABO on to the superhighway I can't help feeling that there's an awful long way to go. ∎

CLASSICAL MUSIC 6 JANUARY 1996

U.S. Internet service provider Prodigy used NZSO on its advertising as an example of the exotic sites that can be visited worldwide on the Internet.

Footnotes

TIMEBAND

1. Thomson, John Mansfield. *Oxford History of Music in New Zealand.* Auckland, Oxford University Press, p.118, 1991.

2. Thomson, John Mansfield. *Oxford History of Music in New Zealand.* Auckland, Oxford University Press, p.154, 1991.

3. Press release, *The Evening Post,* 10 November 1976.

CHAPTER 1: THE PLAYERS

4. *Concert Pitch,* Interview: "Lets Talk: Old Times" with Peter Glen, Frank Gurr, Haydn Murray, No. 22, October 1986 .

5. *Concert Pitch,* No. 21, June 1986, p.23.

6. *Concert Pitch,* No. 24, June 1987, p.2.

7. *Concert Pitch,* No. 27, June 1988, p.21.

8. *Pacific Way* magazine – undated.

9. *Concert Pitch,* No. 27, June 1988, p.22.

CHAPTER 2: NO STRINGS ATTACHED?

10. *Concert Pitch,* No. 32, January 1990

11. *Adam Report on Broadcasting,* (Chairman: Professor Kenneth Adam), 1973.

12. Hawthorne, James. *The Revolutionising of Radio Broadcasting 1988* (British *Listener* Lecture). Editorial in *NZ Listener,* Vol. 123, 1 April 1989.

13. *Adam Report.*

14. Ibid.

15. *Adam Report.*

16 . *The Dominion,* 22 October 1991.

17. Case for the Rehousing of the New Zealand Symphony Orchestra, 1991 (NZSO report).

18. *Nelson Evening Mail* (editorial), 12 September 1991 .

19. *The Dominion,* 5 December 1991.

20. *The Dominion,* 1 May 1992.

21. *Concert Pitch,* No. 35, p.19, March 1991.

22. Case for the Rehousing of the NZSO. (NZSO Report)

23. *The New Zealand Herald,* December 1990.

24. *The Dominion,* date unknown, 1991.

CHAPTER 3: MAESTROS

25. Tonks, Joy. *The New Zealand Symphony Orchestra, The First Forty Years.* Auckland, Reed Methuen, 1986, p.9.

26. Ashley Heenan, interviewed by Joy Tonks.

27. Hambleton, Keith, ed., *Concord of Sweet Sounds.* Wellington, 1977.

28. *Symphony Quarterly,* No. 7, October 1995.

CHAPTER 4: SEVILLE AND OTHER MUSICAL JOURNEYS

29. *The Sunday Morning Herald,* 14 October 1974.

30. *The Australian,* 22 October 1974.

31. Cable from ABC, Adelaide to BCNZ.

32. *The Sydney Morning Herald,* 20 October 1974

33. *The Sydney Daily Mirror,* 16 October 1974.

34. *Canberra Times,* 21 October 1974.

35. *The Evening Post,* 29 June 1992.

36. *Metro,* Issue No. 128, February 1992.

37. *Export News,* 14 July 1992.

38. Ibid.

39. *ABC,* newspaper, Seville, June 1992.

40. *El Correo de Andalucia,* June 1992.

41. *The Evening Post,* June 1992.

CHAPTER 5: A CHANGE OF KEY

42. General Manager's Taskforce: Brian Morris (office manager), Rex Collins (travel manager), Joy Tonks (personnel manager).

43. *The Evening Post*, 19 November 1994.

44. *The Evening Post* (feature), 5 December 1994.

45. *The Evening Post*, 19 April 1995.

46. *The Evening Post*, 30 May 1995.

47. *The European Magazine*, 24-30 August 1995.

48. *Work of Art: In Bed with the Orchestra*, television documentary, 1993.

49. *The Evening Post*, Letters to the Editor

50. *The Evening Post*, 12 April 1995.

51. Ibid.

52. *The Listener*, Letters to the Editor, 3 June 1995.

53. *The Listener*, Letters to the Editor, 24 June 1995.

54. *The Listener*, article by Brian Rudman, 24 June 1995.

55. *The Listener*, Letters to the Editor, 29 July 1995.

56. *The Sunday Star Times*, 27 August 1995.

57. *National Radio*, 29 August 1995.

58. *National Radio*, September 1995.

59. *The Listener*, 24 June 1995.

60. *National Radio*, Interview with Kim Hill, 29 August 1995.

61. *The Press*, Christchurch, 8 September 1995.

62. *The Dominion*, 31 August 1995.

63. *The Evening Post*, 20 November 1995.

64. Ibid.

65. *The Evening Post*, 22 November 1995.

66. *The Evening Post*, 20 November 1995.

CHAPTER 6: PACK-OUT

67. *Concert Pitch*, No. 36, July 1991, p.20.

CHAPTER 8: THE CONCERTMASTERS

68. Jensen, Owen. *NZBC Symphony Orchestra*, London, AH & AW Reed, 1966.

69. Heenan, Ashley. Leaflet with recording, *Vincent Aspey*, Kiwi Pacific Records, 1984.

70. Article by Jeff Scholes, publication and date unknown.

71. Ibid.

72. *The Evening Post*, article by Hans Kuiper, 1969?

73. Ibid.

74. Tribute on behalf of the New Zealand Symphony Orchestra, Memorial Concert, 23 March 1975.

75. *The Dominion*, 24 May 1984.

76. *Concert Pitch*, August 1984.

77. Tonks, Joy. *The New Zealand Symphony Orchestra, The First Forty Years*, Auckland, Reed Methuen, 1986.

78. *The New Zealand Times*, 20 January 1985.

79. Newspaper article, reference unknown.

80. *Concert Pitch*, No. 22, p.6.

CHAPTER 9: MAKING MUSIC

81. *Symphony Quarterly*, No. 6, July 1995, p.7.

82. *Symphony Quarterly*, No. 7, October 1995, p.l9.

83. *Symphony Quarterly*, No. 7, October 1995, p.39.

84. "Alex Lindsay Awards", *Symphony Quarterly*, No. 7, October 1995, p.20.

CHAPTER 10: THE GUEST ARTISTS

85. *Concert Pitch*, No. 23, January 1987, p.4.

86. *The Dominion*, 14 March 1988.

87. *The Dominion,* 16 March 1988.

Appendix A

Current and Former Permanent Members of the National Orchestra, NZBC Symphony Orchestra and the New Zealand Symphony Orchestra (including service in NBS String Orchestra, NZBC Concert Orchestra, Orchestral Trainees/Schola Musica and temporary engagements).

VIOLIN

ALDRICH, Ralph; Jan 56-Jul 58. ANDERSON Lesley; Oct 46-Jun 48. **ARMSTRONG,** Donald; Mar 77-Aug 78, Assoc Concertmaster Jan 87-, trainee from Jan 74. ARMSTRONG, Janet; Jan 91-. ARMSTRONG, Nancy; Jan 71-Aug 71. ASPEY, Barbara; May 63-Sep 65. ASPEY, Vincent*(leader); Oct 46-Feb 73, NBS String Orchestra from Dec 39. ASPEY, Vincent* (Jnr); Jan 58-Apr 60, May 63-Oct 65, Jan 69-Apr 74. AVERI, Sandra; Jun 49 - May 51, Jan 52-Mar 59, Sep 66-Oct 67, Mar 72-May 89. BACKHOUSE, Ronald; Apr 73-Feb 90. **BADLEY** (SUZUKU), Satomi; Jan 89-. BILLING, Bonnie; Clare; Aug 48-0ct 69. BITTAR, Henri*; Sep 65-Oct 66. BLAKE, Mascot; Oct 46-Jan 52. BONETTI, Antoni; Mar 53-Feb 60. BREWERTON, Emma; Temp Jan-Nov 90, Feb-Dec 92, Mar-Dec 93. trainee Feb 86-Feb 88, Feb 89-Jan 90. BULLOCK, June; Jan 70-Jun 86. BURWARD-HOY, Kenneth* (+viola); Jun 65-Dec 66, Jun 71-Aug 76, trainee Jan 62-Apr 64. BUTCHER, Natalie; Jun 49-May 53. CALLAGHAN (Tongs), Sharon; Sep 87-Jan 92, trainee from June 87 (+temp). CHISHOLM, John*; (Assistant Concertmaster); Oct 70-Dec 84. CHRISTELLER, Eva; Oct 46-May 48. **COCHRANE,** Dianna; Sep 94-. COOPER-SMITH, Moya; Oct 46-Feb 48. **CORMACK,** Justine; Jan 90-Aug 91 (+ Cont) Aug 94-. COTTLE, Christine; Jan 74-Nov 78, Jun79-Jun 80. CUNCANNON, Anthony (+ viola) Jan 82-Apr 86. DAVIS, Joyce; Oct 46-Feb 72. DIXON, Vivien; Apr 53-Mar 58. **DODDS,** John (principal); Jan 55-Dec 57, Jan 67-. DOMANESCHI, Franco*; Jan 66-Nov 89. EDRIDGE, Judith; Mar 50-Apr 58. **EGEN,** Lisa (+ viola); Dec 88-, trainee Feb 86-Feb 88 (temp + contr). ELLWOOD, Harry; Oct 46-May 48, NBS String Orchestra from Dec 39. ENGEL, Henry (+ viola, librarian); Oct 46-Dec 67, NBS String Orchestra. ENGLISH, Colleen; Nov 54-Jul 72. ENGLISH, Gordon; Oct 46-Jun 54, Jul 55-Jul 72. **EVANS,** Ursula; Feb 91- (+ temp). **EVANS,** Sharyn; Jun 72-, trainee from Jan 69. FOSTER, Alan; Jan 71-Feb 93. FRANCIA, Haydea; Sep 65-Apr 67. **FREED,** Jane; Apr 83-, trainee Feb 61-Apr 64 (+ temp). GALAMBOS-WINTER (KALL-HAGEN) Clare; Feb 51-Dec 83. GARRITY, Frederick; Aug 48-Feb 49. **GEZENTSVEY,** Yury (principal); Feb 85-. **GILLING,** David May 87-. GOLDSTEIN, Jennie; Oct 79-Sep 87. **GRAY,** Elspeth; Feb 92-, trainee Feb-Nov 88. GREEN, Peter; Jan 67-Nov 76. GREY, Geoffrey (piano + celeste), Sep 58-Apr 59. GUETTA, Andre; Jun-Oct 66. HALEY, Denis; Oct-Dec 52. HANNA, Ritchie; Jun 57-Apr 65. HANSEN, Leif*; Mar 59-Jan 63, Jan-Aug 64. HAZELWOOD, Donald (exchange Concertmaster); Oct-Nov 81. HEALD Anna; Apr 67-May 86, Concert orch. from Apr 62. HELLRIEGEL, Karl; Oct 46-Dec 50. HEMINGWAY, Joyce; Sep 47-Nov 48. HENRY, Frances; Oct 46-Sep 50. HIGGS, Susanjane; Mar 84-Nov 89. HOPKINSON, Mary; Apr 48-May 51, Apr 62-Aug 76. **JACKSON**, Rebecca; Sep 91-. JANE, DOMANESCHI, Franco*; Jan 66-Nov 89. Philip; Feb 76-Nov 89. **JARA,** Ronald Feb 66-. JENSEN, Elsa; Jan 61-Nov 66, Mar-Dec 74. JONES, Wilfred*; Apr. 60-Feb 64. **KASZA,** Andrew; Mar 89-. KERNERMAN, Morry (concertmaster) Jul-Sep 84. KHOURI, Susan; Nov 64-Aug 65, Concert Orchestra from Mar 64. KOWARSKI, Stanislav; Aug 60-0ct 61. LATCHEM, Malcolm*; Feb 56-Aug 57. LATY-SCHEW, Victor; Oct 51-Mar 55. LAVIN, Desmond; Oct 46-Mar 55, Nov 64-Dec 73. LAWSON, Eric* (deputy leader); Mar 48-Mar 71. LEYLAND, Coralie; Feb 62-Feb 64 Concert and National Orchestra. LINDSAY, Alex* (violin); Oct 46-0ct 47, Mar 56-Apr 63, (concertmaster); Aug 67-Dec 74. LINDSAY (CONNAL), Angela; Sep 61-Dec 63, Jul 68-May 84, trainee from Feb 61. LUPP, Thelma; Jul 47-May 48. McCONACHY, Rees; Oct 46-Oct 51. McLEAN (BLOY), Leela; Oct 48-Jan 50, NBS String Orchestra from Dec 39. MacPHAIL, Rosemary; Apr 78-Dec 78. **MAJOR,** Dean; Jan 79-, trainee from Feb 75. **MANAGH,** Stephen; Jan 73-Oct 89, Jun 93-, trainee from Feb 70. **MAURICE,** Donald; Aug 91-Feb 92 + Temp. MILLER, Felix; Oct 46-Jul 47. **MILLER,** Simon; Nov 86-, trainee Jan-Oct 74. **MONAGHAN,** Michael; Jan-Oct 71, Jul 75-Aug 76, Aug 88-, trainee Jan 68-Sep 69, Mar 70-Jan 71. MONAS, Maurits Oct 62-Nov 69. MONCADA, Ruben; Feb-Dec 66. MORGAN, Irene; Mar 71-Dec 94. MORRIS, Gwen; Oct 46-Apr 48. MURRAY, Haydn; Oct 46-Nov 7, NBS String Orchestra from Dec 39. NEGUS, Joan; May 48-May 55. NIELSON, Age; Sep 51-Apr 57. **O'FLAHERTY,** Stephanie; Jul 85-Mar 88, Jul 89-. OKNER, Natan; Mar 66-Sep 68. OUTTRIM, Zita*; Aug 48-Feb 49, Mar-Dec 55, Nov 66-Aug 90. OXLEY, Frank (+ oboe); Nov 64-May 65, Concert Orchestra from Feb 64. PALMER, Helen (+ keyboard); Feb 55-Dec 57. PANTING, Richard; Aug 67-Jul 69, Apr 84-Feb 89. PASCOE, Jane; Jan 74-Feb 75. **PATCHETT,** Elizabeth; Aug 93. PEARL, Ruth* (leader); Apr 62-Nov 64 Concert Orchestra; PERKINS, Laurel (+ viola); Jan 58-Nov 64. **PERKS,** Robin; Jan 65-Mar 67, Dec 75- trainee from Jan 64. PINI, Carl* (concertmaster trial Sep-Nov 84). PITT, Wendy; Apr 62-Sep 64, Concert and National Orchestras, trainee Feb 61-Jan 62. POPLE, Edward; Feb 64-Jan 75. POPLE, Fiona; May 69-Apr 76. PRIETO, Sergio; Feb-Oct 66. PUCHER, David; Temp Aug-Dec 84, Feb-Nov 86, Jan-Nov 87, Jul-Oct 88, trainee Jan 79-Dec 82. **RADAICH** (ADAMS), Juliana; Apr 75-. RIGG, Valerie* (principal); Jan 67-Sep 86. **RIZOS,** Lucien; Jan 74-Dec 88, Apr 90-. ROSNER, Francis*; ar 48-Sep 62. **ROSS,** Matthew; Sep 94-. **ROWE,** Katherine; Mar 87. RUIZ, German; Feb-Oct 66. RUSHBROOK, Rosemary; Apr 68-Aug 69. SASLAV, Isidor* (concertmaster); Aug 86-Dec 92. SCHAFFER, Peter* (concertmaster) Jun 76-Jul 84. SCHORSS, Erika; Jan 47-Dec 73. SECKER, Anthea; Jan 76-Sep 83, trainee Feb 72-Dec 75. SEDDON, Muriel; Feb 65-Mar 75. **SMITH,** Wilma; Jan77-Aug 78, (Concertmaster) Sep93-. STAPLETON, Claire; Sep 80-Oct 86, Mar 90-Jun 91, trainee Jan 79-Jan 80. STEER, Michael; Jun 86-Sep 95, trainee Jul 81-Dec 83. SUTTON Marjorie; Apr 65-May 66. SUTTONN, Reginald; Oct 46-Oct 70. TACHE, Marian (principal); Apr 86-Jan 87. THOMAS, Helga; May 69-Mar 70. TIBBLES (SICELY) Margaret* (principal); Oct 46-Dec 80. VAN DRIMMELEN (CRAVEN) Glenda; Mar 77-Oct 93, trainee from Jan 74. WALLACE, Ethel; Oct 46-Mar 57, Mar 58-Jul 63. WHITMORE, Carl; Oct 46-Dec 50. WHITTINGTON, Audrey; Aug 51-Aug 66. WILLIAMS, Marion; Jul 58-Sep 61, Jan 69-Feb 89. WILSON, Barbara; Feb 48-Apr 57. WONG, Mable (+ viola); contr. Jan 95-.

VIOLA

ADAMS, Glynne* (+ violin); Jun 50-Mar 51, Sep 55-Nov 66. ANNALS, Clare; Temp. Apr 86-Nov 87, May-Jul 88, trainee Feb 83-Feb 86. ATKINSON, Clarence; Jan 55-Jun 58. AUSTIN, Faith; May 80-Mar 90. BAMFORD, Georgia; Jun-Dec 49, Mar 50-Oct 82. **BARBER,** Peter; Jan 79-, trainee from Jan 75. BAXTER, Harold; Oct 46-Dec 49. BERMAN, William; Oct 75-Mar 80. BOWCOTT, Alison; Nov 74-May 94, trainee (violin) from Jan 71. COSTANTINO, Sandro; Jan 91-. **CUNCANNON,** Michael; Jan 77-. **DEBNAM,** Anna; Jan 90-, trainee Feb-Nov 86. DRAFFIN, Anne; Feb 88-Mar 89. EKHOLM, Susan; Aug 71-Oct 74. FEDEROFF, Ivan; Jul 50-Oct 61. **GARITA,** Jenaro; May 94-. GILLIES, Duncan; Aug 49-Jul 50. HEBER, Karel; May 67-Sep 71. HENNINGS, Graham; Jan-Sep 77. **HEUSER,** Norbert; Mar 75-. HOFFEY, Frank; Oct 46-Oct 48, NBS String Orchestra from Dec 39. HUBSCHER, Otto; Oct 46-Dec 50. JOHNSON, Hilary; Jan 68-Jul 69. KUWASHIMA, Mary-Wynn; Apr 70-Sep 74. LAVIN, Edna; Jan 50-Dec 54. LEGGE, Kenneth; Sep-Dec 51, Aug 52-Dec 53.

CELLO

BACKES, Hermann; exchange Jul 87-Jul 88. BONNY, Emile; Oct 48-Feb 54. BURRY, Fleur; Jan 58-Apr 61, + temp. BURWARD-HOY, Virginia*; May 73-Aug 76. CHARLES, Basil; Jul 54-Apr 58, Apr 62-Aug 88. **CHARLES** (NORTON), Blanche; Mar 70-, trainee from Jan 68. **CHICKERING,** David; Aug 93-. **CHISHOLM,** Allan (Assoc Principal) Aug 74-. **CHISHOLM,** Vivien; Oct 71-, trainee Jun 69-0ct 71. DAVIS, Robert; Oct 66-Oct 69. DIPROSE, Margaret; Jan 63-Dec 73, trainee from Feb 62. FERWERDA, John; Temp Oct 64-Dec 65. FRANCIA, Carlos; Sep 65-Apr 67. **GORDON** (ADAMS), Vivienne; Feb 56-Aug 57, Nov 64-. HYATT, John; Jan 53-Jun 54, Jan 57-Mar 58, Dec 58-Jun 93. HYATT (TODD) Judith; Jul 55-Nov 61, Jan 63-Jun 64, (+ temp) Apr 88-Jun 93. **IBELL,** Robert; Jul 93-. JOHANSEN, Lars*; Sep 61-Mar 64, trainee from Feb 61. KALLHAGEN, Karl; Jan 50-Dec 54. **KANE,** Christopher; Jan 91-. LANGE, Hilda; Feb-Jun 61. LANGER, Peter Apr 56-Sep 64. McLEAN, Sam; Oct 46-Dec 49, Aug 53-Aug 60. **MEIJERS,** Annemarie; Jan 94- (+temp). MOFFETT, Valmai; Oct 46-May 50,

LINDSAY, Wendy; Mar 67-Ju174 Aug 93-. McKENZIE, Carol; May 55-Apr 80. McLAUCHLAN, Jean; Feb 52-Feb 54, Oct 75-May 88. McLEAN, William*; Oct 46-Jul 49, Feb 54-Oct 68 + NBS String Orch from Dec 39. MEIER, Freda; Oct 46-Feb 54. MOORE, Talya; Sep 72-Dec 73. MOUNTFORT, Charles; Jan 75-Oct 93, trainee from Jan 72. **MOUNTFORT,** Lyndsay; Jan 83-Dec 86, Jan 91-. trainee from Jan 80. MUNRO, Alexander; Oct 46-Jan 55. MUNRO, Jean*; Oct 61-Dec 66. NEWMAN, Helen; Jan 65-Mar 66, trainee from Jan 64. NORTH, John (+ violin); Feb 65-Dec 72. O'NEILL, Donald; Jun 73-Aug 75, trainee from Jan 73. PARSONS, Ngaio; Oct 46-Dec 71. PHILLIPS, John; Oct 46-May 52. POPE, Sarah; Aug 71-Jan 75. **PRENTICE,** Belinda*; Jul 89-, trainee Jan 80-Dec 82 (+ Temp). **ROSE,** Phillip; Feb 94-. SAUNDERS, Gavin; Oct 53-Apr 54, Nov 54-Jun 55, Aug 66-Mar 70. **SHILLITO,** Brian; Mar 73-Nov 74, Jan 81-. SIMMONS (GEARD), Linda; Oct 68-Dec 69, Jan 72-Feb 90, trainee from Mar 67. TURNBULL, Elizabeth; Jan-Aug 72, trainee Sep 69-Jan 72. VAN BUREN, Anthony; Jul-Aug 89 (+ temp). **VAN DRIMMELEN,** Peter Sep 87-. WAKELY, Brian; Apr 58-Jun 93. WATSON, Anthony; Jul 58-Dec 61, Nov 64-Dec 69, Concert Orch Apr 62-Nov 64. **YENDOLL,** Vyvyan* (principal); Jan 65-, Concert Orchestra from Jul 62. YOUNG, Timothy; temp. Sep 86-Aug 87, May-Jul 90, trainee from Feb 85.

*Current players are indicated in bold type. First dates by each name refer to National Orchestra, NZBCSO and NZSO, unless otherwise stated. *Also appeared as soloist. Temp: temporary contractors for 12 months or more. Some early records are incomplete.*

APPENDIX **219**

Apr-Nov 55, Jan 56-Feb 72. MORGAN, Anthony Jan 65-Oct 67. MURPHY, Joyce; Jul 54-Aug 56 (+ temp). O'CARROLL, Maureen; Aug 50-May 52. **O'MEEG-HAN,** Brigid; Jan 77-Oct 78, Aug 89-. OSTOVA, Greta*; Oct 46-Apr 54. PANTING, Felicity; Apr-Oct 68, Jan-July 69. **SALMON,** Christopher; Jan 64-, trainee from Feb 62 + Concert Orch. SIMENAUER, Wilfred* (co-principal); Jan 65-Dec 93. TANNER, Claude (principal); Oct 46-Mar 55, Apr 58-Dec 68, NBS String Orch. from Dec 39. TAYLOR, Harold; Oct 46-Jul 53. TAYLOR, June; Oct 46-Dec 47. WALLACE, Joan; Jan 66-Jul 68. WILKINSON, Farquhar* (principal); Jan 53-Jul 92.

BASS
ADAIR, Robert; Jul 88-. BARSBY, William; Oct 46-Dec 67, NBS String Orch from Dec 39. BERG, Robert; Jan 72-Apr 75, Apr 76-Feb 86. BLOM, Peter; Mar 66-Jul 67. BOTHAM, Harry* (principal); Jan 60-Nov 64. **DE COLVILLE,** John; Jul 68-Aug 69, Apr 74-. DE RUITER, Adrian; Oct 50-Mar 63. DICK, Benjamin; Jan 65-Apr 72, Concert Orch. from Jul 64. DILIBERTO, Frank; Jan 72-Nov 73. DRONKE, Adolf; Oct 46-Jan 50. ENGEL, Carl; Oct 46-Nov 54. EVANS, Anne; Feb 65-Feb 67, Concert Orch. May 63-Apr 64. **GIBBS,** Stephen; Nov 74-. GOLD, Dale* (principal); Oct 6-. HEMING-WAY, Julian; Sep 47-Nov 48. JARMAN, Glenys; temp Jan 67-Dec 68. JENSEN, Gail; Jan 63-Jul 65, Jan 66-Nov 67, trainee from 59, Concert Orch. from 62. **JOHNSTONE,** Barry*; Jan-Dec 70, Feb 74 ,trainee Mar 67-Jul 69. **JONES,** Victoria; Oct 79-,trainee Jan 78-Jan 79. LATYSCHEW, Vladimir; Oct 51-Dec 71. LUDWIG, Gay Lee; Jan 70-May 71. McKENZIE,Judith; Jan 76-Apr 77, trainee from Jan 74. McNEILLY, John; May 49-Mar 64. NEWSON, Geoffrey; Jan 47-Nov 48. NEWSON, Gerald; May 65-Aug 67. PERKINS, Brian; Jan 70-Apr 75. POTTER, Robert; Jul 86-May 88. RIVE, Anthony; Jan 72-Sep 79, trainee May 68-Jan 70, Jun 70-Jan 72. **SANDLE,** Nicholas; Oct 73-, trainee from Jan 70. SHIELDS, John; Jan-Dec 75. SHIFFRON, Alex; May 67-Oct 68. SUTHERLAND, Donald; Oct 46-Jan 50. THOMAS, Gerhard; May 69-Mar 70. TOBECK, Ralph; Jul 49-Nov 50. VAN GELLEKOM, Johann; Jul 52-Nov 58, Jan 60-Apr 62, Jan 63-Oct 64, Concert Orch. Apr-Sep 62. WALSH, David; Nov 66-Feb 68. WOOD-ALL George (principal); Apr 71-May 74. WOODALL, Shelley; May 72-May 74.

FLUTE
AINSWORTH, Cyril (principal); Oct 46-Oct 47, Feb 54-Feb 67. BLOOM, David; Jul 66-Apr 68. BUNT, Felicity; Jan 73-Apr 87. CATER, Victor; Oct 46-May 48. GALLAHER, Wallace; Apr 53-Feb 54. GIESE, Richard* (principal); Mar 62-Aug 86. HARVIE, Edwin (Jack); Mar 50-Apr 68. HOPKINSON, James* (principal); Mar 49-Mar 62. **LUTHER-JARA,** Nancy* (principal) Apr 73-. MAUDE, Deborah; Oct 87-Dec 91 (+ temp). MULLINS, Margaret; Nov-Dec 64, Concert Orch. from Mar 64. **NEWTON,** Nicola; Jul 93-. NICKALLS, Patricia; Mar 48-Jan 55. POORE, Frank* (principal); Jun-Sep 47 (+ temp). POORE, George; Oct 46-Mar 50. SKINNER, Amelia*; Nov 66-Apr 73(+ temp). **STILL,** Alexa* (principal); Jan 87-. WHITE, Jennifer*; Nov 64-Dec 72, trainee and Concert Orch. Feb 62-Nov 64 (+ temp).

OBOE/COR ANGLAIS
BOOTH, Norman*; Jan 47-Mar 65. BRICKELL,

Andrea; Jan 65-Dec 66. CUMMINS, Joy; Sep 55-Dec 56. DUDDRIDGE, William; Jul-Oct 53. FERLETTI, Luigi (principal); Jan 66-Jan 92. FIELD, John; Jan 57-Jul 58, Concert Orch. Jul-Oct 64. GIRVAN, Eric (+ cor anglais); Jan 50-Jul 53, Sep-Nov 54, May-Dec 59. GIRVAN, Robert*; (+ double bass + saxophone); Nov 46-Dec 73. HARRIS, Ian (+ cor anglais); Apr 65-Dec 74. HELMERS, Carol (exchange) Mar-Sep 89. HENDERSON, Guy (principal); Oct 53-Jul 55, Jul 58-Jul 67. KUWASHIMA, Hironao (principal); Sep 69-Sep 71. MOORE, De Vere*(principal) Jan 72-Dec 74. OOSTERDYK,Tom; **ORR,** Robert; Nob 94- (+ temp). **POPPERWELL,** Stephen; Aug 75-. ROBB, Frank; Oct 46-Oct 48. SHELDON, J; Oct 46-Aug 48. STEAD, Ngaire; Jan 51-Dec 60. WEBB, Ronald*(principal); Aug 61-Aug 69, Jan 75-Dec 93. WILTON, Peter; Mar 70-Sep 71, trainee from Jan 68.

CLARINET
DRAIN, Pauline; Sep 66-Jul 68. GOLD, Alan (principal); Jan 61-Dec 93. GURR, Frank* (principal); Oct 46-May 48, Apr 56-Feb 89. HAMER, Walter*; Nov 64-Jun 94. KHOURI, Murray*; Nov 64-May 66, Concert Orch. from Jan 64. KYNG, Peter*; Apr 55-Apr 56. McCAW, John*; Oct 46-Jun 48. O'CONNOR, Thomas (+ percussion); Oct 48-Dec 55. **SCOTT,** Mary; Jan 92. **STURM,** Marina; May 95- (+ contr). **VERNON** (NICHOLSON), Rachel, Jun 95-. WATTERS, Patrick; Aug 48-Nov 60. WEATHERBURN, Ronald*; Jan 56-Oct 86. WILSON, Ken*; Oct 46-Mar 55.

BASSOON
ADLER, Jonathan; Jun 76-Mar 79. **ANGUS,** David; Sep 81-. BLACKMAN, Anthony; Jul 73-Feb 78. BOOTH, eorge; Oct 46-Dec 62. CROCKETT, John; Jul 62-Mar 67 and Concert Orchestra. EVANS, Harold*; Jan 63-Mar 66, May-Sep 67. **GILL,** Liam; Mar 81-. GIRVAN, Robert*; Nov 46-Dec 73. HEMMINGSEN, Colin* (principal); Oct 74-Dec 75, Mar 78-Feb 92. HOUGH, James; Jan-Jun 81. McEWEN, Mark; Mar 79-Jan 81. MACKIE, Melbon; Jan 48-Sep 69. MUSSON, Peter*; Jun 56-Oct 58, Apr 59-Mar 67. NOBLE, John; Jan 71-Dec 72. RUBACH, Keith; Jan 75-Mar 77. SKINNER, Gordon*; Apr 62-Aug 63, Jun 66-Mar 67, Jan 68-Sep 4, Jan 76-Jul 80 (+ temp.) SUTTON (KLOOGH), Noeline; Nov 64-Oct 75, trainee from Jan 61, Concert Orch. from Apr 62. **TILSON,** Lawrence; Sep 93-.

HORN
ALLEN, Edward* (principal); Jun 84-. **ANDERSON** (nee CLARK), Heather; Apr 81-Jul 83, Sep 95-. BEZEMBINDER, Fritz; Apr 66-Jun 67. BURCH, Robert; Jan 55-Apr 87. CRIPPS, David*; Aug 83-Apr 84. DAY, Donald; Oct 46-Jul 48. FEW, Raymond; Mar 61-Feb 64, Concert Orch. Apr-May 64. GARRY, Bert; Oct 46-Dec 54. GIBBS, Guy; Oct 58-Jun 65. GLEN, Peter*; Oct 46-May 82. GRAYDON, Michael; Mar 48-Mar 50. GUSE, Alan*; Oct 63-Dec 64. HARRIS, Ross; Nov 69-Dec 70. **HILL,** Gregory; Sep 87-. HUGHES, Bruce; Jan 47-Oct 57. LAMBERT, Marcel*; May 65-Feb 80. LAMBERT, Rene; Sep 65-Aug 69. NEWMAN, Roger; May -Dec 65. **RYAN,** William; Jan 69-, trainee from Jan 68. SADLER, Barrie; Oct 48-Jan 49. SCHAFFER, Zoe; Jun 76-Jul 84. **SHARMAN,** Peter; Apr 84-. SHEARER, John; Jul 49-Jul 50. STENTIFORD, Graeme; Apr 63-Nov 64, trainee from Feb 63, Concert Orch. from Apr 63. VAN DER MEER, Leonardus; Nov 55-Mar 58. WHITE, Edward; Jun 67-

Jan 95. WINTLE, Prier; Oct 50-Nov 55, Oct 57-Dec 60 (+ temp)

TRUMPET
CAMPBELL, Lew; Sep 61-Jul 63. CARPINTER, Stewart; Nov 52-Jul 53. **CARTER,** Mark; Contract Jun 95-. DUNCOMBE, George; Jun 66-Oct 86. **EVANS,** Gilbert; Nov 64-, Concert Orch. from Mar 64. FRIEDMAN, Stanley* (principal); Jan 87-Jun 92. GERASIMUCK, Vladimir; Feb 51-Aug 61. GIBBS, Michael*; Jun 53-May 94. GLEN, Joseph; Aug 47-Aug 55. **KIRGAN,** Michael; Sep 95-. LAUDERDALE, John; Feb 64-Oct 77. Concert Orch. from Dec 62. LEW, Yoram; Jul-Dec 94. LOPER Jim (+ horn); Jan-Sep 74 (+ temp). McFARLANE, Norman; Jun 94-May 95. MacKINNON, Albert*(principal); Jan 65-Dec 91. **MOYER,** Thomas; Jun 95-. TABER, John (principal); Jul 63-Mar 66, Jan 93-Sep 95 (+ cont). WEBB, Gordon* (principal); Cont. Aug 55-Feb 64.

TROMBONE
AEPLER, Heinz; Nov 64-Oct 70, Concert Orch. from Mar 63. BROWN, Harold; Oct 46-Dec 50. **BROWNE,** Graeme; Feb 89-. DIXON, Neil*; Oct 56-Feb 89. EVANS, Keith* Passim. **MAUNDER,** Peter; Jan 91. McIVOR, John* (principal); Jan 54-Nov 90. OWERS, Ralph*; Oct 46-Mar 59. SHANAHAN, Tom; Apr 51-Jun 54, Mar 59-Oct 86. **TADDEI,** Marc (principal); Jun 87-. TIBBLES, John*; Oct 46-Aug 56.

TUBA
CONNORS, Maurice*; Oct 48-Dec 70. SCHNACK, Christopher*; Apr 71-Apr 76. **YOUNG,** Kenneth* (principal + conductor in residence); Apr 76-.

TIMPANI/PERCUSSION
ANDREWS, Edward; Jan 49-Dec 67. BRAIN, Gary OBE*(co-principal); May 65-Jul 89, trainee from Jan 64. BRINSDEN, Roy; Oct 46-Dec 50. **CLAYTON,** Matthew; Sep 94-. DEAN, Trevor* (principal); Jan 65-Dec 88, trainee from Feb 62. GADD, Norman* (principal), Feb 52-May 85. GARZA, Edward; Feb 65-Mar 67. **JONES,** Herbert; May 67-. LEWIS, Andrew (principal timpani); contr. Apr-Jun 95, Oct 95-. MALASHENKO, André; Jan 91-Dec 94. **McKINNON,** Bruce (principal percussion); Feb 89-. STIGTER, Hendrik; Aug 52-Nov 71. VENABLES, David; Mar 67-Nov 92.

HARP
ANDERSON, Mary*; Apr 64-Dec 66. CARTER, Winifred*; Feb 47-Sep 54 (+ temp). COMER, Leslie*; Jan 55-Dec 62. CHRISTENSEN, Anna; temp. Jun-Jul 84, Mar-Sep 85, Oct 86-Feb 89. CHRISTENSEN, Jan; Sep 79-Oct 86. HARRIS, Rebecca*; Oct 67-May 79. **MILLS,** Carolyn (principal); Feb 89-. ST JOHN, Rosemary*; temp. Feb-Nov 67.

KEYBOARD
CHEESMAN, Oswald* (+ percussion); Oct 46-Sep 49. COOPER, Diane (+percussion) Feb 89-. CUNNING-HAME, Loretto* (+ violin); Jan 61-Mar 63, Apr 68-Nov 87. POLLARD, Bessie* (+ percussion); Feb 47-May 51. SLACK, Althea Harley* (+ studio strings) Oct 46-Jul 49. WALKER, Jocelyn*; Passim.

Appendix C *Orchestral Bursaries Awarded.*

Year Awarded	Name and Instrument	Type of Bursary	Year Awarded	Name and Instrument	Type of Bursary
1963	ADAMS, Glynne (viola)	–	1978	FOSTER, Alan (violin)	NZSO Study Award
1964	WEATHERBURN, Ronald (bass clarinet)	Refresher	1979	RIGG, Valerie (violin)	NZSO Study Award
	WILKINSON, Farquhar (cello)	Refresher	1980	JOHNSTONE, Barry* (doublebass)	NZSO Study Award
1965	GURR, Frank (clarinet)	Refresher	1981	FERLETTI, Luigi (cor anglais)	NZSO/British Airways Study Award
	WEBB, Ronald (oboe)	Training	1982	POPPERWELL, Stephen* (oboe)	NZSO/British Airways Study Award
1966	BRAIN, Gary (percussion)	Training	1983	YOUNG, Kenneth* (tuba)	NZSO/British Airways Study Award
	HYATT, John (cello)	Refresher	1984	GORDON, Vivienne* (cello)	NZSO/British Airways Study Award
	POPLE, Edward (violin)	Training	1985	MANAGH, Stephen* (violin)	NZSO/British Airways Study Award
1967	Not awarded		1986	JONES, Victoria* (double bass)	NZSO/British Airways Study Award
1968	ENGLISH, Gordon (violin)	Refresher	1987	HEUSER, Norbert* (viola)	NZSO/British Airways Study Award
	STIGTER, Hendrik (percussion)	Refresher	1988	Not awarded	NZSO/British Airways Study Award
1969	BURCH, Robert (horn)	Refresher	1989	PERKS, Robin* (violin)	NZSO/British Airways Study Award
	MACKIE, Melbon (bassoon)	Training	1990	CUNCANNON, Michael* (viola)	NZSO/British Airways Study Award
1970	LAUDERDALE, Jack (trumpet)	Refresher	1991	Not awarded	
	YENDOLL, Vyvyan* (viola)	Refresher	1992	Awarded, postponed to 1993	
1971	Awarded, taken up in 1972		1993	ROWE, Katherine* (violin)	NZSO Study Award
1972	SALMON, Christopher* (cello)	Refresher	1994	EVANS, Ursula* (violin), postponed meanwhile	Lexus Study Bursary
1973	DODDS, John* (violin)	Refresher	1995	McKINNON, Bruce* (percussion)	Lexus Study Award
	GIBBS, Michael (trumpet)	Refresher			
1974	GIESE, Richard (flute)	Refresher			
1975	BUNT, Felicity (flute)	Training			
	RYAN, William* (horn)	Refresher			
1976	DOMANESCHI, Franco (violin)	Refresher			
1977	Not awarded				

Appendix D

Guest conductors, soloists and narrators who have performed with the Orchestra. Groups, orchestras and operas (with or without the orchestra), as at 1 January 1996.

CONDUCTORS

ALLEN, Bernie 80-85;(S) ALLEN, Clyde 82; ANCERL, Karel 61; ANTONINI, Alfredo 73; ASPEY, Vincent 57-60; ATLAS, Dalia 89; ATZMON, Moshe 87; BAINTON, Edgar 47, 48, 50; (S) BAKER, Tony 74; BARATI, George 69; BARLOW, Stephen 93; BARNETT, John 70; BEDFORD, Steuart 81 ;BERGEL, Erich 76, 78, 83; BISHOP, John 57; BISHOP-KOVACEVICH, Stephen 89, 91; BLACK, Stanley 72, 74; BONNEY, Maurice 64, 65; BONYNGE, Richard 76, 86; BOOTH, Barry 83; (P) BOWLES, Michael 50-53; BRAITHWAITE, Nicholas 77,83,86,87,92-95;(P) BRAITHWAITE, Warwick 47, 53, 54; BRION, Keith 83; BRUSEY, Harry 56, 58; (S) BURGES, Peter 55; (S) BURSTEIN, Ulrich 71, 73; CALLAWAY, Sir Frank 68; (S) CAMPOLI, Alfredo 76; CARR, Edwin 67, 70, 71, 73, 74, 81, 85-87; CASTRO, Juan Jose 52; CAVDARSKI, Vanco 71, 73, 74, 78, 80, 92; CHANNELL, Russell 78; CHEESMAN, Oswald 52, 55, 56, 58-62, 65-75; CHOO, Hoey 84; (S) COLOMBI, Hans 51, 55; COMTE, Catherine 91; COSMA, Edgar 63; (S) COX, Charles 55, 57; CRAFT, Robert 61; DANKWORTH, John 91, 94; DAVIES, Claude 56; DAVIES, Meredith 71, 82; (S) DECH, Gil 53; (P) DECKER, Franz-Paul 66, 76, 80, 83-85, 87-95; DE LA MARTINEZ, Odaline 92, 95; DELOGU, Gaetano 78, 92; DOMMETT, Leonard 78; DORATI, Antal 73; DOWNES, Edward 88, 90; DUSCHENES, Mario 87, 89, 91, 92; (S) ESTALL, Stephen 68, 71, 72; (S) FARIS, Alexander 63; (S) FARQUHAR, David 65-67, 69, 71, 75; (S) FEDEROFF, Ivan 51, 55, 59; FELICIANO, Francisco 84, 87; FIEDLER, Arthur 66, 68; FIELD-DODGSON, Robert 55, 57, 58, 60, 72; FISCHER, Eduard 64; FISTOULARI, Anatole 69; FLYNN, Patrick 94, 95; (S) FOSTER, Alan 80, 88; FOSTER, Lawrence 70; FOU, Ts'ong 89; FRANCHI, Dorothea 65, 66, 75; FRANKS, Dobbs 66-68, 76, 77; FREDMAN, Myer 76, 93, 94; FREMAUX, Louis 84; FRUHBECK DE BURGOS, Rafael 80; FUENTE, Herrera de la 66; FURST, Janos 82, 87, 90-92, 94, 95; GALLIERA, Alceo 63, 67; GALWAY, James 86; GAMBA, Piero 69, 81, 84, 87; GARCIA, Russell 73, 74; GEORGIADIS, John 79, 80; GLOVER, Jane 93; GODFREY, Peter 67, 70-72, 74, 75, 83, 85, 87; GOODWIN, Ron 75, 76, 78, 81, 83, 84, 87, 90, 93; GOOSSENS, Sir Eugene 47; (S) GRAY, Terry 83; GRIFFITHS, Vernon 53, 55; GRIN, Leonard 85; GROVES, Sir Charles 76, 80, 82, 84, 87; HALASZ, Michael 95; HANDFORD, Maurice 78; HANDLEY, Vernon 93; HANGEN, Bruce 75, 76; HATCH, Tony 90; HAWKEY, William 67, 70-72; HEENAN, Ashley 65, 68-71, 73, 75, 78; HEINZE, Sir Bernard 51, 56; HELTAY, Laszlo 64-66; (S) HOFFMAN, Heinz 67; HOLLINRAKE, Prof H 53; (P) HOPKINS, John 58-63, 68, 69, 72, 74-83, 85-90, 92; HOUSTOUN, Michael 95; HUGHES, Owain Arwel 80; INOUE, Michiyoshi 75, 77-81, 83, 86, 88, 92; JACKSON, Stanley 67; JENSEN, Owen 56, 66, 67, 69; JOHANOS, Donald 93; (S) JONES, Wilfred 63; JORDANIA, Vakhtang 85; JORDANS, Hein 68, 71, 74; JOUBERT, John 79; KAMU, Okko 81, 90; KASPSZYK, Jacek 95; KOJIAN, Varujan 88, 91, 92; (S) KOMLOS, William 57; KOSTELANETZ, Andre 70, 76; KOVACIC, Ernst 95; KRIPS, Henry 62; KRIPS, Josef 59; (S) KRUG, Gerald 70; LANCHBERY, John 83, 86; LAW, Brian 92, 93; LAWRENCE, Ashley 88; LAZAREV, Alexander 94; (P) LEHEL, Gyorgy 83,86, 89; LEWIS, Henry 79; LILLY, Ralph 56,58; LINDSAY, Alex 54, 55,57,60-62, 67-74; LITTON, Andrew 93; LOUGHRAN, James 89, 94; LUSCOMBE, Harry 49, 50, 55, 60; LYNDON-GEE, Christopher 94; MAKSYMIUK, Jerzy 95; MALKO, Nicolai 57, 58; MARRINER, Sir Neville 92; MASSON, Diego 82; (P) MATA, Eduardo 93; MATHESON, John 72, 75, 82, 84-86, 88, 92, 94; (P) MATTEUCCI, Juan 64-69, 72-74, 86; MATTHEWS, Thomas 67; (S) MAUNTY, Leon de 50; MEASHAM, David 76; MONTGOMERY, Kenneth 83; MOORES, Michael 77, 79; MORIYAMA, Shungo 94, 95; MORRIS, Brett 94, 95; (S) NALDEN, Charles 51, 52, 57-59, 72; NEWSON, Keith 58; OLIVER, Stanley 54, 55; OSSONCE, Jean Yves 94; PEKAREK, Rudolf 61, 63; PETERS, Victor 56; (S) PLATT, Peter 72; POLIANICHKO, Alexander 95; PORCELIJN, David 94; POST, Joseph 60, 71; (P) PRIESTMAN, Brian 72-75; PRUDEN, Larry 56, 57, 63, 66, 75, 76; RAHBARI, Alexander 93; REMOORTEL, Edouard VAN 71; RICHARDSON, Don 74; (S) RITCHIE, John 56, 66, 69, 70-72; (P) ROBERTSON, James 54-57, 62, 63, 69, 73, 76, 81; ROBINSON, Stanford 67; ROLLER, A Clyde 64, 70, 82, 83; ROSEN, Albert 79, 81; ROSENMAN, Leonard 89; SALOMON, Doron 82, 84, 85, 89; SANDERLING, Kurt 81; SANDERLING, Thomas 83, 86; SARBU, Eugene 89; (S) SCHAFFER, Peter 83; SCHENCK, Andrew 88, 91; SCHOLES, Peter 93, 95; SCHONZELER, Hans-Hubert 83; SCHUMACHER, Richard 68; SEAMAN, Christopher 71, 81; SEDARES, James 92 93 94 95; SEGAL, Uri 71, 75, 77, 79, 80, 86; SEGERSTAM, Leif 89; SEREBRIER, Jose, 85-86; SHALLON, David 91, 95; SHAO, En 95; SHAPIRRA, Elyakum 78, 86; SHOSTAKOVICH, Maxim 88, 93; SINGER, Jacques 71; SKROWACZEWSKI, Stanislaw 88; SMETACEK, Vaclav 65, 72; SOUTHGATE, Sir William 75-77, 79, 82-88, 90-95; SPEIRS, Jack 80; STEINITZ, Paul 70; (S) STIASNY, Walter 73; STRAVINSKY, Igor 61; SUSSKIND, Walter 67, 70, 74, 76, 79; TALMI, Yoav 89, 90, 94; TEMIANKA, Henri 66; THOMAS, Patrick 80, 82; THOMSON, Bryden 90; (S) TILL, Maurice 51; TINTNER, Georg 53, 55, 64, 77-79, 95; TOMLINSON, Ernest 93; TOOGOOD, Selwyn 56; TORTELIER, Yan Pascal 94; TURNOVSKY, Martin 75, 87; (P) TYRER, Andersen 46-49; VALDES, Maximiano 83, 89; VAUGHAN, Terence 51-53, 78; VETO, Tamas 92; VINTEN, Michael 89; VIS, Lucas 93; WALDEN-MILLS, William 55, 56; WALLBERG, Heinrich 90, 91, 92; WALLENSTEIN, Alfred 70; WILLCOCKS, Sir David 77, 80, 85, 88 94; WILSON, Ray 56, 60, 68-70; WRIGHT, Denis 59; WYSS, Niklaus 80; YAMPOLSKY, Victor 86, 88, 90; YEO, Lindsay 76; (S) YOUNG, Graeme 73; (S) YOUNG, Kenneth 85, 87-90, 92-95; (S) ZWARTZ, Peter 62, 64, 80;

PIANO

AIMAND, Pierre Laurent 82; ALBULESCU, Eugene 87-89; ALEXEEV, Dmitri 88, 91; ALPENHEIM, Ilse von 59, 73; (S) ANDERSON, Jean 59; ARRAU, Claudio 62, 68, 74; ASHKENAZY, Vladimir 69, 73, 82; ATKINSON, Leslie 56, 57; AUSTIN, Katherine 82; AVELING, Valda 57 (harpsichord); BACHAUER, Gina 62, 64; BADURA-SKODA, Paul 56; BANOWETZ, Joseph 89; (S) BARNETT, Kathleen 67; BEAUCHAMP, Richard 70, 72, 89; BERNATHOVA, Eva 60, 65; BETTS-VINCENT, Elsie 47; BIRET, Idil 84; BIRNIE, Tessa 63, 65, 73, 76; BISHOP-KOVACEVICH, Stephen 68, 79, 89; BLACK, Stanley 72, 74; BLACKSHAW, Christian 85; BLANK, Freda 53; BLOCH, Joseph 62; BLOOM, Olive 52, 57; BOLET, Jorge 64, 87; BOLLARD, David 66; BONAVENTURA, Anthony di 70; BRADFORD, Vera 51; BRENDEL, Alfred 63, 71; BRONSTEIN, Ena 68; BROWN, Gwenyth 57, 65; BUCHBINDER, Rudolf 69; BUECHNER, David 95; CARTER, Shirley 48, 52, 53, 67; CHEESMAN, Oswald 47, 57, 62-64; CHERKASSKY, Shura 61, 69, 81; CHIEN, Alec 87; CHOU, Chia 83; CHUNG, Myung-Whun 74; CISLOWSKA, Tamara Anna 95; CLARKE, Julie 54; CLARKE, Sheryl 73, 74; CLARKEN, Peter 65, 66; COHN, Hilde 52; COLLIER, Helen 62, 63, 67, 73; COOKE, W 49; COOPER, Imogen 87, 90; COOPER, Peter 48, 53, 60, 62, 68, 71, 73; CUMING, Christine 75, 87; CUNNINGHAME, Loretto 59, 61; DALBERTO, Michel 80; DONOHOE, Peter 89, 90, 93; DOSSER, Lance 55, 56, 59; DOUGLAS, Barry 88, 92; DOWNING, Dorothy 52, 66; DUPHIL, Monique 83, 84, 91; EDGAR, Alison 55-57; EVROV, Nikolai FALLOT, Monique 57; FARRELL, Richard 48, 51-54, 56; FAUST, Sylvia 52; FIELD, Keith 52, 53; FISCHER, Annie 68; FOLDES, Andor 59; FOU, Ts'ong 65, 70, 75-77, 83, 92; FOWKE, Philip 94; FRAGER, Malcolm 82; FRANKL, Peter 75-77, 80, 81, 85, 90; FRASER, Ian 94, 95; FURKUSNY, Rudol 67; GALBRAITH, David 55-62, 65-67, 69, 70, 72; GAVRILOV, Andrei 92; GRAFFMANN, Gary 67; GRAINGER, Percy 82 (piano roll); (S) GRICE, Jeffrey 76, 88; (S) GUERIN, David 78, 83, 86, 87; HAEBLER, Ingrid 64; HALL, Cara 49-51, 54, 55; HARLEY-SLACK, Althea 47; HARRISON, Eric 63; HAUTZIG, Walter 80, 83; HAVILL, Joan 74, 77; HELMANN, Aleksandr 48; HENDERSON, Lca 82; (S) HESSE, M 51; HOBSON, Ian 82, 84; HOLLANDER, J 49; HOLLANDER, Lorin 72; HORSLEY, Colin 47, 50, 55, 65, 72; HOUSTOUN, Michael 71-75, 77, 78, 82-95; IRONS, Diedre 78, 79, 81, 83-87, 89, 92, 94; ISTOMIN, Eugene 69; JABLONSKY, Peter 94; JAMES, David 69, 75, 80, 83, 86, 87, 91; JENNER, Ernest 51, 53, 54; JOHNSONE, Elaine 69; JOHNSON, Lola 61, 65, 68-72; JOHNSTON, Valda 54; JONES, Maureen 62, 64, 70; JOYCE, Eileen 58; JURY, B 49; KAHAN, Jose 66; KALICHSTEIN, Joseph 78; KATCHEN, Julius 55, 63; KATIN, Peter 76; KENTNER, Louis 53, 66; KERSENBAUM, Sylvia 78; KOGOSAWSKI, Alan 76; KOHLER, Irene 55, 56, 62; KONTARSKY, Alfons and Aloys, 74, 79; KRAUS, Lili 47, 59, 63, 70, 73, 79; LAMB, Martin 69; LAMBERT, Raymond 57; LANDER, Alison 74; LARROCHA, Alicia de 73, 77, 95; LAWRENCE, Michael 82; LEE, Dennis 86; LEE, Julian 74; LILAMAND, Charles 54; LILL, John 71, 74; LISLE, Rae de 69, 77, 78, 81, 82, 85; LIST, Eugene 67; LOFTHOUSE, Thornton 56 (harpsichord); LORENZ, Phillip 68; LORTIE, Louis 94; LOWENTHAL, Jerome 71; LYMPANY, Moura 66, 72; LUPU, Radu 74; McCARTHY, William 77; McDONALD, Judith 58-61, 63-66, 72; (S) McEWAN, Desiree 56; McMILLAN, Hugh 75, 77; McSTAY, Janetta 54-69, 74-76; MAGILL, Paul 52, 53; MALCUZYNSKI, Witold 56; MAPP, Richard 72, 73, 75, 86, 88, 91-93; MARGAN, Barry 68; MARTIN, Charles 48; MATTHEWS, Denis 63; MAYS, Sally 87; MENUHIN, Hephzibah 55; MILLER, Rosemary 66; (S) MOORES, Michael 77; NORTON, Christopher 75; O'BYRNE, Patrick 87; O'CONOR, John 93; OGDON, John 64,68; OHLSSON, Garrick 74; OROZCO, Rafael 77; ORTIZ, Cristina 76,78,81, 95;

Appendix compiled by John Gray and updated by Murray Alford 1986-95. (S) Studio performances; (P) Principal conductor.

OUSSET, Cecile 86, 91; PAGE, Frederick 54, 56, 60, 67, 71, 80; PENNARIO, Leonard 67,70; POENTINEN, Roland 90; POGORELICH, Ivo 84; POLLARD, Bessie 52; PONTI, Michael 73,76,79; POWER, Shirley 58,61, 63,64,69; (S) RAE-GERRARD, Colleen 61, 62,64 67, 69; RALF, Eileen 67; RANKI, Dezso 80; REID, Ormi 52; RICHTER-HMSER, Hans 76; ROBERTSON, James 55,56; ROGE, Pascal 75, 80, 86, 93; ROLLER, Moreland-Kortkamp 70; ROSEN, Charles 75; ROSTAL, Peter 83; RUDY, Mikhail 95; RYCE, Joel 58; SAARINEN, Gloria 65, 68, 73; SALZMAN, Pnina 51; SANDOR, Gyorgy 78; SANGIORGIO, Victor 91; SASLAV, Ann 87-89; SAYER, Brian 65; SCHAEFER, Paul 83; SCHIFF, Andras 83; SEREBRIAKOV, Paul 65; SERKIN, Rudolf 75; SERR, Harriet 88; (S) SHEPPARD, Doris 68; SHIRLEY, Henry 58, 62; (S) SKILLEN, Molly 55; SIKI, Bela 54, 60, 62, 84; SIMON, Abbey 61, 67; SIMPSON, George 55, 59, 62; SLENCZYNSKA, Ruth 70; SMETERLIN, Jan 54; SMITH, Cyril and SELLICK, Phyllis 65; SOLOMON, 46, 54; SPASOVSKI, Raymond 86; SPIVAKOVSKY, Jascha 55, 57; STEPHENSON, Diana 56, 61-63; SUSSKIND, Walter 67, 70; TAN, Melvyn 80; TANKARD, Geoffrey 55; TAYLOR, Kendall 69; TCHAIKOWSKY, Andre 67, 71, 73, 75, 77; TILL, Maurice 51-64, 66, 69, 71, 72, 74, 85; UCHIDA, Mitsuko 83; VASARY, Tamas 68; VEALE, Doris 54; VESMAS, Tamas 83, 85, 88; VOGAN, Sharon Joy 82-84, 87 90 91; WALKER, Jocelyn 52-56, 58-60, 62, 63, 65, 66, 68, 73; WATSON, Gordon 58, 71; WEHR, David Allen 92, 93; WEMYSS, Elizabeth 53; (S) WHITEHORN, G 54; WILD, Earl 78; WILDE, David 76; WILLIAMS, Janet 82; (S) WILSON, Sonja 71; WINDSOR, Raymond 47; WOODWARD, Roger 75, 79, 81; YANKOFF, Ventislav 55; ZELLAN-SMITH, Georgina 72, 73; ZELTSER, Mark 82;

HARPSICHORD

VIGNOLES, Roger 86;

VIOLIN

ANTHONY, Adele 88; BEAUFAND, Brigitte de 54; BELKIN, Boris 80, 84, 86, 90; (5) BUNT, Belinda 76; CAMPOLI, ALfredo 50, 70, 72, 76; CHERNIAVSKY, Leo 50; CLARE, Maurice 53-55, 58, 62, 64; COHEN, Raymond 66; CUSHING, Selwyn 95; DAVIDOVICI, Robert 84, 88; ERLICH, Devy 59; FUJIKAWA, Mayumi 77; GADD, Charmain 65, 66; GOLDBERG, Szymon 77; GOREN, Eli 61, 63; GRISHMAN, Alan 58; HAENDEL, Ida 58, 92; HASSON, Maurice 75, 78, 86; JASEK, Ladislav 60, 66-68, 70-72; KABAYAO, Gilopez 61; KENNEDY, Nigel 87 90; KIMBER, Beryl 58, 65, 67, 69; KLIMOV, Valeri 62; KOGAN, Leonid 62; KOVACIC, Ernst 95; KRYSA, Oleh 94; LIN, Cho-Liang 82, 88; LLELEWYN, Ernest 50, 51; LOVEDAY, Alan 53, 71; MENUHIN, Sir Yehudi 51, 62; MENZIES, Mark 88; MILANOVA, Stoika NALDEN, David 56; ODNOPOSOFF, Ricardo 57; OISTRAKH, David 58; OLEG, Raphael 92; OLEVSKY, Julian 69; OZIM, Igor 59; PAUK, Gyorgy 65, 76, 78, 92; PEPPER, Joseph 60; PETERS, Jane 95; PIKLER, Robert 47 (+ viola); RICCI, Ruggiero 62, 66, 80, 81, 89; ROSEFIELD, Gillian 63; ROSENBERG, Sylvia 68, 72; ROSTAL, Max 55; SARBU, Eugene 83, 85, 89, 93; SEGERSTAM, Hannele 89; SENOFSKY, Berl 64; SHAPIRO, Eudice 62; SHKOLNIKOVA, Nelli 63; ST.JOHN, Scott 94; STERN, Isaac 47, 71; SUBRAMANIAM, Dr L 92; SZERYNG, Henryk 68, 76; TAKEZAWA, Kyoko 90;

TAWROSZEWICZ, Jan 91, 94; TEMIANKA, Henri 66; UGHI, Uto 64; VARGA, Tibor 63; WANG, Zheng-Rong 93; (S) WIECK, Michael 63, 65; (S) WILK, Maurice 58; WILKOMIRSKA, Wanda 76; WOODCOCK, Ronald 57, 58, 71, 73, 74; ZEITLIN, Zvi 67;

VIOLA

IRELAND, Patrick 61, 63; (S) KARLOVSKY, Jaroslav 66; PIKLER, Robert 47, 53 (+ violin); STILES, Winifred 54, 55; ZIMMERMANN, Tabea 95;

CELLO

BECK, Harold 56; BEST, Donald 95; BUSH, James 95; COETMORE, Peers 49; COHEN, Robert 86; DU PRE, Jacqueline 70; FALLOT, Guy 57, 63, 71; FOURNIER, Pierre 67, 69; GOTTLIEB, Victor 62; HELMERSON, Frans 90; ISSERLIS, Steven 94; IVASHKIN, Alexander 94; KENNEDY, John 51; KIRSCHBAUM, Ralph 76, 78; PLEETH, William 61, 63; POPLE, Ross 80, 87; ROSTROPOVICH, Mstislav 88; SALTZMANN, Theo 51; SCHIFF, Heinrich 89; STARKER, Janos 91; VANDEWART, Marie 70; WALLFISCH, Raphael 92, 94; WEBBER, Julian Lloyd 83; WHITEHEAD, James 59.

DOUBLE BASS

KARR, Gary 92

WOODWIND / BRASS

ADLER, Larry 55, 61 (harmonica); AMADIO, John 50 (flute); COLLINS, Michael (clarinet) 95; CULLIFORD, Ingrid (flute) 87; DRAHOS, Bela (flute) 88; GALWAY, James 83, 86 (flute); GOOSSENS, Leon 54 (oboe); (S) HAMID, Barney 81 (trombone); HARDENBERGER, Hakan (trumpet) 90; HEMKE, Fred 66 (saxophone); HILL, Thomas 73 (trombone); HOPKINS, George 55, 56 (clarinet); JAMES, Ifor (horn) 87; MALCOLM, Andrew (oboe) 93; MARTIN, Marya 81, 83, 91 (flute); MASON, Errol 83 (cornet); McVEAN, Marion (bagpipes) 93; MITSUHASHI, Kifu (shakuhachi) 89; ROBERTSON, John 56, 56, 68 (trumpet); ROBINSON, John 82 (clarinet); SCHOLES, Peter 92 (clarinet); SMITH, Ken 52, 54-58, 71 (trumpet); SMITH, Lindsay 71 (trumpet); TANCIBUDEK, Jiri 52 (oboe); TARR, Edward 79 (trumpet); TUCKWELL, Barry 77 (horn); WION, John 73, 77 (flute); ZUKERMAN, George 72, 76, 88 (bassoon).

GUITAR

BEHREND, Siegfried 71, 85; BREAM, Julian 83, 89; (S) COURT, Suzanne 83; GHIGLIA, Oscar 73; MARSHALL, Matthew 92; WILLIAMS, John 77.

PERCUSSION

ALBULESCU, Nicolae 87; CHENOWETH, Veda (Marimba) 71; GLENNIE, Evelyn 94; GOPINATH, Mr (Indian drums) 92; TENA, Lucero (castanets) 95.

ORGAN

ALAIN, Marie-Claire 78; AVERI, Peter 58, 64, 89, 91, 94; BATE, Jennifer 76; GIBBS, Janet 86; HOLLOBON, Graham 79; JENNINGS, Anthony 80; MARTIN, Charles 51; PEETERS, Flor 75; SKERRETT, Geoffrey 56, 66; STEWART, Betty 79, 81; THALBEN-BALL, George 71; WEIR, Gillian 68, 71, 81, 83, 84, 86.

HARP

NALDEN, Charles 56; ROBLES, Marisa 92

SOPRANOS

(S) ALCOCK, Jean 59; ALDERSLEY, Patricia 83; ANDREW, Milla 76; BAILLIE, Isobel 48; (S) BANNISTER, Ainslie 75, 89; BECKER, Pepe 94; BENTLEY, Greta 82; BERGEN, Beverley 73-76, 78, 84, 85, 87; (S) BERRY, Betty 71, 73, 74; BIGGS, Elizabeth 87-89; BLACKBURN, Violet 59; BONSALL, Richard 71 (boy soprano); BOYD-WILSON, Edna 55, 56, 62; BRONHILL, June 75; BRYERS, Rhonda 73, 84; (S) CAMPAGNA, Clorinda di Leonardo 70; CANTELO, April 69, 73; CANTLON, Lynne 75, 77-84; CHRISTIE, Eve 93; (S) CONNAL, Rosamunde 65; (S) CRAIGH, Kathleen 82; CROUL, Pettine Ann 70, 72; CURTIN, Phyllis 68; DALLEY, Beryl 58, 61, 70; DE LOS ANGELES, Victoria 56; DIXON, Wendy 79-84, 85, 88; DOBBS, Mattiwilda 59, 68; DRAKE, Dora 48, 54; EDMUNDSEN, Darryn 89, 90; EDWARDS, Rena 61; (S) ELLIOTT, Victoria 66; ELLWOOD, Daphne 61, 70, 71; EVANS, Anne 89; (S) EYRE, Joyce 52; FARLEY, Carole 86; FERNER-WAITE (previously WAITE), Nicola 79, 82, 83. 85-88, 93; FINDLAY, Margaret 89; FITCHETT, Pauline 59, 61, 72, 75, 78, 82; FOLEY, Mina 50, 53; FRETWELL, Elizabeth 78; (S) GAMBLE, Merle 52, 55; (S) GREEN, Barbara 73; GREEN, Frances 79-80, 82-84; (S) GREEN, Suzanne 74; GREGORY, Jane 86; GORDON, Rosemary 59, 60, 62, 63, 69, 70, 75-78; (S) GRAHAM, Lesley 82; GRIEBLING, Lynne 77; (S) HADDEN, Fay 79; HANNAN, Eilene 94; HARRIES, Kathryn 89; HELLAWELL, Elisabeth 62-68, 70, 73.75; (S) HICK, Elaine 68; HOPKINS, Dorothy 54-55; HUNT, Margaret 61, 65, 72; HYNES, Elizabeth 85, 94; JANSEN, Nicola 88; (S) JONES, Carol 74; KENNAWAY, Joan 78; KOPAHE, Deborah Wai 94; KOPPEL-WINTER, Lone 77; LATISCHEVA, Lily 53-54; (S) LAMB, Raewyn 56; (S) LANDIS, Marie 52; (S) LANGFORD, Mary 57; LEE, Ella 64; MACONAGHIE, Fiona 90; (S) MacDONALD, Catherine 82; (S) McDONALD, Heather 82, 85, 87; MacFARLANE, Betty 74; McGREGOR, Jennifer 94; McGURK, Molly 66; (S) McKENZIE, Airdrey 73; McMASTER, Marion 55; MAIR, Emily 65-73, 75,76, 78, 82, 89; MAJOR, Dame Malvina 69, 71, 75, 76, 79,80, 82,84, 85, 88, 91-95; MAJOR, Vincente 57, 58, 60, 65-67, 70; MALLOY, Louise 76, 78, 80-84; MALONEY, Alison 66-73, 76; MANDER, Phyllis 51; (S) MANNING, C 52; MARC, Alessandra 90-92; MARSHALL, Lois 60, 71; (S) MARTIN, M 56; (S) MOULDER, Helen 78, 81 83; MURPHY, Mary 57; O'BRIEN, Mary 58, 60, 65, 70; (S) OLSEN, Marion 78; ORAHEL, Dora 53, 55, 56; (S) PACEY, Ann 77; PARKER, Linda 50, 53, 54; PARKIN, Joy 59; PASCUAL, Heather 79, 82; PETRIE, Fiona 79; PHILLIPS, Gabrielle 56; PHILLIPS, Sybil 52, 55-59; PIERARD, Catherine 87, 91; PONS, Gerda 67, 68; RAYMOND, Glenda 56, 57; RICHARDSON, Marilyn 68; RITCHIE, Anita 55; ROBERTSON, Sally 73, 75; ROBINSON, Marie 58; SANDERS, Gina 92; SCHWARZKOPF, Elisabeth 67; SHAW, Angela 59, 63, 65, 67, 71-76; SHAW, Maureen 69, 71; SHAW, Patricia Anne 72, 73; SMITH, Janice 62; (S) STEELE, Suzanne 63; STREICH, Rita 60, 66, 68, 72; SUTHERLAND, Dame Joan 76, 86; TAYLOR, Heather 72, 73, 81; TE KANAWA, Dame Kiri 65, 67, 70, 72, 74, 90, 92, 93; TIRBUTT, Irene 74; TROTT, Gillian 81; WELCH, Noreen 73; WILLIAMS, Camilla 62; WOLL-ERMAN, Jenny 95; (S) WOOLMORE, Pamela 54,57; WOZTOWICZ, Stephania 66; WRIGHT, Patricia Ann 74,95

MEZZO-SOPRANOS / CONTRALTOS

ALEXANDER, Shelley 85; ATKINSON, Molly 58; BAKER, Dame Janet 68; BEGG, Heather 64-67, 79, 82, 88, 91; BELLINGHAM, Judy 85,89; BRIDGE, Corrine 54,58,65,66,68,76, 80, 81; CAIGOU, Lorna 72; CARROLL, Carmel 89, 95; CUNNINGHAM, Isabel 87; DOLUKHANOVA, Zara 66, 69; EDWARDS, Flora 73, 74,77-84, 87, 89; ELLIOTT, Deirdre 88; ELMS, Lauris 62, 63, 67, 70, 76, 79; FINNILA, Birgit 74; FORRESTER, Maureen 69; GALE, Muriel 56; (S) GRAHAM, Alice 55, 56, 58; GRAY, Marion 69, 72, 78; GREEVY, Bernadette 77, 84, 90, 93; GUY, Maureen 71; HARRINGTON, Jan 87, 89; HARRIS, Lorna 81; (S) HITCH, Dorothy 73, 74; HOWARD, Joan 68, 73, 75; HOWE, Janet 48; HUIZER, Nel 87, 88; JONES, Beatrice 55; LAWREY, Patricia 72, 74-76, 78, 80, 81; LOADER, Linden 81; McCRACKEN, Valda 63, 71, 73; McKELLAR, Honor 59-61, 63, 73-75; MEDLYN, Margaret 89, 91, 93-95; MEYER, Kerstin 63; MOLLER, Anthea 68, 70-82, 85-87, 90, 91; PAYNE, Patricia 73, 83, 90; PRATT, Mary 48, 53, 55-59; PRICE, Patricia 68, 70, 71; QUINN, Rosemary 79; (S) RAWLINSON, Bertha 56, 58, 87; ROACHE, Collene 70, 71, 73, 75; ROSS, Mona 57; (S) ROWLEY, Marjorie 56; SHEARER, Linda 80; TATANA, Hannah 62; TAYLOR, Florence 65; (S) TE WIATA, Beryl 82; THOMAS, Nancy 63; THORPE, Lesley 57; VAN NES, Jard 89, 94; (S) VAUSE, Joan 57; WALKER, Sarah 82, 86; WATTS, Helen 70; WATTS, Joyce 72; WAUGH, Irene 90, 92; WILDE, Hon Fran 95; YOUNG, Anne 80, 83; YOUNG, Christina 55.

COUNTER-TENORS

COKER, Geoffrey 95.

TENORS

ANDREW, Jon 62, 71; ANDREWS, Leslie 58, 62, 63; AUSTIN, Anson 70, 77, 90, 92, 94, 95; BAILLIE, Peter 63, 65, 66, 70, 75, 82; BENFELL, Anthony 72-83, 85, 87, 88, 90, 91; BOHAN, Edmund 73, 85; BONIFANT, Owen 56; BONN, Justus 50; BURCH, Michael 72, 73; CARTER, Frank 72, 74, 80-83; CHANDLER, Bruce 61, 63, 66, 69, 72, 73, 78; CHEW, John 52; CORNISH, Ken 76, 78, 81, 91; DOIG, Christopher 85-88, 91, 95 (previously baritone); DORIZAC, Leslie 80-83; DOWD, Ronald 51, 53-55, 58, 64, 72,73; DRISCOLL, Edward 74, 75,78; EVANS, Glyn 93; FACOORY, Paul 95; FINNIGAN, Terence 57; GALLIVER, David 64; GOLD, Andrew 54, 57; (S) GOODSON, Newton 57, 59; GORDON, Robin 53, 55, 57-59; GREAGER, Richard 68, 83, 95; HAYASHI, Makoto 94; HERBERT, William 59; HORNBLOW, Philip 87, 88; KELLAWAY, Cecil 70, 71, 76; KEUBLER, David 92; LARSEN, Maurice 76; LEWIS, Keith 93; LEWIS, Richard 57; METCALFE, George 59, 66-71, 75; (S) MILEY, John 78; MITCHINSON, John 71; O'HAGAN, Patrick 73; OLIVER, Robert 78; OPIE, Raymon 50, 55, 66, 69-70, 79; PARKER, David 72, 73; PATON, Iain 86; PEERCE, Jan 67; PHILLIPS, Richard 82; POWER, Patrick 73-75, 94; SERVENT, Arthur 48; SIGNAL, Noel 62, 67, 68, 72-74; THOMPSON, John 58-60; TIZARD, Dixon 50; VAN KESTEREN, John 85, 94; WALMSLEY, Alfred 48; (S) WEAVING, Jon 63; WEST, Thomas 48, 55.

BARITONES/BASSES

ALLMAN, Robert 77; (S) BARNETT, Leo 73; (S) BARRY, Patrick 78; (S) BLISKO, Kosta 54; BORG, Kim 61; BROWN-LEE, John 55; BUNT, Lucas

65,67,68; CARSON, Bruce 72, 73, 75-82, 84, 85, 91; (S) CHRISTELLAR, Gerald 54, 68, 71; (S) CLIFFORD, Grahame 78, 80, 81; (S) CORTIS, Marcello 61; CREAGH, Roger 73, 76, 77, 81-83; (S) CRYER, Max 77; DAWE, Robert 93; DE LAUTOUR, Geoffrey 58, 59, 78-81, 83; DICKSON, Grant 62, 66-71, 80, 89, 90; DOIG, Christopher 73, 74 (now tenor); DRAKE, Brian 48, 71; ESTES, Simon 72, 74; FALKNER, Keith 56; GORTON, Graeme 61, 63-65, 71-76; GREEN, Richard 87; HAGEGARD, Hakan 80; HANNA, Tom 58; HANSFORD, Brian 66, 67; HARVEY, Howard 82; HARVEY, Stewart 49-51; HAWLEY, Timothy 78-80, 82, 83; HENDERSON, Kerry 95; (S) JOHNSON, William 70; KENNAWAY, Lyell 79; (S) KETTER-IDGE, Paul 73; LACKNER, Christopher 74; LEIGH-TON JONES, Michael 88,91, 95; LEMKE, David 95; MACANN, Rodney 70, 76, 90-92, 94; MACAULEY, Ken 54, 56; MALAS, Spiro 72; MALTHUS, Frank 59, 71; MANGIN, Noel 59, 60, 74, 76, 79, 81, 87, 90; (S) McDONALD, John 61; McDONALD, Lex 50,54; McINTYRE, Sir Donald 68, 75, 78, 82, 89-92; MILLER, Derek 87; (S) MILLER, Niven 58, 87; (S) MOFFAT, Brian 74; MORA, Barry 72-75, 80, 85, 95; MORTON, Ian 59, 67; MUNRO, Donald 55-58, 60-62; NAYLOR, Charles 59, 62, 64-70, 72-75; NEAL, Paul 65, 68, 69, 75; (S) PARKER, John 66; PERSON, Paul 74; PRESCOTT, Martin 59; QUIRK, John Shirley 81, 84; REX, Tony 70, 71; RHODES, Ted 88; (S) RIDDIFORD, Michael 78; ROGATSY, Laszlo 55-57; (S) RUSSELL, Peter 76; SAKURAI, Naoki 94; SANDLE, Tony 87; (S) SHANKS, Owen 78; SHARP, Winston 55-57; (S) SKINNER, David 81, 83; SOUZAY, Gerard 59, 64, 79; TAYLOR, Maurice 71-74, 76-79, 81-83; THOMAS, Martin 81, 83; TODD, Philip 75 (previously tenor); VERCOE, Anthony 57; WALDEN, Ninian 55, 56, 58,

60; WALKER, Norman 52; (S) WARD, David, 80, 82; WARREN-SMITH, Neil 77; (S) WATTIE, Nelson 62; WESTON, Richard 87, 91; WHELAN, Paul 88, 93; (S) WILKINS, Bruce 74; (S) WILSON, Martin 57; WILSON, Roger 79, 81-83, 84, 92; YARNELL, Bruce 72; Yl, Kwei Sze 53, 60; (S) YOUNG, Robert 59.

POPULAR VOCALISTS
DANKWORTH, Jacqueline 94; DIETRICH, John 90; DOBBYN, Dave 94; FINN, Neil 94; GRIFFEL, Kay 90; MATTY, J 94; McNEILL, Malcolm 88, 91, 94; MOR-RISON, Sir Howard 94; TE WIATA, Rima 95; TRENT, Jackie 90; WARD-LEALAND, Jennifer 94; WOOD, Steve Allan 95.

SPEAKERS/NARRATORS/ACTORS/ COMPERES
ANDREWS, Leslie 71; AUSTIN, William 55-57, 60, 62, 69, 74; BANAS, John 69, 80; BARLOW, Simon 80; BISHOP, John 57; BRADLEY, Tom 74; BOTTOM-LEY, Ellen 68; CALLEN, John 80; CATHIE, D 47; CLEMENTS, Stephen 88; COLUMBUS, Ray 71, 72, 74; COOKSON, B 52; CURNOW, Allan 62; DENNETT, Peter 88; DENNISON, Stu; ELLIOTT, Tim 64; FRASER, Ian 73, 74; GOODYER, Jan 69; GUNN, Jason 92; GWYNNE, Peter 69; HADLOW, Mark 93; HAIGH, Michael 79; HAMBLETON, Keith 79; HAR-COURT, Miranda 88; HARRIS, Rolf 83; HAWES, Peter 88; HENWOOD, Ray 74, 78, 79; HOWIE, Ramsay 47; KEARNS, Bernard 67, 88; KELLY, Desmond 88; LINER, Philip 82; MASON, Bruce 66, 72; McCARTHY, William 77, 81; McKENZIE, David 90; OHLSON, Olly 82; O'SULLIVAN, Matthew 70; PARKER, Bob 83; PETHERBRIDGE, Louise 79, 89; READ, Peter 67, 75; SAUL, Nitza 85; SINCLAIR, Peter

73; SMART, Dulcie 88; SMITH, Merv 81; SMYTH, Patrick 72; SOLON, Ewen 72; THOMPSON, Mervyn 73; TILLY, Grant 88; TINKHAM, David 62; TOO-GOOD, Selwyn 72; TRIMMER, Jon 93; VERE-JONES, Peter 69, 73, 75, 76, 79, 80, 82; WADDELL, Jane 80; WAKEM, Beverley 79; WALKER, P 52; WALKER, William 88; WALLACE, Craig 80; WARE, Darryl 80; WATSON, Roland 47; WEIR, Dick 74; WHITE-HOUSE, Davina 67, 69; WILSON, Susan 79; WOODS, Mildred 73, 79; YEO, Lindsay 79, 92.

GROUPS (with or without the Orchestra)
ALMA TRIO 54, 58 (Maurice Wilk (v1), Gabor Rejto (vcl), Adolf Baller (pf); CANTERBURY TRIO 94; COUNT BASIE ORCHESTRA 71; CZECH WIND QUINTET 59; DUKE ELLINGTON ORCHESTRA 70; FROM SCRATCH (Auckland) 81; KYNGES COMPANYE, The (Auckland) 81; MEMBERS OF THE ROBERT MASTERS QUARTET 56 (R Masters (vl), Muriel Taylor (vcl), Kinloch Anderson (pf); MUSIC PLAYERS 70, 74,76; NEW ZEALAND BRASS QUINTET (Wellington) 81; NEW ZEALAND JAZZ ORCHESTRA (Wellington) 73, 81; NEW ZEALAND PERCUSSION ENSEMBLE 78, 82 (G Brain, T Dean, H Jones); NEW ZEALAND STRING QUARTET 89; PIATTI PLAYERS (Wellington) 73, 81; ROYAL NEW ZEALAND BALLET – SWAN LAKE 88, CINDERELLA 91, PINEAPPLE POLL & PETROUCHKA 93, ROMEO & JULIET 94, CINDER-ELLA 95; RUDOLF NUREYEV AND MEMBERS OF THE PARIS OPERA BALLET 88; TANIWHARAU CULTURE GROUP 79; TRIO DI MILANO 82 (A Stafanato (vl), R Filippini (vcl), B Carino (pf); TURNOVSKY TRIO 91 (E Elbulescu (pn), Sam Konise (vl), Christopher Kane (vcl); SALT LAKE CITY

MORMON TABERNACLE CHOIR & BRIGHAM YOUNG UNIVERSITY FACULTY BRASS AND PERCUSSION ENSEMBLE 88; VIENNA BOYS CHOIR 59; YOUNG VIENNA TRIO 66 (Peter Guth (vl), Heidi Litschauer (vcl), Rudolf Buchhinder (pf).

ORCHESTRAS/OPERAS
ACADEMY OF ST MARTINS-IN-THE-FIELD 74 (conductor Sir Neville Marriner); AUCKLAND OPERA – DER FLIEGENDE HOLLANDER 92 (conductor John Matheson); AUSTRALIAN OPERA (conductor Richard Bonynge); BOSTON SYMPHONY ORCHESTRA 60 (conductor Charles Munch); CLEVELAND ORCHESTRA 73 (conductor Erich Leinsdorf); CZECH PHILHAR-MONIC ORCHESTRA 59 (conductors Karel Ancerl, Ladislav Slovak); ENGLISH CHAMBER ORCHES-TRA 69 (conductor Daniel Barenboim); ISRAEL PHILHARMONIC ORCHESTRA 66 (conductor Antal Dorati, Zubin Mehta); ITALIAN GRAND OPERA CO. 49 (conductors Franco Ghione, Manno Wolf-Ferrari, Umberto Vedovelli); NEW ZEALAND INTERNATIONAL FESTIVAL OF THE ARTS OPERAS – DIE MEISTERSINGER VON NURN-BERG 90, SALOME 92, MADAME BUTTERFLY 94; NEW ZEALAND OPERA 69, 71 (conductors James Robertson, Vanco Cavdarski, Alex Lindsay); NHK SYMPHONY ORCHESTRA 64 (conductors Yuzo Toyama, Hiroyuki Iwaki); POLISH NATIONAL RADIO ORCHESTRA 63 (conductors Jan Krenz, Jerzy Katlowicz); SHANGHAI PHILHARMONIC SOCIE-TY 75 (conductor Tsao Peng); WELLINGTON CITY OPERA – TURANDOT 94, PETER GRIMES 95.

Appendix E

Major New Zealand Compositions and Commissions and Year First Performed/Recorded by the NZSO.

BESSER, Jonathan
Four Symphonic Dances 94

BLAKE, Christopher
Symphony – The Islands 96*; *Till Human Voices Wake Us* 86.

BODY, Jack
23 Pages 71; *Little Elegies* 85; *Melodies for Orchestra* 83; *Resonance Music* (guitar and percussion) 74.

BUCHANAN, Dorothy
Sinfonietta 90.

BURCH, Robert
Concertino for Horn and Strings with Piano 88

CARR, Edwin
Electra Dances 60; *Elizabethan Lyrics* (choir) 81; *Five Pieces* 67; *Gaudeamus Overture* 91; *Mardi Gras Overture* 56; *Nastasya* (opera) 73; *Pacific Festival Overture* 86, *Piano Concerto* 63; *Piano Concerto No. 2* 87; *Poems* 90; *Promenade Suite* 85; *Scherzo* ("Night Music") 58; *Seven Medieval Lyrics* (chorus and orchestra) 74; *Sinfonietta* 85; *Snow Maiden* (ballet) 71; *Symphony No. 1* 82; *Symphony No. 2* ("The Exile") 84; *Symphony No. 4* 93; *The Song of Solomon* 89; *The Twelve Signs* 74; *Three Tableaux* 67; *Waikato Song* 88.

CRESSWELL, Lyell
A Modern Ecstasy (portions) 87; *Aria* (solo strings and percussion) 74; *Concerto for Violin* 71; *Music for Strings with Horns* 79; *O!* 83; *Salm* 79; *The Magical Wooden Head* 90; *Threnody for Mrs S...* (narrator and orchestra) 73; *Voices of Ocean Winds* 90.

DE CASTRO-ROBINSON, Eve
Fractions 84; *Overture* 95; *Peregrinations for Piano & Orchestra* 88.

FARQUHAR, David
An Irish Faustus 66; *Anniversary Suites No. 1* 69 and *No.2* 80; *Echoes and Reflections* 86; *Elegy* (strings) 69; *Epithalamion* (strings) 59; *Evocation* (for violins) 75; *Fives – Concerto for Dancers and Instruments* 71; *Harlequin Overture* 59; *Harlequin Overture* 69; *Measure for Measure* 67; *Ring Around the Moon* 60; *Symphony* 60; *Symphony No. 2* 83; *The Leaden Echo and the Golden Echo* 69; *Three Scots Ballads* 65; *Unicorn for Christmas, A* (opera) 74.

FARR, Gareth
Lileth's Dream of Ecstasy 96*; *Pacific Piece, A* 96*.

FRANCHI, Dorothea
Do-Wack-A-Do 65; *Rhapsody for Viola* 53; *Twelfth Night* 66.

HARRIS, Ross
Double Music (children and orchestra) 79; *The Hills of Time* 81.

HEENAN, Ashley
Cindy (strings) 52; *College Overture* 56; *Jack Winter's Dream* (narrator, voices and orchestra) 57; *Maori Suite* (soloist, chorus and orchestra) 73; *Scottish Dances* 75; *Three Sea Songs* (voice and orchestra) 55; *War and Peace Suite* 78.

LILBURN, Douglas
Allegro (strings) 58; *Aotearoa Overture* 53; *Birthday Offering A* 56; *Diversions* (strings) 61; *Drysdale Overture* 87; *Festival Overture* 55; *Landfall in Unknown Seas* (narrator and strings) 55; *Prodigal Country* 87; *Song of Islands A* 47; *Suite for Orchestra* 57; *Symphony No. 1* 51; *Symphony No. 2* 53; *Symphony No. 3* 62.

McLEOD, Jenny
Three Celebrations for Orchestra 87.

PRUDEN, Larry
Akaroa ("South Island Sketches") 75; *Dances of Brittany* 57; *Harbour Nocturne* 59; *Lambton Quay* 59; *Soliloquy* (strings) 56; *Taranaki Overture* 76; *Westland – A Back Country Overture* 66.

RIMMER, John
At the Appointed Time 73; *December Nights* 72; *Explorations/Discoveries* 74; *Expo Ballet* 70; *Ring of Fire* 84; *Symphony* 70; *Viola Concerto* 82.

RITCHIE, Anthony
A Bugle will Do 96*; *Concerto for Flute and Orchestra* 95; *Piano Concerto* 84; *The Hanging Bulb* 93.

RITCHIE, John
Concertino for Clarinet 60; *Slane* 84; *Suite for Strings* 58; *Turkey in the Straw* (strings) 81.

SHIRLEY, Henry
Piano Concerto in F Minor 58.

*SOUTHGATE, Sir William
Cassation (clarinet, piano and percussion) 81; *Concerto for Trombone* 81; *Symphony No. 1* 87; *Symphony No. 2* (*Music from the Old World*) 88; *Trio Sonata* (percussion) 78.

SPEIRS, Jack
Cantico del Sole 89; *Fanfares* (renamed *Fiorature*) 69; *Three Poems of Janet Frame* 80.

TREMAIN, Ronald
Symphony (strings) 77; *Three Mystical Songs* (soprano and strings) 58.

WATSON, Anthony
In Memoriam 72; *Movement* (strings) 71; *Prelude and Allegro* (strings) 66.

WHITEHEAD, Gillian
Resurgences 89.

WILSON, Ken
Concerto for Clarinet 64; *Variations for Orchestra* 62.

YOUNG, Kenneth
Brass Quintet No. 1 81; *Concerto for Tuba* 79; *Fanfare* 82; *Sinfonieffa* 85; *Symphony* 88.

COMPOSERS OF MISCELLANEOUS COMPOSITIONS
Abbot, C; Allen, B; Allen, S; Austin, L.D; Baker, A; Banks, D; Charles, J; Cheesman, O; Cousins, J; Cree-Brown, C; Crotty, G; Crowe, P; Daverne, G; Dyett, K; Elton, A; Finlay, H; Galway, V; Garcia, R; Gray, T; Griffiths, V; Grindley, M; Hamilton, D; Harris, I; Harvey, M; Jarman, C; Jensen, O; Jones, L; Keay, N; Ker, D; Ladd, J; Laird, W; Lodge, M; Luscombe, H; McDonald I; Mews, D Sr; Moss, B; Norman, P; Nguyen, C; O'Brien, B; Powell, K; Rive, T; Sanders, N; Saunders, M; Senior, W; Sheppard, D; Small, C; Smith, S; Vaughan, T.

*Appendix compiled by Ashley Heenan OBE, updated by Murray Alford 1986-95. * Performance in Anniversary Year.*

Appendix F

All CDs listed and some cassettes are currently available from NZSO Merchandising. Please phone Freephone 0800 656 881, or Fax: 04 384 2824. CD Index prepared by Joy Aberdein.

COMPACT DISCS

American Diva Alessandra Marc (soprano)	Operatic Selections	Delos DE 3108
Samuel Barber Andrew Schenck (conductor)	Symphony No. 2 etc	Stradivari Classics SCD-8012
Samuel Barber & Gian Carlo Menotti Andrew Schenck (conductor)	Sebastian, Amahl, Souvenirs etc	Koch 3-7005-2
Samuel Barber Andrew Schenck (conductor)	Fadograph, Medea, Third Essay	Koch 3-7010-2H1
Bizet Donald Johanos (conductor)	Symphony in C Major, Jeux d'enfants	Naxos 8.553027
Ernest Bloch James Sedares (conductor)	Three Jewish Poems Two Last Poems (Maybe), Evocations	Koch 3-7232-2H 1
Britten Myer Fredman (conductor)	Sinfonia da Requiem Four Sea Interludes, Passacaglia, An American Overture	Naxos 8.553107
Edwin Carr Franz-Paul Decker/ John Matheson/ Edwin Carr (conductors)	Three Orchestral Works Gaudeamus - Overture Symphony No. 1 Symphony No. 2 The Exile	Corellia CRA.1005
Gary Daverne Kenneth Young (conductor)	Selection (with accordion, choir)	BMG VRCD 0841
Delius Myer Fredman (conductor)	Selection incl. Brigg Fair, Irmelin: Prelude	Naxos 8.553001
Norman Dello Joio James Sedares (conductor)	Triumph of St Joan, Variations Incl. Barber/Adagio for String	Koch 3-7243-2H1
The Heart of the Ballet Varujan Kojian (conductor)	Popular Selection Kiwi Pacific	CD SLC-222
The Heart of the Symphony Victor Yampolsky (conductor)	Popular Selection	Kiwi Pacific CD SLC-215
Bernard Hermann/Alex North/ Frank Waxman James Sedares (conductor) & Orchestra David Buechner (piano)	Selection Piano	Koch 3.7225-2H1
Paul Hindemith Franz-Paul Decker (conductor)	Mathis der Maler Symphony Nobilissima Visione Symphonic Metamorphosis	Naxos 8.553079
Kiri at Aotea John Hopkins (conductor)	Selection	Kiwi Pacific CDK ML-2
Lilburn Ashley Heenan/ John Hopkins (conductors)	Symphony No. 2 Diversions for Strings	Jerusalem Records SCD 8004
Lilburn Ashley Heenan/ John Hopkins (conductors)	The Three Symphonies	Kiwi Pacific SLD-90
Lilburn John Hopkins (conductor)	The Three Symphonies	Continuum CCD 1069
Massenet Jean-Yves Ossonce (conductor)	Orchestral Suites – Hérodiade Suite No. 1, Scenes Hongroises Scenes Dramatiques	Naxos 8.553.24
Massenet Jean-Yves Ossonce (conductor)	Orchestral Suites – Scenes Pittoresques, Scenes Napolitaines, Scenes de Feerie, Scenes Alscienne	Naxos 8.553.25
Donald McIntyre sings Wagner John Matheson (conductor)	Selection	CD SLD -39
Max Reger Franz-Paul Decker (conductor)	Mozart Variations Op.132 Hiller Variations Op. 100	Naxos 8.553079
Respighi Andrew Schenck (conductor)	Tritticio Botticelliano, The Birds, Stradivari Classics, Ancient Airs, Dances Suite No. 3	SLD 8013
Miklos Rozsa James Sedares (conductor)	Theme, Variations and Finale Opus 13A, Hungarian Nocturne etc.	Koch 3-7191-2H1
Miklos Rosza James Sedares (conductor)	Symphony in three movements The Vintner's Daughter	Koch 3-7244-2H1
Symphony Showcase Kenneth Young (conductor)	Selection	Continuum NZSO 100
Randall Thompson Andrew Schenck (conductor)	Symphony No.2 in E minor Symphony No.3 in A minor	Koch 3-7074-2H1

Randall Thompson — Symphony No.1, incl — Koch 3-7181-2H1
James Sedares (conductor) — Morton Gould/Fall River Legend

Wagner Excerpts — Selection — Manu Classic CD 1317
Heinz Wallberg (conductor), Alessandra Marc (soprano)
Christopher Doig (tenor), Donald McIntrye (bass baritone)

STEREO RECORDS (some also on cassette)

Vincent Aspey — Bruch Violin Concerto No. 1 — Kiwi-Pacific
John Hopkins (conductor) — Mendelssohn Violin Concerto — SLD 64
Vincent Aspey (violin) — Concert performances (1962) — 1984

Birth of a Nation — Film by D.W. Griffiths — Label X
Film score: Joseph Carl Breil — (Stereo Digital) — LXDR 701/2
Clyde Allen (conductor) — 1985

Charles: UTU — Music from soundtrack — EMI UTU 1
William Southgate (conductor) — 1983

Cheesman — Wayleggo, Treasury Island — Kiwi-Pacific
Oswald Cheesman (conductor) — SLC 74 — 1969

Festive Overtures — Includes Lilburn's — EMI MALP 6008
John Hopkins (conductor) — Festival Overture — 1959

Going Places — Short popular pieces — EMI HSD 1068
Ron Goodwin (conductor) — 1978

Goodwin — A New Zealand Suite, etc — EMI EJ 2601721
Ron Goodwin (conductor) — 1984

Ron Goodwin Conducts — Light music, including — HMVNZ22
Carnival, Skyliner, etc

The Great Classics — Orchestral excerpts — Deutsche Grammophon DGG 2 — 1976
John Hopkins (conductor)

Heenan — War and Peace — Kiwi-Pacific
Ashley Heenan/ — Jack Winter's Dream — SLD 81
John Hopkins (conductors) — 1987

Invitation to the Dance — Short popular pieces — Tartar TRL 020
John Hopkins (conductor) — 1982

Jack Winter's Dream — Play for voices by — Kiwi-Pacific
Ashley Heenan (composer) — James K Baxter — SLD40 1978
John Hopkins (conductor)

Lilburn — Aotearoa Overture and Symphony No 3 — Kiwi-Pacific
Farquhar — Symphony No. 1 — SLD 14
John Hopkins / Juan Matteucci (conductors) — 1968

Lilburn — Prodigal Country — Kiwi-Pacific
Sir Charles Groves / — Drysdale Overture — SLD 86
John Hopkins (conductors) — Birthday Offering — 1987

Lilburn — A Song of Islands, — Kiwi-Pacific
John Hopkins (conductor) — plus other short pieces by — SLD 79
other orchestras — 1986

Lilburn — Symphony No 1 — Kiwi-Pacific
John Hopkins (conductor) — Festival Overture — SLD 75
Suite for Orchestra — 1985

Lilburn — Symphony No. 2 — Kiwi-Pacific
Farquhar — Evocation — SLD 48
Watson — Prelude & Allegro — 1976
Rimmer — At the Appointed Time
Ashley Heenan, David Farquhar
Brian Priestman (conductors)

Lilburn — Symphony No. 2 — Stradivari
NZSO/Ashley Heenan (conductor) — Aotearoa Overture — SCD 8004
NZSO/John Hopkins (conductor) — Diversions for Strings — 1988
Heenan/Schola Musica
Ashley Heenan (conductor)

Louise — Opera arias and duets — CBS 236066
Louise Malloy (soprano) — 1982
Anthony Benfell (tenor)
Patrick Thomas (conductor)

Mahler — Symphony No. 4 — EMI ASD 9001
Malvina Major (soprano) — 1976
Uri Segal (conductor)

Pruden — Overture Taranaki, — Kiwi-Pacific
NZSO, Schola Musica, — Akaroa, etc — SLD 66
Skellerup Band — 1983
Walter Susskind John Matheson/
John Hopkins (conductors)

Wagner — Opera Monologues — Kiwi-Pacific
Donald McIntyre (bass) — SLD 39
John Matheson (conductor) — 1975

SCHOLA MUSICA

Canzona — Music for Strings and Voices — Kiwi-Pacific
Lilburn — SLD 67
Patricia Lawrey, Anthea Moller, — 1982
Peter Vere-Jones (soloists)
Ashley Heenan (conductor)

Lilburn — Kiwi-Pacific & — NZ Composers
Instrumental Music 1945 -1957 — Schola Musica Duo — Foundation
(double album) — Schola Musica Duo — SLD 57
Ashley Heenan (conductor) — 1981

Ashley Heenan (conductor) — Schola Musica Quartet — SLD 58
1981

Music For Strings — Music by J. Ritchie, A. Ritchie, — Kiwi-Pacific
Ashley Heenan / — C. Moon and J. Elmsly — SLD 71
John Ritchie (conductors) — 1984

Music For Strings (Vol 3) — Music by D. Lilburn, J. Rimmer — Kiwi-Pacific
Composers Edition — D. Farquhar, J. Ritchie, P. Crowe — SLD 77
Ashley Heenan, John Rimmer — W. Lehmann — 1984
Wilfred Lehmann (conductors)

NZBC Schola Musicum — Music by D. Lilburn, — Kiwi-Pacific
Ashley Heenan (conductor) — A. Heenan, L. Pruden — SLD 37
1 974

Patricia Lawrey — Music by Scarlatti and — Kiwi-Pacific
Schola Musica — Vivaldi — SLD 52
Patricia Lawrey (Mezzo) — 1979
Ashley Heenan (conductor)

Schola Musica Ashley Heenan (conductor)	Music by Boyce, Handel, and Bach	Kiwi-Pacific SLD 53 1977
NZBC Schola Musicum Ashley Heenan (conductor)	Handel-Heenan Concerto-Grosso in F Major Opus 3 No 4 Fantasia on Byrd's "Miserere mihi"	EMI PR 750 (45 rpm) 1974

NATIONAL YOUTH ORCHESTRA OF NEW ZEALAND

The Best of National Youth Orchestra 1972 -1974 Michael Houstoun (piano) Ashley Heenan (conductor)	Souvenir Recording (Box album) Includes works by Bach, Brahms, Beethoven, Mahler, Tchaikovsky, Ravel	NZSO 1975
National Youth Orchestra Return Concert Christchurch, 1975 Keith Spragg (clarinet) Ashley Heenan (conductor)	Lilburn: Aotearoa Ritchie: Concerto for Clarinet Other works by Haydn, Kodaly, Ho Ching-Chih, Ting Yi	Radio NZ 1975
National Youth Orchestra in China National Youth Orchestra & Members Shanghai Philharmonic Soc. Recorded in Peking by Radio Peking	Incl: White-haired Girl Children of the Grasslands, etc.	Radio NZ (45 rpm) 1975

Appendix G *Bibliography*

DAY, Patrick
The Radio Years, A History of Broadcasting in New Zealand, Volume One. Auckland University Press, Auckland, 1994.

DOWNES, Peter & HARCOURT, Peter
Voices in the Air, Methuen/Radio New Zealand, Wellington, 1976.

HALL, J.H
The History of Broadcasting (1920-1954), Broadcasting Corporation of New Zealand, Wellington, 1980.

HAMBLETON, Keith (ed.)
Concord of Sweet Sounds, The New Zealand Symphony Orchestra at 30, Broadcasting Corporation of New Zealand, Wellington, 1977.

HEENAN, Ashley,
NZBC Schola Musicum, New Zealand Broadcasting Corporation, Wellington, 1974.

HURST, Maurice,
Music and the Stage in New Zealand (1840-1943). Charles Begg & Company, 1944.

JENSEN, Owen
NZBC Symphony Orchestra, AH & AW Reed, Wellington, 1966.

JILLETT, David, Farrell
A Biography, Benton Ross, Auckland, 1985.

SIMPSON, E.C
A Survey of the Arts in New Zealand, Wellington Chamber Music Society, Harry H Tombs, Wellington, 1961.

THOMSON, John Mansfield
Biographical Dictionary of New Zealand Composers, Victoria University Press, Wellington, 1990.

THOMSON, John Mansfield
The Oxford History of New Zealand Music, Oxford University Press, Auckland, 1991.

TONKS, Joy
The New Zealand Symphony Orchestra, The First Forty Years, Reed Methuen, Auckland, 1986.

Orchestral Books:
BLANDFORD, Linda
The LSO, Scenes from Orchestral Life, Michael Joseph Ltd, London, 1984.

BUTTROSE, Charles
Playing for Australia; A Story About ABC Orchestras and Music in Australia, Australian Broadcasting Commission, Sydney, 1982.

HURD, Michael
The Orchestra, Facts on File, New York, 1980.

JEFFERSON, Alan
Inside the Orchestra, Keith Reid Ltd, Devon, 1974.

KENNEDY, Michael
The Halle, 1858-1983, A History of the Orchestra, Manchester University Press, 1982.

KENYON, Nicholas
The BBC Symphony Orchestra (1930-1980), British Broadcasting Corporation, London, 1981.

PETTITT, Stephan J
Philharmonia Orchestra: A Record of Achievement, 1945-1985, Robert Hale, London, 1985.

PREVIN, Andre
Orchestra, Macdonald and Jane's, London, 1979.

SAMETZ, Phillip
Play On! 60 Years of Music-Making with the Sydney Symphony Orchestra, Australian Broadcasting Corporation, Sydney, 1992.

SHORE, Bernard
The Orchestra Speaks, Longmans, Green and Co. Ltd, 1938.

VIGELAND, Carl A
In Concert: On Stage and Off Stage with the Boston Symphony Orchestra, William Morrow & Corp, Inc. New York, 1989.

Journals and Miscellaneous Publications
Concert Pitch magazine
New Zealand Symphony Orchestra, January 1980–July 1981, Issues 1-36. Editors: Carol Brownlie, Keith Hambleton, Joy Tonks.

Concert Pitch Newsletter
December 1991–October 1992. No.s 1-3; editor Joy Aberdein.

Symphony Quarterly magazine
April 1994–October 1994. Vols. 1-7; editor: Joy Aberdein.

Various publications of New Zealand Broadcasting (NZBS, NZBC, BCNZ), and New Zealand Symphony Orchestra.

Taped Interviews
Past and present players, administrators, conductors and soloists of the orchestra (National, NZBC Symphony) and New Zealand Symphony Orchestra.

Index

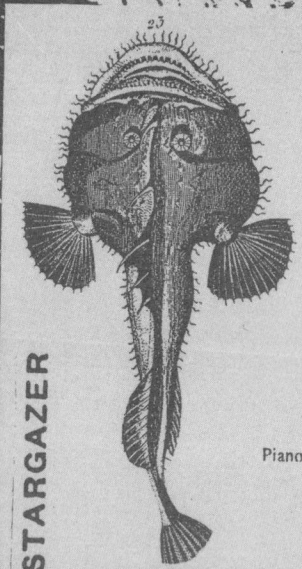